MURDER
IN THE
GARMENT
DISTRICT

MURDER
IN THE
GARMENT
DISTRICT

THE GRIP OF ORGANIZED CRIME AND THE
DECLINE OF LABOR IN THE UNITED STATES

DAVID WITWER AND
CATHERINE RIOS

THE
NEW
PRESS

NEW YORK
LONDON

Requests for permission to reproduce selections from this book should be made through our website: https://thenewpress.com/contact.

Published in the United States by The New Press, New York, 2019
Distributed by Two Rivers Distribution

ISBN 978-1-62097-463-6 (hc)
ISBN 978-1-62097-464-3 (ebook)

CIP data is available.

The New Press publishes books that promote and enrich public discussion and understanding of the issues vital to our democracy and to a more equitable world. These books are made possible by the enthusiasm of our readers; the support of a committed group of donors, large and small; the collaboration of our many partners in the independent media and the not-for-profit sector; booksellers, who often hand-sell New Press books; librarians; and above all by our authors.

www.thenewpress.com

Composition by dix! Digital Prepress
This book was set in Minion

Printed in the United States of America

10 9 8 7 6 5 4 3 2 1

CONTENTS

MURDER
IN THE
GARMENT
DISTRICT

INTRODUCTION

M ost Americans have little firsthand knowledge about unions, and they know even less about the history of organized labor. Ironically, this is especially true for most working-class Americans. Often what they know about the subject comes through a mandatory orientation session when they get a job at one of the giant, non-union businesses that dominate today's economic landscape. At Walmart, the nation's largest employer, all new hires watch a video that conveys the company's view of organized labor. The video features a handful of contented-looking actors portraying Walmart associates. And their message is fairly straightforward: "We don't think that a labor union is necessary here." Other large corporate employers, such as Target and Delta Air Lines, follow a similar corporate strategy.[1]

In conveying that message, these videos offer a succinct explanation of unions along with a brief summary of labor history. As one of the purported Walmart employees puts it, "Funny thing is I always thought that unions were kind of like clubs, you know, or you know charities that were out to help workers." The video quickly moves to correct that impression. "The truth is that unions are businesses, multi-million-dollar businesses, that make their money by convincing people like you and me to give them part of our paychecks." These videos also make it clear that this union enterprise is a failing business model. Both the Walmart and Target videos include a dramatic chart that illustrates the arc of twentieth-century labor history. A jagged line, descending from near the top of the chart's left-hand side, records organized labor's former strength in this country, a time in the

1940s and 1950s when a third of the workforce belonged to unions. Back then, a Target employee explains, unions provided necessary protections, but now that role has become obsolete. "Workers know that all the good things these unions once did are now law." This dubious historical claim goes unchallenged by the other Target employees in the film, who simply nod and smile in agreement.

In this version of labor history, union membership has fallen because workers don't want to pay costly union dues for protections they get for free from the government. To illustrate this point, an ominous downward chart line shows how membership rates have fallen dramatically over the course of the last couple of decades. "Because union membership has dropped over the years to less than 8 percent of the private employers' [workforce]," Walmart's video explains, "unions are fighting to survive." "The fewer members their business has," one Target employee observes, "the less money they collect." And these orientations emphasize that it is the workers' money that these unions are after, and their unscrupulous organizers are willing to do almost anything to get that money. In her book *Nickel and Dimed*, Barbara Ehrenreich describes sitting through one of these Walmart orientations: "You have to wonder—and I imagine some of my teenage fellow orientees may be doing so—why such fiends as these union organizers, such outright extortionists, are allowed to roam free in the land." [2]

These corporate campaigns depict unions as fading, obsolete businesses; they also paint them as corrupt. In Walmart's training films "unions are portrayed as essentially corrupt and parasitical institutions," according to the labor historian Nelson Lichtenstein. [3] Recently, as Delta Air Lines sought to fend off an organizing campaign by the International Association of Machinists (IAM), it funded the creation of a website to convince its employees to reject the union, which the website described as "a 'family' business that is not about its members." Delta asserted that many of its employees had already rejected the IAM, and concluded: "Here are a few reasons why you should do the same." Reason number one featured a mugshot of a cartoon cutout figure holding a sign that reads "Guilty." The text below that figure asserts, "In the last five years alone, 12 IAM officials have been convicted of stealing over $1 million in nine different states."[4] This emphasis on corruption is a major theme in such anti-union websites, which tend to document criminal cases involving union officials in meticulous detail. The Center for Union Facts, for example, attacks unions representing employees in health care and manufacturing as well as teaching and other public employee unions. It describes itself as an "online empire exposing big labor," and much of what it exposes has to do with instances of corruption. Most recently its main webpage featured an ongoing account of "The Latest Corruption Scandals in the UAW [United Auto Workers Union]."[5]

A central message for these corporate campaigns is that their employees should be wary about turning over a share of their hard-earned paychecks to these unscrupulous, failing businesses—aka unions. Instead of paying dues to a corrupt union, Delta urges its employees to consider the other great things they could buy with the $700 a year they might spend on dues. Workers might use that same money to buy a "new video game system with the latest hits" or "buy a few rounds of beer" for their buddies while watching a football game.

Critics have been quick to highlight the absurdities of Delta's argument. An article in the *Los Angeles Times* noted that while non-union Delta flight attendants averaged $58,341 a year in 2017, their unionized counterparts at United earned $62,461 and at American they made $62,366. Seen in this context, the $700 in dues money looks like a good investment. Indeed, statistics show that workers who pay union dues tend to reap significant economic advantages from their membership in organized labor. The Bureau of Labor Statistics reports that the median annual earnings for unionized workers is $52,700 versus $42,000 for non-union workers. Workers who belong to unions are more likely to receive employer-provided health insurance and pension benefits, and enjoy more vacations days. For women and minorities, the benefits of union membership are even more noticeable. A government study found that women union members earn on average 33 percent higher wages than non-union women workers; African American unionized workers take home 35 percent more in wages, and for Hispanic workers the increase is an impressive 51 percent.[6]

These union-gained advantages make it clear that organized labor still has an important role to play in protecting the well-being of American workers, despite the assertions made in corporate orientation videos.

But the corporate-sponsored version of labor history does get one central point right: unions have been on the decline. And their plummeting role has been particularly apparent in a manufacturing sector that had once been at the center of union strength. The story of one iconic American product offers a snapshot of this decline, and its impact on workers.

In 2012, thousands of workers who labored for Hostess Brands food corporation, the maker of the Twinkie, went on strike. In our current era of union weakness, such strikes have become relatively rare. That year there were just nineteen strikes nationwide that involved over 1,000 workers, and the total number of workers active in those strikes numbered about 148,000. Walkouts have become rare because unionized workers today are afraid to strike. Their unions are weak, and the employers hold almost all of the cards. By comparison, in the early 1950s, when, as Walmart has noted, organized labor accounted for nearly a third of the workforce and was reaching its zenith in power, workers felt secure enough to stage walkouts that extended the reach of their unions and won important gains in wages and workplace conditions. In 1952, for instance, there were 470 strikes in the United States that involved almost 2.8 million workers. Throughout the 1950s, the number of strikes each year ranged between four hundred and five hundred, but in recent decades, as organized labor faded in strength, that number plummeted. By 2009, only five strikes involving 1,000 workers or more occurred that year across the entire country; in 2017, there were seven.[7]

The walkout at Hostess, which involved Bakery Union members supported by Teamster truck drivers, quickly demonstrated the cause for labor's timidity in this era. The private equity firm that controlled Hostess chose to shut the entire corporation down rather than come to terms with their striking employees. A total of 8,500 workers lost their jobs. By 2013 another private equity firm had snapped up key portions of Hostess, including the Twinkie brand, and rehired a fraction of the Hostess workforce as non-unionized employees. When the four hundred workers at the Twinkie factory in Schiller Park, Illinois, voted to rejoin the union, the new owners simply shut their factory down and threw them out of work. For Mark Popovich, fifty-six years old, a lifelong union member and a Democrat, it was a cataclysmic event that led him to turn elsewhere for protection of his rights and interests as a worker. In 2016 he cast his first ever vote for a Republican—presidential candidate Donald Trump.[8]

The current fragile state of the labor movement has important social and political repercussions. Several observers, including the Economic Policy Institute, have noted how, "to a remarkable extent," the growing level of economic inequality in the United States has coincided with the historic decline in rates of union membership.[9] At the same time, disempowered and embittered workers have turned away from their traditional political allegiances, fostering the acidic political divisions of today.

To understand how we got here, it is necessary to go back to the era when unions were at their peak and explore the forces that emerged then to undercut their position. The 1950s marked a pivotal turning point for organized labor. The defeats that unions suffered then did not lead to an immediate decline in membership numbers, but important shifts in public opinion were accompanied by a significant legislative defeat. Perhaps worse, the labor movement was tarred with a lasting stain of impropriety and corruption that continues to mar its appeal to the working class and provides useful fodder to anti-union campaigns. As Steven Greenhouse, the labor reporter for the *New York Times*, recently observed, "Some people say unions should be written off as hopelessly corrupt."[10] Together these reversals set the stage for the subsequent slide of unions into the increasingly marginal role they occupy today. "It is hard to overstate," Greenhouse writes, "how much America's labor unions have declined in power, prestige, and in the public's consciousness."[11] Sixty years after the events described in this book, it is no longer necessary for anti-union forces to murder an organizer in order to control their workforce; the balance of power allows them to disregard labor concerns, and simply starve workers into submission.

1

A MURDER IN THE GARMENT
DISTRICT: POWER AND PRESSURE

May 9, 1949, was a typical day in the Garment District, twenty densely packed city blocks sprawled across midtown Manhattan, with Seventh Avenue cutting diagonally through the heart of it. While tourists strolled down the glamorous boulevard, lined with stately buildings that contained the showrooms and offices of well-known fashion houses, a turn onto one of the narrow side streets revealed a very different side of the neighborhood. On Thirty-Fifth Street between Seventh and Eighth Avenues, trucks lined up along the curb on both sides of the street, choking off through traffic and so closely parked that their tailgates couldn't be opened. Drivers loaded and unloaded garments from side doors, using the sidewalk as an ad hoc public loading dock. Pedestrians wove their way through the nearly impassable sidewalks, dodging stacks of boxes as men pushed clattering dress racks through the walkways. Towering above, sixteen-story loft buildings closed in on the action of the street. These lofts were full of small-scale workshops whose low wages, often compared to "coolie" wages,[1] earned this part of the Garment District the nickname "Chinatown." From this tightly bound district, 80 percent of the nation's dresses were produced.[2]

The International Ladies' Garment Workers' Union (ILG) was pushing to organize the District's intractable Chinatown shops. On this afternoon, one organizing crew included a forty-year-old father of four from Brooklyn named William Lurye. He was, according to *Time* magazine, "a mild-looking, curly-haired little fellow who would give a man the shirt off his back, people said." Lurye had taken a temporary leave from his job as a presser and had signed up to work on the organizing committee. In doing so, he had accepted a stiff pay cut from his usual weekly earnings of $180 to the $80 paid to organizers. His motivation was apparently clear, as Lurye came from a union family that had fought in some of the era's most notorious labor battles. His father had been a union leader in Chicago during the Capone era. Gangsters muscling in on the unionizing ragpickers—an industry of impoverished scavengers—had killed one of his colleagues as they attempted a street execution of the elder Lurye, opening fire in broad daylight. Two of Lurye's siblings worked on staff positions at the ILG, and he served on the executive board of his local union.[3] Joining the organizing team seemed a matter of course, a union and family duty.

A few minutes before four in the afternoon, Lurye went into the lobby of 224 West Thirty-Fifth Street to use a payphone and check in with union headquarters. The busy commercial whirl of the district rolled through the building's interior, as buyers and salesmen came in and out of the building elevators to visit the garment companies' showrooms and workshops. On this particular afternoon, a man was in the lobby peddling neckties to people passing by. Two phone booths stood near the elevators, across from a cigar stand with the usual assortment

Will Lurye around the time of the 1948 ILG anti-racketeering organizing campaign. *Seafarers International Union*

of candy, cigarettes, newspapers, and magazines. Hand-lettered "Out of Order" signs hung on the pay phones, placed there by a couple of bookies who ran a brisk business taking bets in the lobby. Ignoring the signs, Lurye sat down in one of the booths and dialed the union's phone number. As he made the call, two men pushed into the booth doors, wedging Lurye into the tight space. Desperately, he fought back as they stabbed him repeatedly, slashing his jugular and piercing his chest with a wound that punctured his lung. As the crimson fluid filled his chest, Lurye was effectively drowning in his own blood.[4]

His attackers fled the scene. Lurye somehow managed to make his way out of the lobby, calling out the name of one of his fellow organizers as he reached the street. He collapsed in front of a fire hydrant, amid the controlled chaos of a typical day of commerce in the District. As he lay on the street, young women, workers from the nearby shops, rushed to his assistance. They balanced their concern for the victim with a wary reluctance to stick their necks out, such that by the time the police arrived no one would admit to having seen anything.

An ambulance rushed Lurye to nearby St. Vincent's Hospital. Questioned there by both the police and union leaders, he could provide few details about his attackers, but described a man who had been following him recently during his organizing rounds. As the night wore on, fellow members of his local pressers' union filled the hospital waiting rooms, lining the halls to donate blood for their union brother. But, with his wife, sister, and union mentor holding vigil through the night for him, Lurye died before dawn the following day.[5]

Staged in the midst of a busy workday, in the crowded center of the Garment District, Lurye's murder was designed to send a message to the union and its supporters. The leadership of the ILG understood it that way. A blind memo in the union records analyzed the possible motives behind the killing with this explanation: "The fear had to be brought right into the market area. Like a political assassination that has to be done in a public place and there be no doubt for what the killing is for, so an organizer has to be assaulted right in the market." Gangsters had planned this attack to curb the union's organizing campaign and to demonstrate their ability to commit such violence with impunity.[6]

In response, the leaders of the Garment Workers' Union moved quickly to mobilize a wave of public outrage over the murder, framing the attack as a dramatic example of the kind of racketeering the union had faced in recent years. The organization's General Executive Board denounced the "brutal murder in broad daylight" of a union "idealist" by "gangsters in the hire of non-union sweatshop employers operating in the dress district."[7] In a defiant show of their own power on the street, the union planned a rally and a funeral procession through the heart of the Garment District, calling 65,000 dressmakers to stage a work stoppage. The resulting demonstration offered a vivid reminder of the ILG's powerful presence in the city. With the hearse carrying Lurye's body at the lead, twenty thousand union members filled Eighth Avenue, marching fifty abreast, shoulder to shoulder, curb to curb. They moved as a silent, solid mass that stretched for two blocks behind the hearse. As many as eighty thousand other workers lined the streets to watch. The march ended in a huge gathering where the attack had occurred, on Thirty-Fifth Street in the center of the District's Chinatown.

Among the speakers at the funeral was Charles S. Zimmerman, the leader of the Garment Workers' organizing campaign and the man Lurye had been trying to call when he was attacked. Present with the family at Lurye's death, Zimmerman told the gathering that Lurye "died in the battle to rid our industry of the hoodlum gangsters and open-shoppers who resort to such tactics in their greed for profits."[8] With the crowd overflowing the Manhattan Center, loudspeakers were used to broadcast his words to the workers packed in the street and crowding the doorframes and windows that lined the avenue.

The event culminated with a speech by the union's president, David Dubinsky. The stout, white-haired Dubinsky spoke with a deep accent that revealed his immigrant roots in the ghettoes of eastern Europe. According to the newspapers, his voice throbbed with emotion as he described Lurye as a martyr, a "noble soldier who had given his life to the advancement of labor's cause." Dubinsky's speech depicted a union at war with mobsters who were brought into the Garment District by unscrupulous businessmen in order to resist the union.[9]

From the union's perspective, it was waging this fight against the racketeers with little assistance from the government. Despite this lack of support, or maybe because of it, Dubinsky vowed to the mass of workers present that the union would continue the struggle, "no matter what the Police Department and the District Attorney do or do not do." Just the previous fall, a series of brutal attacks against union organizers had resulted in a lackluster investigation that ironically led to the arrests of the injured Garment Workers' Union leaders and union pickets. The union clearly intended to do whatever it could to publicly pressure the police and district attorney to act with more vigor and integrity this time around. Pulling 65,000 dressmakers out of the shops for the day, marching down Eighth Avenue, making dramatic speeches—all of these actions were part of a well-thought-out publicity campaign, designed to move public opinion in ways that would put pressure on government officials. Dubinsky continued this tack, promising that the union would cooperate with the authorities in their search for the killers. It would also back those efforts with its own financial resources. The union posted a $25,000 reward for information that would lead to the arrest and conviction of those involved in the murder, the equivalent today of a quarter million dollars. In a large, printed advertisement announcing this reward in the *New York Times*, the union declared that it was "as much interested in uncovering the instigators of this horrible crime" as it was in "finding the actual assassins."[10]

In the end, though, no one was ever convicted of Lurye's murder. His killers and the men who had instigated the crime went unpunished. Writing in the *New York Post*, the columnist Murray Kempton noted the significance of this outcome, how it demonstrated the vulnerability of organized labor and the apparent immunity of organized crime. Reviewing the brutality of the murder one year after it had occurred, Kempton noted, "That is how a man died organizing for the most powerful union in the biggest labor town in the world."[11] And indeed, the episode demonstrates how the odds were stacked against union leaders. Even in an era when unions were close to their zenith in terms of economic and political influence, many union leaders faced the dilemma of how to respond to the challenge of organized crime. Unable to rely on the government, they made other accommodations, and in so doing left the labor movement open to charges of complicity in the very racketeering that they had hoped to resist.

The story of Lurye's murder fits alongside a larger pattern of violence confronting union officials in this era. From New York City to Chicago, Detroit, and St. Louis, many faced a similar dilemma, one arising from their relative vulnerability and the stark realization that neither the government, nor society at large, seemed to have much of an interest in protecting them from mob violence. In the story of labor racketeering in the post–World War II era, this vulnerability was a fundamental piece of the puzzle. It was a tragic weak point for a labor movement whose size and power would be hard for most Americans today to appreciate. In 1949, almost a third of the workforce belonged to unions, with membership reaching into 28 percent of American households. Key manufacturing industries that stood at the heart of that era's economy, such as automotive and steel, were firmly organized, as were the crucial transport sectors. Organized labor maintained a potent alliance with the Democratic Party that had reshaped the country's political landscape ever since the mid-1930s. Magazine articles written in the postwar era included headlines such as "Bigger Big Labor," and invoked terms like "leviathan" to describe a huge and powerful union movement that appeared to be poised to become even more powerful.[12]

Despite labor's size and power in the post–World War II era, some of its vulnerable leaders had to make compromises. Close historical ties between businessmen and criminal groups in particular economic sectors made it impossible to organize in those industries without reaching an accommodation with mobsters. In these same sectors, labor leaders were vulnerable to assault and murder from gangsters seeking to control their organizations and milk the union's funds. With no help from indifferent police and federal officials, threatened union officials' only option often involved turning to other gangsters for protection, making accommodations in the process. Anti-union forces seized upon such instances of accommodation to equate organized labor with organized crime, depicting all unions as little better than criminal organizations, and fostering a long-term negative public perception of the labor movement.

In the years that followed Lurye's murder, labor racketeering—or the misuse of organized labor's power for criminal ends—would become one of the major issues in Cold War America, culminating in a set of well-publicized congressional hearings at the end of the 1950s. Those hearings starred a young Robert F. Kennedy, the general counsel of the Senate investigating committee, and James R. Hoffa, the head of the Teamsters Union, but they also featured a rogues' gallery of gangsters and mobbed-up union officials whose testimony fueled public anxiety about the menace of labor racketeering. In hearings and in the news media, concern about this issue was framed in ways that echoed the alarm over domestic communism—both were portrayed as dangerous domestic threats to a country menaced by the Soviet Union. Conservatives and anti-union forces sought to harness those concerns to their efforts to restrict a union movement that had come to include one-third of the nation's workforce and that had built a powerful political alliance with the Democratic Party. To delegitimize aspects of union power, labor's opponents labeled aggressive union tactics as a form of racketeering. But this era's discourse of anti-racketeering had such potency, and tapped so effectively into public anxieties, that union leaders and rank-and-file members could wield it to promote their interests as well. Unions invoked anti-racketeering to justify militant strike actions and strong union contracts. They equated the employers with whom they contended to mobsters, and depicted picket-line contests as valiant efforts to curb the spread of nefarious racketeering. The ILG organizing campaign that immediately preceded the murder of Will Lurye was crafted around these very issues.

Racketeering and corruption were, in this way, contested terms, which both anti-union and pro-union forces could adopt to serve their ends. And, as Lurye's murder demonstrated, racketeering amounted to more than just political rhetoric. Organized criminal groups had come to exert a powerful influence in particular economic sectors, and part of their power lay in their ability to mount these kinds of assaults. It was this pattern of attacks, and the problematic responses offered by the state and by organized labor, that helped to give labor racketeering its potency and fueled the political contests that would revolve around this issue. The story of Lurye's murder was the opening

ILG strike of 1948, New York. *Kheel Center, Cornell University*

moment in a larger narrative about America's encounter with labor racketeering in the Cold War era.

That encounter played a pivotal role in the history of the labor movement in the United States—a movement that had over the preceding two decades transformed the lives of millions of working people and laid the foundation of America's middle class. The public debate over racketeering was a watershed, the moment where the balance of public opinion and the political landscape shifted to the fundamental detriment of organized labor. Just as conservatives in this era had conjured the threat of communism to delegitimize efforts to expand the New Deal, so they invoked the menace of racketeering to offer a frightening vision of how union power might threaten the nation's security. Labor leaders struggled with only limited success to respond to concerns about the misuse of union power; the erosion of labor's public image undercut the foundations of union growth in the post–World War II era. In the wake of congressional hearings, new legislation banned key union organizing tactics. But even more significantly, the labor movement suffered a loss of prestige. In response to the hearings in

1957, *Time* magazine asserted that "the role of unionism in a peace-time economy was called into question as rarely before."[13] The result was, the magazine asserted, a "historic change in the political climate in which organized labor lives and breathes." This book is about how that historic change came to happen.

The prologue to the labor racketeering crisis was the rebirth of the labor movement itself. In the 1930s the labor movement—which had historically played a limited role in the United States—achieved an unprecedented level of power in the nation's economy. American workers searching for security in the midst of the Great Depression responded with enthusiasm to union organizing efforts, and they joined waves of strikes that cracked open traditionally anti-union industries and established labor organizations in former citadels of employer strength. Labor's new economic power was accompanied by comparable gains in the political sphere. Nowhere was this more true than in the women's garment industry in New York City. Here, the power shifted during the summer of 1933 with a strike called by a moribund, bankrupt union—the International Ladies' Garment Workers' Union. The organization's membership had fallen below forty thousand nationwide, which represented only a fraction of the three hundred thousand workers in the industry. The union's finances were so weak in early 1933 that it had stopped operating the elevator at the national headquarters to save money. Unable to pay its phone bill, the Dress Joint Board, a collection of local unions with members involved in dressmaking, could no longer make outgoing calls.

But new hope emerged as Franklin Roosevelt took office and the New Deal promised more support for unions, including a clause in the National Industrial Recovery Act that guaranteed labor's right to organize. In New York City, the union's Dress Joint Board seized the moment and pulled together a volunteer cadre of 1,500 activists and staff members. On August 16, 1933, they launched the biggest and most successful strike in the union's history. The city's 1,200 dress shops were shut down completely and tens of thousands of dressmakers flooded into the union.[14] The desire of rank-and-file workers, 70 percent of them women, to join the ranks of the labor movement made this a pivotal moment. "We had estimated that 30,000 workers might go out, or at most 35,000," recalled Zimmerman, the head of one of the dressmakers' local unions. "The actual outpouring was in the neighborhood of 70,000, [including] shops we had never been near, shops that did not have a single union member. We did not have halls enough to hold them, so we had to take [over] an armory. It was enormous, just enormous."[15]

Similar victories followed in emerging centers of dress manufacturing in Philadelphia, Los Angeles, and elsewhere, and in other sectors of the women's garment industry, such as children's dresses and the undergarment trade. By 1934, the ILG had two hundred thousand members and was now the third-largest organization in the American Federation of Labor.[16] This pattern continued through the prosperous years of World War II, so by the mid-1940s the ILG had four hundred thousand members, half of them living in New York City. Other industries followed, as the ranks of organized labor swelled in the years of the Great Depression and during World War II. Across the country about 35 percent of all non-agricultural wage earners belonged to a union at the end of the war. In New York City, there were over a million union members, and they constituted between a quarter and a third of the city's total workforce. Ladies garment manufacturing was the largest industry in America's biggest city, and the ILG was the city's largest union.[17]

The ILG used its power to try to reshape the economic landscape, struggling against basic tendencies in this fragmented, highly competitive business, where women's dresses were produced by about 750 manufacturing firms and jobbers. Especially in the lower-priced dress market, jobbers had come to predominate the production process. While a manufacturer had their own shop and crew of inside workers, a jobber typically arranged to have a particular dress style made by contractors, providing them with the cut fabric, patterns, and sample dresses. This contracting system enabled dressmaking firms to hold down their costs and meet the fluctuating production demands that resulted from sudden changes in fashion. Dress firms could therefore save the overhead cost of maintaining their own factories and workforces. The contractors in turn could set up a small garment factory with little more expense than it took to rent a loft space and acquire

enough sewing machines to staff it; the garment materials were sup-
plied to them by the jobbers. As a result, the dress industry included
about 1,600 contractors operating small shops, with an average thirty-
six workers per shop. Competition was keen; often the difference of
a few cents in price determined success or failure. Firms went out of
business frequently and, because the initial investment could be quite
small, new firms were emerging all the time.[18]

Through contracts negotiated in the mid-1930s, the union worked
to stabilize the garment industry. It negotiated contracts that called
for uniform wage rates across the industry and established a standard thirty-five-hour work week. The goal was an objective, uniform
wage system that eliminated labor costs as a venue of competition
within the industry.[19] Similarly, the ILG instituted a system of controls
over the process of garment contracting in an effort to eliminate the
ruthless competition between small firms that had historically led to
sweatshop conditions in the industry. After 1936, each jobber was limited to working with a set of contractors that the union had registered
to him. He could not send his work out to another contractor unless
he could demonstrate that his existing contractors were operating at
capacity. In this way, the union sought to ensure that contractors received a more dependable stream of orders and in turn could provide
their workers with steadier employment.[20]

The union's achievements, however, created new problems. To the
extent that union contracts created a level of uniformity in the industry, they also provided an opportunity for firms to find a way to
circumvent the union's controls. With greater flexibility and lower
labor costs, these firms could make a bigger profit and still undersell
their competition. By the late 1930s, some District garment makers
were turning to individuals with ties to organized crime who could
help them evade union controls for a price. From the union's perspective, the pivotal figure involved in such arrangements was Abe Chait.
Described as a "big hulking six-footer," the fifty-year-old Chait owned
an important garment trucking firm and reportedly had interests
in several other firms in the District. He also stood at the center of
a web of organized crime networks that were active in the garment
industry.[21]

Chait had assumed a role previously held by Louis "Lepke" Buchalter, a prominent Jewish gangster in the Garment District, who had been executed after his murder conviction in 1944. Sometimes referred to as "the Judge," Buchalter headed a criminal group that was based in the Lower East Side's Jewish immigrant community, a community that for a long time had played a leading part in the city's garment industry. Buchalter's gang had formed key connections with elements in the Garment District's business community and its labor unions. Such connections were not new in the Garment District. Since early in the twentieth century, various employers and union factions had hired different gangsters to wage battles on the picket line. Referring to the prominent role acquired by a Lower East Side Jewish gangster, Benjamin Fein, the historian Jenna Weissman Joselit observed that already by 1915, "Dopey Benny and his ilk had become an integral aspect of the Jewish [Garment District] economy, influencing conditions in the marketplace and threatening the integrity of the labor movement." [22]

Like his predecessor Buchalter, Chait's influence centered on trucking. Truckers played a pivotal role in the ladies garment manufacturing process, enabling jobbers and manufacturers to hold costs down and meet fluctuating production demands by shipping their cut fabric out to the small garment contractors scattered across the New York metropolitan region. By the 1940s, ILG leaders had discerned a particular group of trucking firms emerging with links to gangsters such as Chait. These firms specialized in helping jobbers and contractors avoid the union's controls. Jobbers could contract with someone like Chait to have garment pieces shipped to out-of-town, non-union contractors who could underbid their unionized counterparts. The mob-connected trucker received a set fee in return for guaranteeing that the union would not discover and therefore not be able to stop this contract evasion. Acting as a broker, truckers like Chait also arranged to provide non-union contractors with a steady supply of work from jobbers in return for a share of their profits, at times even providing initial financing to someone who wanted to set up such a shop. Many of these non-union contracting shops were appearing outside New York City, in places like northeast Pennsylvania. Their growth drew money and jobs away from the Garment District, the heart of the union's strength. As one union official warned in 1939, "Legitimate jobbers and contractors are squeezed out of business."[23]

The union now faced a serious threat. A group of jobbers had emerged in the low-priced dress sector of the industry who operated in defiance of the union contract with apparent immunity, using truckers like Chait to evade union oversight, and to ship their goods right through union picket lines. More and more shops were operating non-union, or were unionized in name only. The latter included jobbers who were offered special contracts by the union, called International Agreements, granting them exemptions from various restrictions and wage requirements included in the standard contract. Such agreements allowed the union to organize mob-connected firms without having to resort to picket lines that were all too often ineffective, but in making such agreements the union undercut its goal of providing stability and uniformity in wage costs. Already by 1939, one of the leaders of a dress manufacturing employers' association warned the union that "the retreat from the coveted goal of uniformity is degenerating into a rout." World War II brought an economic boom to the Garment District that blunted concerns about these trends, but at the war's end tighter economic times emerged, especially for firms making dresses for the lower-priced market.[24]

By the late 1940s, unionized dressmakers in the Garment District warned the union that it had to address this situation and that it had to do so soon. Among those issuing these warnings was Sidney Blauner, whose firm, Lombardy Dress Company, was one of the largest unionized manufacturers of lower-priced women's dresses. He and his father, Max Blauner, an immigrant from Austria, had founded the firm in 1929. They were established Garment District insiders who had experienced firsthand the menace of racketeering. In the mid-1930s, targeted by the racketeer Lepke Buchalter, their firm had paid $40,000 in protection money to the gangster. When the district attorney uncovered records of those payments, Max Blauner had been forced to testify at Buchalter's extortion trial or else face a perjury charge over his grand jury testimony.[25]

A decade later, the son wrote to the head of the ILG's Dress Joint Board complaining about how other firms were taking away his

business, selling the same dresses he made for less than he could produce them given the conditions imposed by his union contract: "This
makes the difference between one fellow staying in business and another fellow being busted out of business, which is me!" [26] Blauner
and his counterparts faced the choice of joining their competitors outside the union fold or giving up their business. "I repeat, once more,"
he wrote in another letter, "YOUR big problem is getting this type of
manufacturer lined up [in a union contract]—not tomorrow, not next
week, not in two weeks, but RIGHT NOW, because if you let guys
like this get away with things like this . . . eventually you'll wind up
without a union." [27]

In 1948, a year before Lurye's murder, the union heeded these calls
and launched an ambitious organizing drive, targeting the mob-
connected jobbers and growing number of non-union contractors. [28]
In doing so, the union leaders were directly challenging the organized
crime figures whose role in the garment industry had been expanding. The gangsters' response provided a symbolic demonstration of
the union's vulnerability. After pickets had begun to target non-union
firms in the Thirty-Fifth Street, Chinatown area, on September 28,
1948, a group of five men walked up to the second floor of the ILG's
Dress Joint Board offices on West Fortieth Street in the middle of the
day. Entering the room that served as the headquarters of the organizing effort, they asked for the head of the campaign, Bill Ross. When
he identified himself, they went after him, pounding him with brass
knuckles, and giving a similar beating to Ross's two assistants who
were also present. They left the three union officials lying on the floor,
bleeding. Ross required seven stitches to his skull. A half hour later,
ILG pickets were ambushed on Thirty-Fifth Street, on the same block
where Lurye would later be attacked. The attackers this time used lead
pipes wrapped in newspapers. The union had warned law enforcement
that there might be trouble, and in fact police did quickly arrive on the
scene at Thirty-Fifth Street—just in time to arrest the four wounded
union pickets. Their attackers somehow managed to slip away. [29]

As it would later do in the wake of Lurye's murder, the ILG sought
to mobilize public support and pressure law enforcement to take
action. The union called for a mass demonstration on Thirty-Fifth

Street, where the attacks had taken place. Fliers declared the union's determination to fight "Open Shoppers and Their Gangster Henchmen," and union leaders spoke of the need for garment manufacturers to "shake off the grip of the racketeers." ILG president Dubinsky and other top union officials met privately with the district attorney and the police commissioner. The prosecutor promised to launch a new grand jury probe into Garment District racketeering. The union's attorney described a meeting between the ILG's top officials and the police commissioner the day after the attack as a "very cordial interview," and he wrote a note to thank the commissioner for his "sympathetic understanding of the union's immediate problem." [30]

But in the weeks that followed, none of the gangsters active in the Garment District was arrested. There were, however, arrests of union organizers and of the union pickets the ILG had recruited from the Seafarers International Union, men known as whitecaps because of their sailor hats. These whitecaps had a reputation for toughness and were used to bolster the ranks of dressmaker pickets in this new climate of violence. A couple of weeks after the assault in the Dress Joint Board headquarters, police arrested forty-two union pickets and later charged three ILG organizers with coercion in response to a complaint from a non-union garment manufacturer. [31] In an era rife with police corruption, this action suggested that the police had received directions to attack the unionists and not the union-busting racketeers.

Meanwhile, individual pickets, the men recruited from the Seafarers Union, were being waylaid by knife-wielding attackers on their way home at night. In one example, Clifford Wilson was jumped by five men as he left his subway station on October 30, 1948. His attackers told him, "This will teach the _____ seamen to keep in their own backyard." They slashed him in the chest and the forehead, and his wounds required fifty-six stitches. [32] After another Seafarer picket, Joseph Carroll, was knifed at the entrance to his subway station in the Bronx, he was brought in for questioning by the Bronx District Attorney's Office. It was the second time Carroll had been attacked; a couple of weeks earlier a group of men had jumped him outside a Garment District subway stop. The DA's staff appeared unsympathetic. They asked why that night Carroll had taken a different route home than his usual one, and observed that his knife wounds could possibly have been self-inflicted. As the *New York Post* noted, "The questioning was directed along a line that almost made it appear that the authorities thought Carroll was a defendant rather than a complainant." [33]

Despite their initial declarations of support, the authorities did little to aid the union's efforts against racketeers in the 1948 organizing campaign. One union official later recalled how during the meeting with authorities, the police commissioner had "banged the table" and declared, "Under my administration I will not permit any gangsterism." "I will do everything I can to stop it," the commissioner asserted. "The next day he sent out the cops and they arrested all our pickets." [34] The situation appeared hopeless and the union soon shut the organizing campaign down. An internal memorandum cited the effects of the attacks on the union staff and pickets, as well as the police response. "As a result of these attacks," the union report concluded, "the police instead of protecting our pickets and officers made it impossible to carry on organization work." [35]

None of this would have come as a surprise to the ILG's president, David Dubinsky. Born in 1892 into a poor Jewish family that lived on the eastern edge of the Russian empire, Dubinsky had become involved in the Jewish labor movement, the Bund, when he was fifteen years old. Arrested twice by the czar's police, he was imprisoned for a year and a half and then sent to exile in Siberia. With his father's help, he used bribery to make his way back to his hometown, and then at the age of nineteen he immigrated to America. He found work as a cutter, the skilled trade that involved wielding a cutting blade through piles of fabric to cut out the pieces of the garment for later assembly. By 1921, he became general manager of the cutters' local union. Because this local played such a pivotal role in the Garment District, Dubinsky was drawn into the union's national leadership, assuming the presidency of the ILG in 1932. [36]

Profiles from the period emphasize the contrast between his diminutive size—he stood five feet, five inches tall—and his outsize personality, described as a "powder keg of explosive energy." Pacing relentlessly around his office, he smoked eighteen cigars a day, until he quit, whereupon he took up chewing them, shredding a half-dozen a day. He could be charming, with a warm, beaming smile and an infectious laugh, but he was also known for his tantrums that "took the form of wall piercing shrieks." A vigorous speaker, whose Yiddish accent became stronger when he became excited, he would wave his arms as he spoke, and as one obituary put it, "His loud voice, which started as a shout, went up from there." Though he kept his union salary modest and imposed similar restraints on the wages of other union staff members, Dubinsky liked the good life. He lived in a "lavish penthouse apartment," according to one magazine profile, and had a taste for flamboyant and expensive neckties, posh restaurants, and pricey liquor.[37]

At the same time, he imposed tight controls over the union, micromanaging as much as he could and keeping a team of accountants literally across the hall from his office to ensure that little happened to the union funds that he didn't know about.[38] Paul Jacobs recalled Dubinsky's looming presence as something the journalist had experienced firsthand in the early 1940s, when he worked as an ILG organizer: "Very quickly we learned that it was D.D., as he liked to be called, who made most of the decisions in the ILG—ranging from where an organizing campaign should be started to how much of a car allowance, if any, should be granted." The union was Dubinsky's life, and he viewed himself as the all-powerful father figure who guided it with a firm but unquestioned hand. There was no room in this life for real friends, and Dubinsky once described himself as a "lone wolf." "All of his colleagues," Jacobs observed, "were really his subordinates and the awe with which they held him was mixed with fear."[39]

By the late 1940s Dubinsky was a national figure who dominated the union with his outsize personality. *Time* magazine featured him on the cover in 1949, and titled its profile of him "Little David, the Giant." His status reflected his leading role in opposing communist influence within organized labor, an issue of growing significance as the Cold War emerged in the late 1940s. He had worked tirelessly to weed communist elements out of his own union, and those efforts were now cited as a model for other union leaders eager to distance their organizations from the menace of Soviet influence. Similarly, Dubinsky had a prominent role in a U.S. campaign to curb communist influence in labor movements abroad. These efforts included covert CIA funding for the Free Trade Union Committee that Dubinsky had helped found and for which he served as treasurer. The Agency even gave him a code name, Mr. Garment Worker, although it would seem to have done little to disguise his identity.[40]

In domestic politics, Dubinsky was a prominent leader among anticommunist liberals. He was one of the founding members of Americans for Democratic Action, an influential political organization of politically progressive Cold Warriors that included such prominent figures as Reinhold Niebuhr and Hubert Humphrey. At the state level, Dubinsky wielded his political influence through an independent party he had founded, the American Liberal Party, which played a strategic role in New York City and New York State elections, often providing the several hundred thousand votes necessary to swing a contest from one side to the other.[41]

At the national level, the ILG president demonstrated the strong political alliance between organized labor and the Democratic Party. Facing a difficult bid for reelection in 1948, President Harry Truman leaned heavily on labor leaders such as Dubinsky, who provided critical financial contributions and worked to rally working-class voters.[42] Truman's reliance on this support comes through in accounts of the rally his campaign held in New York City on October 28, days away from the 1948 election, in which Truman staged a surprise upset over Thomas Dewey. The president's campaign entourage toured Manhattan starting from Grand Central Station and proceeding to Seventh Avenue and the heart of the Garment District, where a reporter from the *New York Times* asserted that the crowd put on the day's "greatest show," one clearly staged by the ILG's ever-meticulous president. The sidewalks were solidly packed with a crowd of garment workers while others in the offices and shops above street level sent down a blizzard of confetti that included colorful fabric scraps as well. Loudspeakers, set at full volume, played "Happy Days Are Here Again." And there in the midst of this tumultuous scene, Dubinsky greeted the president from a platform at the corner of Thirty-Eighth Street and Seventh Avenue. Truman's procession paused long enough for the president to borrow a loudspeaker and shout, "Thanks, Dave, for this great welcome." Dubinsky was literally on a first-name basis with the president. At the evening's rally, held in Madison Square Garden, Truman sat next to Dubinsky on the stage.[43]

Despite his prominent status, Dubinsky remained a union leader in a country where labor officials were peculiarly vulnerable to threats and violence. He had certainly known fear himself, and as a union official he had experienced personal danger. In Russia that meant being hunted by the czar's police. In New York City, as the head of a local union crucial to the garment industry, he had personal encounters with gangsters. In his later life, he described turning down one notorious gangster, Curly Holtz, who asked him to rescind a fine that the cutters' local had imposed on a union member who had worked for a non-union firm. According to Dubinsky, he suffered no violence as a result of this refusal, but it is also true that in 1926 he applied for a gun permit. At the cutters' local he kept a gun in his desk drawer at the union office. He also took to carrying a pistol with him, concealed in his sleeve, as he walked to and from the subway station during his daily commute.[44] His precautions were not foolish. In 1930, another official in the cutters' local, David Fruhling, had begun tracking down information on the payments that garment firms were making to gangsters for protection. He was attacked and stabbed several times as he was leaving his house on his way to work. As Dubinsky later recalled it, the attackers had carved up Fruhling's face and left him blind in one eye. The victim ended up leaving his union position and in fact got out of the garment industry entirely.[45]

In response to the assault on Fruhling, Dubinsky and other Garment Workers' Union leaders demanded to meet with the District Attorney's Office to push the authorities to take action against what appeared to be a rising tide of racketeering. According to a news report on this meeting, the district attorney "invited union officials to return with more specific information regarding employers who have been victimized and he asked them to help identify the racketeers preying upon the industry." The prosecutor promised that once they had done that—essentially conduct their own grand jury probe but without grand jury powers—then he would assign an assistant district attorney to go ahead with the case. It wasn't the most supportive offer.[46]

Decades later, Dubinsky recalled another aspect of the episode, one that had left an enduring impression of the problematic role of the state. After leaving the district attorney's, "I come to my office," he remembered, "I get a call." It was a prominent gangster, who told Dubinsky, " 'You went to the District Attorney. He couldn't help you.' They already knew from the District Attorney and they related some of the conversation that I had." The link between the prosecutor's office and the gangsters was so tight that they knew what Dubinsky had said within minutes of his conversation there. "That was their connection," Dubinsky explained. And the same held true elsewhere in the law enforcement establishment. "They had it all over." In the early 1950s, Dubinsky would tell an FBI official that he had absolutely no faith in local law enforcement, which he believed was too closely tied in with elements of organized crime.[47]

After Lurye's murder in May of 1949, New York mayor William O'Dwyer asked to meet with Dubinsky; the Garment Workers president refused. Dubinsky sent instead one of his subordinates, Sasha Zimmerman. In the ensuing conversation, Zimmerman voiced the frustration and the anger that Dubinsky must have felt in face of disingenuous official claims of concern. "I went down to see him," Zimmerman told an interviewer. "He wanted to know what happened. You can imagine how I felt at that meeting. Terribly disturbed. I told him, 'Mr. Mayor, we came down here [after the attacks in September 1948] and we warned you and told you and we asked for your assistance. We told you something worse will happen.' " The only result, Zimmerman observed, had been an implicit show of support for the racketeers. " 'You sent down the cops and they arrested all our pickets. What are you asking now, what happened? You knew what's going on. We told you. You didn't do anything.' "[48]

In the Cold War era, Dubinsky and other labor leaders occupied a contradictory place in American society. In the wake of the rebirth of the labor movement, they led powerful organizations that represented millions of American workers. Indeed, in terms of the share of the workforce that belonged to unions, this era marked the peak of the labor movement in U.S. history. The International Ladies' Garment

Workers' Union epitomized this status. It was the largest union in New York City and it played a dominant role in the city's most important industry. That economic power underlay Dubinsky's political status as a key figure in the alliance between the Democratic Party and organized labor. The president of the United States courted his support. Dubinsky's role even extended into the realm of foreign relations; he and other anti-communist labor leaders worked hand in glove with government agencies such as the CIA to wage the Cold War. He was on the cover of *Time* magazine. And yet, the Garment Workers' Union could not count on basic security for its officials and organizers. Gangsters and thugs could walk right into union headquarters and beat up the head of the union's organizing drive. Or worse, they could stab an organizer to death in the heart of the crowded Garment District in the midst of a typical working day. The ILG might rally tens of thousands of workers against the menace of racketeering, but without basic security for its officials the union's ability to curb this threat was limited. Lurye's murder demonstrated that fact.

A couple of decades later, in an interview with the labor beat reporter A.H. Raskin, Dubinsky discussed the vulnerability of union officials. A transcript stored in the union archives suggests that even then, well after he had retired from union office, Dubinsky was careful in his responses to questions about his past experiences with racketeering; at his request, the microphone was turned off at key moments in this discussion, and some of Dubinsky's responses on the transcript refer to points he made during those off-the-record exchanges. In one section, Dubinsky mentions how in the 1920s, the notorious gangster Dopey Benny Fein had "wanted to go after" the ILG president at the time, Benjamin Schlesinger. Dubinsky implied that this episode was unusual, because in general, he asserted, gangsters did not "go after high officials" such as the president of a national union. But as his anecdote made clear, the possibility always existed. And meanwhile, local union officials, business agents, and managers were completely vulnerable.[49]

In this era of union power, all union officials were vulnerable to threats and violent assaults. This weakness had significant repercussions, fostering corrupt accommodations and leaving a powerful post–World War II labor movement vulnerable in ways that its opponents would exploit in the decade that followed. The resulting exposures derailed unions just at the moment that should have marked an era of dramatic growth, leaving the movement haltered by new restrictions and doomed to a steep decline in the decades that followed.

2

SHOTS IN THE DARK:
VIOLENCE AND APATHY

Eleven months before William Lurye was murdered, someone fired a shotgun through the kitchen window at the home of Walter Reuther, the president of the nation's largest union, the United Auto Workers (UAW). Reuther had come home late from a meeting at the union's Detroit headquarters. He had finished eating the dinner set aside for him by his wife and had just gone to the refrigerator to get some fruit salad for dessert when the window was shattered by a load of 00 buckshot—enough to drop a deer at fifty feet. A moment before, the UAW president had turned in response to a comment from his wife, a gesture that probably saved his life. The bulk of the blast just missed him, shredding a kitchen cupboard instead. Four of the pea-sized buckshot pellets hit his shoulder, shattering his arm bones and nearly tearing his arm from his body. Another pellet ricocheted through his chest. Although he survived, Reuther was hospitalized for months, enduring incredible pain; the damage to his arm was so severe that doctors warned him he would never be able to use it again.

It was a narrow escape for the UAW leader. Police investigators later determined that the gunman had been waiting in the dark in the bushes behind Reuther's house. The UAW president's usual evening routine was to park his car on the side street that ran along his home's corner lot and enter the house through the back door. For no particular reason, on this occasion he parked in the driveway and came in the front. Had he followed his routine, the assassin would have caught him point blank outside his back door.[1]

The attack on Reuther had many similarities to Lurye's murder. In both cases, investigators traced the origins of the attacks to organized crime. In both cases, the response by law enforcement was both conflicted and ineffectual. As a result, no one was ever convicted of either crime. There were other cases just like these in this same period. In retrospect a pattern is evident: organized crime groups deployed violence against union officials with impunity, assured of an apathetic response on the part of the government. In a search for security, labor leaders had to turn elsewhere. Where they turned depended upon the resources available to them, resources that would vary from union to union and according to their rank within the organization. This pattern—gang violence and an apathetic state response—underlay the prevalence of labor racketeering in the Cold War era. It festered in those parts of urban America where gangsters could prey on union officials with impunity.

At the time of the attempted assassination, April 1948, Walter Reuther was one of the most prominent labor leaders in the United States. He had been elected president of the UAW two years earlier, and in 1952 he would become the head of the Congress of Industrial Organizations (CIO); with four and a half million members, the CIO included most of the unions that had organized the mass production sector of the economy. In the post–World War II era, Reuther championed an expansive vision for organized labor. "We are not going to operate as a narrow economic interest group," he pledged.[2] Instead, Reuther envisioned a future in which representatives of labor, government, and business worked together to plan economic growth and promote a more even distribution of wealth. Although his most ambitious plans remained unrealized, he achieved dramatic victories for his autoworkers. These included steady wage gains with built in cost-of-living increases, retirement plans, health care coverage, and a system of supplemental unemployment benefits to guarantee laid-off workers the equivalent of 95 percent of their regular salary. He demonstrated the ways that unions could dramatically improve the economic lives of working Americans.[3]

He also symbolized the power of the labor movement that had been reborn in the 1930s. Conservatives in the Cold War era viewed Reuther as the embodiment of their worst fears about the danger that organized labor presented to the traditional outlines of America's free enterprise system. Indeed, the head of the Automobile Manufacturers' Association famously dubbed Reuther "the most dangerous man in Detroit because no one is more skillful in bringing about the revolution without seeming to disturb the existing forms of society."[4] Despite such epithets, Reuther was not a revolutionary; he was instead one of the most vociferous anti-communists in the labor movement. Like Dubinsky of the Garment Workers' Union, Reuther's anti-communism had emerged after a youthful career of left-wing activism. Reuther's father, a German immigrant who had settled in West Virginia, had been a union leader and an active member of the Socialist Party, and he urged his children to dedicate themselves to the cause of the working class. Walter trained as a skilled tool and die worker, moved to Detroit in 1927, and took an active part in the local branch of the Socialist Party. Laid off from his job at Ford Motor Company in 1932, he and his brother Victor set off to work their way around the world, hiring on as sailors for their boat passage and then picking up work where they could as they made their way across Europe and Asia. They spent eighteen months working in an auto plant in the Soviet Union, a formative experience for them both. It showed them firsthand the possible achievements of a mobilized working class as well as the menace of a totalitarian system.[5]

When the brothers returned to Detroit in 1935, they joined efforts to build a new union in the auto industry. Walter Reuther moved steadily up the ranks of the union's leadership, jockeying among a series of political factions that included a powerful Communist wing in the union's bureaucracy. In the process he became convinced that the Communist Party played a nefarious role within the union, "making political capital of workers' legitimate demands" only to advance the party's goals, not the needs of the union's membership. Reuther had come to see the Soviet Union as a menacing totalitarian state and the Communist Party in the United States as little more than its agent. One of his first acts after solidifying his control of the UAW in 1947

was to purge the union's staff of anyone with Communist ties. Within
the CIO he pushed hard to expel those unions that had not similarly
purged themselves of Communist influence.[6]

But if his politics resembled Dubinsky's, Reuther's personality was
the polar opposite. Where Dubinsky was an ebullient bon vivant,
Reuther was commonly depicted as something of an abstemious au-
tomaton. A 1948 profile in the *Saturday Evening Post* described him
as a "tensely wired man of almost ascetic personal habits." He did not
drink or smoke or play cards. He worked sixteen-hour days and for
relaxation he liked to read policy analyses. His life was the union. The
Post asserted, "The whole of Reuther's working life revolves around
the labor movement and its projection into the political field—very
little else is discussed in his office or his home." These traits may have
made him a successful union leader, but one gathers that it limited his
appeal on a social level. *Newsweek* referred to him as "impersonal and
machine like." The *Saturday Evening Post*'s reporter, simply asserted,
"He has little sense of humor and less sense of fun." He also defied
the stereotype of the high-living union boss. Keeping his salary relatively low, Reuther lived a frugal lifestyle. He ate lunch at his desk
in the Detroit office, bringing a sandwich from home. When traveling
to Washington, DC, for union business, he favored a Swedish smor-
gasbord restaurant, where he stuck to the extremely economical all-
you-can-eat buffet.[7]

"A formidable crusader," as one journalist described him, Reuther's
ambition was legendary. In 1946, Reuther met with President Harry
Truman and Philip Murray, who at the time was the president of the
CIO. After Reuther left, Truman allegedly turned to warn Murray,
"Phil, that young man is after your job." To which Murray responded,
"No, Mr. President, he really is after *your* job." Even Reuther's appearance seemed to reflect this intensity. At five foot seven, he still had the
build that reflected his past as a high school athlete, muscular with a
deep chest. His broad face was framed by sandy red hair and punctu-
ated by pale blue eyes that "narrow to slits when he is angry."[8]

For a month after the attack, however, those pale blue eyes did little more than stare at the white ceiling of Reuther's hospital room,
his whole upper body encased in a plaster cast and his injured arm

Walter Reuther and President Harry S. Truman. *Harry S. Truman Library*

held up by a system of pulleys. The pain was intense but his doctors were wary of giving him sedatives lest it impede the healing process, and so he slept less than two hours of every twenty-four-hour period. Periodically he was given electric shocks to keep his arm from stiffening. The doctors told him that although they had been able to avoid amputating his arm, he would never regain the use of it. But with the same relentless drive he had devoted to his career, Reuther proved them wrong, squeezing a rubber ball with his withered arm for hours at a time to regain the use of the limb. By the spring of 1949, he had recovered enough to resume his regular union duties.[9]

In the meantime the union had taken precautions to guard Reuther against another attack. His family was relocated to a more easily protected house with bulletproof glass installed in the ground floor windows. A fence was erected, floodlights installed, and two guard dogs acquired. Reuther traveled in an armored car and was constantly accompanied by armed bodyguards. During this period the union staff received over forty permits to carry weapons.[10]

Even with these precautions, the following year an assassin fired

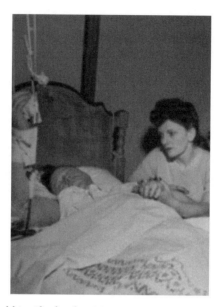

Walter Reuther and his wife after the 1948 assassination attempt. *Walter P. Reuther Library*

a shotgun through the living room window of his brother, Victor Reuther, the UAW's director of education. The attack was like a rerun of the attempted assassination of Walter. The assailant had hidden in the dark, in the bushes outside the window; he fired both barrels of a twelve-gauge shotgun loaded with 00 buckshot. This time the blast hit the victim's head and right shoulder and, though Victor Reuther survived, his surgery required four pints of blood and he lost his right eye.[11]

Six months after that, in December 1949, a bomb containing thirty-nine sticks of dynamite was planted at the UAW headquarters in Detroit, apparently timed to go off when Walter Reuther would be in the building. It was enough dynamite to have leveled the building had the bomb gone off. This time a news reporter received an anonymous tip and the bomb was discovered, unexploded. One of the fuses had burned out, just an inch away from reaching the detonation point.[12]

"Who's After the Reuthers?" *Business Week*'s headline wondered.[13] In the context of the Cold War, initial suspicion centered on the

Communists. *Newsweek*'s analysis was typical in this regard. In a June 1949 article the magazine laid out four groups of potential suspects. These included employers, who may have resented the Reuther's organizing efforts, and the Ku Klux Klan, upset over Reuther's efforts to combat discrimination against African Americans. There was also the possibility that racketeers involved in running numbers gambling in the auto plants were behind the attack. But *Newsweek* concluded that the most likely culprits were the Communists. "The Communists had more reason to hate the Reuther brothers than any of the other groups." [14] *Time*'s story echoed this conclusion, noting, "Detroit Police suspected that the deadly attempts against the Reuthers stemmed from their successful anti-communist crusade within the UAW." [15] On the floor of Congress, a senator from Michigan, Homer Ferguson, repeated this assertion as a statement of fact: "The Communists to be frank are involved in this." [16]

The victims themselves remained uncertain about who was behind it. Walter Reuther told reporters, "It could have been management, a communist, a Fascist, or a screwball. I can't put them in order." [17]

One might have expected the police investigation to provide answers, but this was not the case, despite what was described as "the greatest manhunt in Detroit's history." [18] Several commentators noted a significant gap between the scale of the police response and the quality of their efforts. During one "mammoth dragnet," over four hundred men were brought in for questioning on apparently an almost random basis. Within three days every single one of them had been released. Local authorities appeared to view the intended targets with a measure of suspicion. [19] Detroit's police commissioner insinuated that the victims knew more than they were willing to admit about the origins of the attack, and claimed his force could quickly bring the attackers to justice, "if the Reuther brothers came to Police headquarters and took a lie detector test." The implication was that the assassination attempts had to do with an internal union feud. At the same time, the local authorities indicated their belief that the most fruitful leads in their probe pointed to a communist role in these attacks. Such claims had a tactical benefit. By blaming the attacks on a communist conspiracy, directed possibly by elements outside the country, the Detroit

Police absolved themselves of responsibility for bringing the culprits to justice.[20]

Police incompetence was only part of the problem. A larger barrier to solving the case stemmed from police corruption, which was endemic in Detroit. An organized system of payoffs set up by mobsters kept police from interfering with the city's main gambling rings. A UAW investigator noted that the individual managing those payoffs was located just two blocks from the police headquarters. The lucrative nature of these arrangements provided a powerful incentive for the police to avoid following any leads in the Reuther case that might pull their probe in the direction of local organized crime figures. Moreover, the man directing the Detroit's Police investigation, Sgt. Albert DeLamielleure, had strong ties to the organized crime figure Santo Perrone, who was the most likely culprit behind these attacks. DeLamielleure could misdirect the police investigation and keep Perrone informed on any leads that did develop. Victor Reuther, for instance, recalled that after he told DeLamielleure about a neighbor who had seen the shooter waiting in a car near his home, the potential witness suddenly started getting a series of threatening phone calls.[21]

This was not the first time DeLamielleure had played this type of role. In 1945 and 1946, UAW activists in a local union that represented workers at Briggs Manufacturing Company were ambushed and beaten in a series of attacks. The attacks coincided with the company's decision to grant a lucrative scrap-hauling contract to the gangster Perrone, a contract which apparently compensated Perrone for helping the company to curb the local union's militancy. The police investigation, again led by DeLamielleure, went nowhere. In one instance a weapon left by one of the attackers at the scene of the crime disappeared straight from the police evidence locker. When a grand jury probe was launched into these attacks, DeLamielleure served as the chief investigator for the judge conducting the probe. He used this position to keep the targets of the probe well informed. Witnesses who shared information with DeLamielleure found themselves subjected to threats and violence.[22]

Reuther and other UAW leaders would have seen nothing new in this pattern of local corruption. In 1938, a couple of thugs, apparently

Detroit scrap dealer Santo Perrone testifying at a Kefauver Committee Senate crime investigation hearing, 1951. *Walter P. Reuther Library*

employed by Ford's notorious Service Department, had invaded Reuther's home and beaten him with a blackjack. The Service Department functioned as a kind of private police force that Ford used in the 1920s and 1930s to combat efforts by unions to organize the company's employees. It was run by Harry Bennett, a former boxer who had served in the navy and had begun working for Henry Ford in the 1920s, eventually becoming one of his most trusted aides. Bennett cultivated strong ties with Detroit's organized crime groups and they in turn maintained close ties with the city administration.[23] These links provided Bennett with a supply of strong-arm men for roughing up union activists, and with contacts in law enforcement who could be counted on to sabotage any efforts to prosecute the attackers.

In Reuther's case, Bennett's Service Department had begun tracking his movements in 1938 after he distinguished himself by leading a strike against one of Ford's key suppliers. The two Service Department thugs who invaded Reuther's home had apparently hoped to catch him alone and take him for a ride, but were surprised to find a group of guests gathered there for a birthday party. The presence of the guests probably saved Reuther's life by forcing his assailants to modify their initial plans. One of the party's guests fled the apartment to call for help while another told the gunmen that they would not allow them to seize Reuther. "You're not getting him out of here," the guest said. "You may shoot some of us, but you won't get out yourselves." The thugs settled for attacking Reuther with a blackjack and then quickly fleeing.[24]

The collusive role of the local authorities soon became apparent. It took the police over an hour to respond when they were called to Reuther's home, and the subsequent police investigation went nowhere. Reuther resorted to using union funds to pay off an underworld informant to track down the attackers himself. The two assailants were quickly identified by several witnesses. But the trial, according to Victor Reuther, was a "farce." The prosecutor allowed the defense to pack the jury and appeared intent on sabotaging his own case, offering little opposition to the defendants' absurd claim that the Reuthers had staged the attack themselves.[25]

Later, in testimony before a congressional committee, Walter Reuther said he had learned that the men responsible for the attack had received prior approval from the city's administration: "The night the Ford gangsters broke into my home, and I was told this, there was a deal between the City Hall, the police department, and Harry Bennett, to have Bennett's gangsters bump me off and drop me in the Detroit River."[26]

The strength of the ties between mobsters and Detroit city officials was demonstrated by an independent grand jury probe that delved deep into Detroit's municipal corruption in this era. In 1940 the mayor of Detroit, the chief prosecutor, the superintendent of the city's police force, and the sheriff of Wayne County—where Detroit was located—were all indicted for taking payoff money from gangsters involved in the numbers racket. The indictments also included eighty-nine policemen. So much of the police leadership was involved that, according to a news report, "in some precincts there weren't enough sergeants left unscathed to man the desks and call the rolls."[27]

The scale of such police corruption had clear implications for union officials: they could not count on local authorities to bring mobsters to justice. The secretary-treasurer of the UAW, Emil Mazey, told a congressional committee in 1951 that "violent acts organized by organized criminals and hoodlums against the leadership of our union have not been solved by the law enforcement agencies in our community." They went unsolved because of this persistent pattern of corruption. "We believe that the law-enforcement agencies were not really interested in solving some of the crimes committed against our union because they were being paid off by the organized rackets."[28]

Given their distrust of local authorities, it made sense for the UAW's leadership to turn instead to the Federal Bureau of Investigation. And one might think that the FBI would be eager to take up a case involving efforts to assassinate the head of the nation's largest union. But it wasn't. The longtime director of the Bureau, J. Edgar Hoover, wanted nothing to do with this case. A skilled bureaucrat, Hoover could, when he wished to get involved, always manage to find a federal violation at stake that justified sending in his agents. And, likewise, when he wanted to keep the Bureau out, he would remind the public of the Bureau's narrow jurisdiction and the need to carefully allocate its limited resources. In this instance he chose the latter path. The conservative Hoover was no fan of organized labor, and he viewed Reuther's left-wing past with a baleful eye that made him especially unwilling to involve the Bureau in this case.[29] Hoping to overcome Hoover's reluctance, the UAW dispatched its top lawyers to take the matter up with the attorney general, Tom Clark, who expressed sympathy and promised to make an immediate appeal directly to Hoover. The next day, Clark met with UAW lawyers and told them Hoover had turned him down. One of the UAW lawyers recalled Clark's exact words: "Fellows, Edgar says no. He says he's not going to send the FBI in every time some nigger woman gets raped."[30] A vile indication of Hoover's racism, the FBI director's comment also indicated the Bureau's disinclination to protect a union official, even one with a national profile like Reuther.

The context of the Cold War, however, provided a potent counterargument. Both of the senators from Michigan, Homer Ferguson and

Arthur Vandenberg, told their fellow congressmen that Communists were behind the attacks on Reuther. On that basis they convinced their fellow senators to vote for a resolution urging the FBI to take up the case.[31] The Justice Department adopted similar language. A memo from the assistant attorney general to the director of the FBI in May 1949 asserted, "Basis for federal entry into the investigation lies primarily in the fact that these acts of violence are quite logically suspected to have arisen out of Communist subversive activity in this country."[32] After the bomb was discovered at UAW headquarters in December 1949, the attorney general ordered Hoover to send in the FBI, and Hoover finally relented.[33]

The result was a limited investigation that the Bureau quietly shut down in February 1952 having made no arrests and naming no suspects. Originally, two squads of agents had been assigned to the case, but after eight months, the bulk of the manpower was reassigned. The UAW investigator assigned to liaison with the Bureau was struck by the lack of expertise and lackluster attitude of the agents working on the case.[34] For their part, the FBI's case file indicates that the agents were equally dubious of the union officials. The Bureau came to the conclusion that the bomb planted at the UAW headquarters was a hoax, set up by a couple of Reuther's top aides, who hoped it would pressure the FBI to become involved in the case. The agents dismissed leads pointing toward the organized crime figure Santo Perrone, which had been collected by a task force of UAW investigators and the Michigan State Police. Instead, like the Detroit Police, the FBI concluded the attacks were the result of an internal union feud.[35]

When UAW officials sought to pressure Hoover to commit more resources to the case, they received no support from the attorney general. By 1950, J. Howard McGrath had replaced Tom Clark as the nation's top law enforcement official. He met with UAW officials, including Reuther, in June and told them he would not ask the FBI to give the case greater priority. One of the union officials who was present asserted in a memo, "McGrath's entire attitude was that this case was a matter for the FBI, and that he could not do anything about it." He would not second-guess the Bureau's handling of the case. Nor, apparently, did McGrath view that an attack on the president of the nation's largest union as a matter deserving any special priority. "The fact that he had not even bothered to get a report on the case prior to our arrival seemed to indicate his total lack of concern with the case." In the midst of the Red Scare, the bulk of the FBI's resources were devoted to fighting communism, and the attorney general suggested that Reuther and his aides should see that as a good thing. According to the UAW summary of the meeting, McGrath "contended that by concentrating on various Commie cases, the FBI might break this case through some Commie angle. He said that the Commie lead was the best hope of breaking the case."[36] In this way, the same Cold War context that offered an argument for dragging the Bureau into the case provided an excuse for the FBI to limit its efforts.

From the union's perspective, the FBI's involvement brought mixed results. On the one hand, after the Bureau entered the case, the efforts to kill Reuther came to an end; the FBI's involvement apparently made the gangster Perrone wary of continuing these attacks. But, on the other hand, as one UAW official put it, the local police apparently viewed the arrival of the FBI as an excuse to "sit further down on their fannies than they [already] had, if that was possible."[37] A year and a half later, the FBI closed the case, making it extremely unlikely that anyone would ever be convicted for these attacks. And, in fact, no one ever was.

Reuther's situation was better than most union officials. A prominent national figure, he and his supporters could exert enough pressure to drag a reluctant FBI into the picture, and the Bureau's entrance at least curbed the violence. Other union officials lacking Reuther's national profile faced a bleaker prospect when targeted by organized crime groups. A series of attacks in Chicago demonstrated both the prevalence of this violence on union officials and how little recourse most victims had.

Louis Peick was an official with Chicago Teamsters Local 705, a large local union composed mainly of truck drivers. On June 1, 1950, he was on his way home from work when two men jumped him, beating him with baseball bats. The attack occurred a year after Lurye was murdered in the heart of New York's Garment District, and a year after someone fired a shotgun through Victor Reuther's living room window. Peick's assailants fractured his skull and broke bones in both of his hands. They also shot him; he had bullet wounds in one hand and in his right thigh. The assailants made no move to rob him and it seems clear that, had they wanted to, they could have killed him. The goal instead was to beat him badly, apparently with the intention of leaving him with wounds that would be evident to everyone. The focus on his hands may have been connected to his role as the office manager of Local 705, a post that included oversight of the union's finances. We can only guess at the actual motives because the police never caught the attackers, and when they questioned Peick about the assault he provided no useful information. He told the police that he didn't know the men. And, according to the *Chicago Tribune*'s report, Peick also "knew of no motive for the assault." [38]

This was the first of what would be a long string of attacks in Chicago targeting local Teamster leaders. Two weeks after the assault on Peick, another Local 705 official, Anthony Cerone, was murdered. Cerone and his wife had been leaving their home and preparing to drive to a family event. He had gone around to the driver's side door of his automobile, which was parked on the street outside his home. Just as he went to open the car door he was hit by another vehicle, an Oldsmobile that had been quietly idling a bit farther down the street. The speeding Oldsmobile dragged Cerone's body for seventy feet and then roared away. It was not a conventional hit-and-run. The Oldsmobile's license plate had been stolen off another car two weeks earlier, exactly one day before the attack on Peick. There was one more circumstantial link between the two episodes: according to Peick, the men who attacked him had driven away in an Oldsmobile. [39]

Still, the Chicago Police were dubious that the connections between Peick's attack and the murder of Cerone were anything but coincidental. When the head of the Police labor detail, Captain George Barnes, was called in, he told the press that the department "leaned to the theory that Cerone's death was an accident." [40]

Other attacks followed. Three months after Cerone's death, Stephen Slahor, the president of another Teamsters local, was pulling into his driveway at the end of the day when a car drove up and one of its passengers began firing a gun at him. In early January 1951, someone put a bomb on the back porch of the building where Sam Conino and his family lived. Conino was an official in Teamsters Local 705, the same one in which Peick and Cerone held office. The blast obliterated the porch, cracked the wall of the building, and blew out the windows of the neighboring houses. Conino and his son were sleeping on the building's second floor when the blast occurred, though they were unhurt. Two weeks later, someone ambushed Albert Ceas, another Local 705 official. In what was becoming a familiar pattern, the gunman was waiting near where the union official had parked his car outside his apartment house, and fired several shots just after Ceas had stepped into the car. Ceas suffered two bullet wounds, one in the arm and the other in the back.[41]

Although the initial victims were all leaders in Local 705, as time passed officials in other locals were targeted as well. In early April 1951, someone placed a bomb outside the apartment of John Ryan, the president of Teamsters Local 786, the building materials drivers' local. A month later, another bomb went off at the home of Thomas Haggerty, the secretary-treasurer of the Teamsters Local 753, the Milk Drivers' Union. Two days later another bomb was left on the front porch of E.T. Redmond, a business agent with Teamsters Local 725, the Parcel Delivery Drivers' Union. The home of the secretary-treasurer of the Laundry Drivers' local was bombed in August 1952.[42]

All of the bombing victims told the police the same thing: they had no idea who was behind the attacks and knew of no motive for anyone to attack them. As the *Chicago Tribune* noted, the union officials "have said repeatedly that they are mystified by the attacks." The head of the Chicago Teamsters Joint Council, Ray Schoessling, told the press that none of the victims had been approached in advance with demands by anyone. "We don't know what's behind all of this," Schoessling said.[43]

In all, eight bombings occurred, including a car bomb that injured a Teamsters business agent and two sticks of dynamite set off at the building used as the Teamsters Joint Council headquarters. The bombs caused no deaths, and except for the car bomb, they did not lead to any injuries. The *Tribune* asserted that this type of bombing, in which explosive devices were set to go off at a victim's home with the intent to cause damage but not to kill the home's residents, was a particular mob tactic known as a "pineapple," which "in gang language is a warning." [44]

But three other attacks were fatal, and two of those involved gruesome torture. Anthony Baldino was the victim of the car bomb attack that occurred in October 1951. Two sticks of dynamite wired up to his car's starter left the vehicle demolished and Baldino shaken, but uninjured. A year later, though, he was kidnapped, driven to a remote spot where he was tied up and beaten severely with a metal rod, and then shot through the head. [45] The murder of John Jankovski, a member of Teamsters Local 705 who was preparing to run for union office, followed a similar pattern. He too had been kidnapped, tied up, beaten, and stabbed repeatedly. One wound was bandaged at the site, apparently in order to keep him alive for further torture. Finally, he was shot four times in the head. [46] It may have been significant that out of all the victims of the bombings, Baldino had apparently been the only one to claim that he knew who was behind the attack. The manner of Baldino's death may have been intended as a caution to the other targets not to make similar claims.

The response from local law enforcement was limited, or as the *Chicago Tribune* put it, "perfunctory." In an editorial published in July 1952, two years after this string of attacks had begun, the *Tribune's* editors asserted, "Both the police and the State's Attorney Boyle have made perfunctory investigations. They seem to take the position, however, that if the union officials don't want to complain and cooperate, the war on the union is a private matter, one of no public concern." Indeed the state's attorney had told the press in January 1951 that without a formal complaint from the victims, his office had not begun an investigation, this despite the wide coverage the attacks received in the local press. A half-hour meeting with the head of the Teamsters Joint Council apparently solved that obstacle. "Now we have an official record," Boyle said. "We are going to get busy." [47]

The results were similar to those achieved by the Detroit Police. The investigation made no apparent progress and local law enforcement appeared reluctant to consider the possible role of organized crime. After one shooting attack in January 1951, Chicago's police commissioner asserted that it could not have been a mob attack because only one shooter had been involved and, if it was the mob, "they would not have missed."[48] Instead the police reportedly focused on looking either for a personal motive behind the attack or for an internal union dispute. As the attacks continued, the official police position remained unchanged. In August 1952, the police commissioner was asked if he believed these incidents were part of an effort by the syndicate to take over the Teamsters Union. He responded, "Nobody has given me any idea who or what was behind these bombings."[49] It was a patently disingenuous statement. Speaking off the record a day earlier, other police officials admitted to reporters that the only group capable of waging this kind of campaign of violence was the Chicago Mafia, usually referred to as the Outfit.[50] Still, local law enforcement officials focused their efforts on pursuing other leads. In the process, they tended to treat the victims as possible suspects themselves, calling for the union officials who had been attacked to come in and submit to questioning while wired up to a lie detector. The state prosecutor's only substantive action was to threaten to bring the union officials before a grand jury.[51]

In retrospect everyone involved appears to have been playacting, pretending not to know what was plainly obvious: the attacks were part of an effort by the Outfit to gain more influence over the Chicago Teamsters Union. In January 1951, the *Chicago Tribune* ran an article about how the top Teamster official in Chicago, William Lee, had reported being accosted by three hoodlums in the fall of 1950. They had approached Lee one evening as he was leaving a union meeting and asked him to get into their car, an offer he had unsurprisingly turned down. As he described the encounter to a radio interviewer, "They said they wanted in." The interviewer asked what that meant, and Lee equivocated; according to the newspaper, he said, "He understood that they wanted on the payroll or something of that kind." Lee said that he turned them down, but there were subsequent threatening phone calls.[52] A close confidante and political ally of Chicago mayor Richard Daley, Lee was assigned an around-the-clock detail of police detectives to serve as his bodyguards. He met with the state's attorney and described his encounter.[53] And yet, in the wake of the mob's approach, the police, the prosecutor's office, and even the members of Chicago's Teamsters Joint Council continued to insist that they had no idea who was behind the attacks.

The veil was lifted two years later when the *Chicago Tribune* ran an eight-part series on the mob's growing influence in the city's labor unions. The newspaper devoted a great deal of space to the events of 1950 to 1952. A *Tribune* reporter interviewed Lee, who described his encounter with the gangsters in the fall of 1950 in more detail, identifying by name two of the men who approached him. Both of them were well-known members of the Outfit. One, Vincent Inserro, known as "the Saint," had gained notoriety in 1951 as one of the chief suspects in an attack on a suburban Chicago resident, Robert Niemeyer, who had complained about the proliferation of illegal gambling in his community. The incident had received coverage in *Life* magazine because of its frightening brutality. The assailants had kidnapped Niemeyer and then beat him with baseball bats, methodically working down from his neck to break every major bone in his body, while avoiding his head, so that he would remain conscious throughout the ordeal.[54]

Just as the newspaper could easily identify who had approached Lee two years after these events occurred, the *Tribune* also named the Outfit figure who had orchestrated these attacks: Joseph Glimco. The paper quoted an unnamed Teamster official who told them, "All our troubles came from Glimco." Long a prominent figure in Chicago's produce market, where he allegedly collected protection payments from the fruit and vegetable merchants, Glimco had become an official in Teamsters Local 703, whose members worked in that market. In the early 1950s, he was apparently moving to expand his influence in the Teamsters Joint Council. Teamster officials told the *Tribune* that by early 1953 Glimco controlled the votes of twelve locals in the Joint Council, and thus could sway about a quarter of the ballots cast in the Council's elections.[55]

But in 1951 and 1952, nobody, especially the officials in the Teamsters locals that were being targeted, was willing to talk publicly about this. The Chicago Police could assert that the Teamster leaders were stonewalling them, because clearly they were. The *Tribune* reported how one of the Joint Council officials "scoffed at reports that syndicate gunmen are assailing the [Teamster] leaders." Another Teamsters official asserted, "We do not think that the syndicate is responsible. If we did, we would be talking about it."[56]

And yet, obviously they did know the mob was responsible, so why didn't these Teamster officials cooperate with Chicago law enforcement officials? The answer is almost certainly because they did not trust those officials. They would have good reason to believe that whatever information they provided to the prosecutor's office would almost immediately be shared with the Outfit. Chicago Police captain Daniel Gilbert, the longtime chief investigator for the State's Attorney's Office, had a close relationship with the Chicago Outfit. He was on the mob's payroll, a fact made public by a *Chicago Tribune* exposé in 1941. One of his subordinates on the police force later described how Gilbert had consistently protected Outfit members who were arrested. He "either speedily released them, or, if the newspapers played them up too big, fixed their court cases."[57]

One example of how Gilbert could fix a case occurred in 1940. A leader in the Bartenders Union, George McLane, had been pushed out of office by the Outfit. In response, he had gone to the press and put pressure on the State's Attorney's Office to bring charges against the prominent gang leaders who were involved. McLane later told the FBI how hours before he was to testify at the trial, Gilbert had threatened him on behalf of the Outfit. Gilbert called McLane into his office and warned him that if he did testify the Outfit would abduct his wife, and each day, cut off one of her body parts and send it to him. Taking the threat seriously, McLane had chosen not to testify.[58] Ten years later, Teamster officials would assume that providing information to this same prosecutor's office would not lead to an effective prosecution. Instead the union official who had offered this information would be targeted for retaliation—not a warning, but the kind of abduction and torture that the Outfit had meted out to other victims.

Unlike the UAW president, Walter Reuther, these Teamster officials were not national figures who could hope to rally an intervention by the federal government. There were no meetings with the attorney general to pressure the FBI into this case. No Senate resolutions occurred. There were no articles in *Time* or *Newsweek*.

The *Chicago Tribune* covered the story, but the newspaper's editorial board was decidedly unsympathetic to the union officials, whom they depicted as no different than gangsters. As one editorial explained, "Unions are peculiarly vulnerable to such hazards because many of them are run by labor bosses with a vested interest in spoliation of the rank and file. It is natural gangsters should see no distinction between themselves and the union bosses when both have the same outlook and interest." The current violence directed at these union officials was unsurprising, according to the *Tribune*, given the fact that union leaders themselves had long encouraged their members to practice "methods of violence" to achieve their own selfish ends. Taking on a somewhat biblical tone, the *Tribune* asserted, "Violence invites violence: He who lives by the sword perishes by the sword. What has been happening in the Teamsters Union is precisely what is to be expected." In other words, they got what they deserved.[59]

The liberal magazine the *New Republic* echoed this sentiment. It was the only national news magazine to cover the attacks on the Chicago Teamsters leaders, printing one article on the attacks in a September 1951 issue. The article's author, Albert Votaw, listed the series of shootings and bombings that had occurred by the summer of 1951. He concluded that the attacks probably signified a move by organized crime to gain control over the Chicago Teamsters. But like the editors at the *Tribune*, Votaw was not sympathetic. In the article's conclusion he cited the Teamsters' history of strike violence, going as far back as a big strike in 1905, and also the union's "habit of selling co-operation," an apparent reference to closed-shop contracts that protected anti-competitive cartel arrangements in local construction trades and other similar industries. Both tendencies, Votaw asserted, explained why the union was "particularly vulnerable to hoodlum infiltration." Votaw ended his piece with a modern update of the *Tribune*'s homily. "As a friend of mine remarked, apropos of these attacks," Votaw wrote, "'It couldn't have happened to a better bunch of guys.'"[60]

The result was that Chicago Teamster officials had limited options. There would be no intervention by national authorities, no announcement of an FBI probe that might curb the attacks, the way it had in Detroit. As local union officials, whose organizations had limited resources, the Chicago Teamsters could not take the same protective measures that the Auto Workers had done to safeguard its national president, Reuther. No teams of bodyguards were available for unlimited periods of time. By 1952, Reuther's family had been relocated to a secluded rural homestead, surrounded by a ten-foot steel fence with a gatehouse staffed by security guards who were constantly present.[61] These were not arrangements that the various Teamster locals could provide for their officials. Instead, Chicago Teamster officials would have to continue to live in the same residences that had been periodically bombed, and face the real threat that gunmen were waiting for them when they left to go to work in the morning, or when they came home in the evening.

Given these circumstances they would have to make some kind of accommodation with the Outfit. The precise nature of such an accommodation is unknown, but we can get some sense of it by looking at the case of Harold Gibbons, a Teamsters official working in St. Louis in this same era.

The son of a Pennsylvania coal miner, Gibbons had moved to Chicago as a young man, taken courses at the University of Chicago, and caught the attention of several well-placed political progressives, including the future U.S. senator Paul Douglas. In 1933, he became involved in a New Deal–supported worker education program, and then began organizing for the American Federation of Teachers. He eventually ended up in St. Louis, where he organized a union composed of warehouse workers as part of a CIO affiliate. He brought the local over to the Teamsters Union in 1949. A tall man, Gibbons was described by those who knew him then as "almost stately looking" and extremely articulate, with what his recent biographer, Robert Bussel, notes was "formidable presence and personality." Organizing unskilled workers, many of them minorities and women, in the face of stiff employer resistance, Gibbons embraced an expansive vision for organized labor. Unions, he believed, should spearhead political and economic changes that met the needs of workers, their families, and their larger communities. To do this, Gibbons experimented with programs and policies that he hoped would mobilize the union's rank and file. As Bussel explains, Gibbons and his closest union colleague,

Harold Gibbons joins Martin Luther King Jr. and Jimmy Hoffa at the memorial service for civil rights activist Viola Liuzzo. *Bowen Archives*

Ernest Calloway, "sought to create a community bargaining table where empowered worker-citizens negotiated with St. Louis's economic and political elites to ensure an equitable distribution of social resources."[62] The union movement they built in St. Louis became a champion of the civil rights movement.

But in the process of building this movement, Gibbons encountered the same kinds of obstacles and dangers that his fellow union leaders were meeting in places like New York City, Detroit, and Chicago. In early 1952, messengers from one of the city's mob bosses, Buster Wortman, told Gibbons that he must put some of the mob's men on his local union's payroll. Wortman already dominated several unions in the St. Louis construction and trucking industry, and this was apparently the first step in a move to play a similar role in the union that Gibbons had built in the warehouse industry. The threat of violence that lay behind Wortman's demand was not something Gibbons could easily dismiss. In September 1950, the home of a St. Louis Carpenters Union official had been bombed. In 1952, the same year

Gibbons received this ultimatum, two officials in the city's Laborers' Union were murdered. Gibbons went to the St. Louis Police for protection and was put off. His request for a gun permit was stalled by the same authorities. He was receiving death threats over the phone and he was genuinely afraid for his life, with good reason. Having nowhere else to turn, Gibbons reached out to a fellow Teamster official who he was told could help him out. This was James R. Hoffa, then a Teamster vice president based in Detroit, but also someone who had developed a relationship with the Chicago Outfit. Hoffa used that relationship, and his influence with the national leadership of the Teamsters Union, to take the necessary steps to protect Gibbons.[63]

The idealistic St. Louis union leader needed to make an accommodation. Organized crime in the person of Buster Wortman presented Gibbons with a real threat, and as he looked around in 1952 he would have seen plenty of evidence that gangsters could make good on those threats with impunity. The violent legacy of organized labor's battles on the picket lines left its leaders in the paradoxical position of having power but no real legitimate status in American society, certainly not the status of their counterparts in business. The *New Republic* had signaled this lack of legitimacy by titling its piece on the wave of attacks on the Chicago Teamsters "Gangs and Goons"; for all his liberal connections and his aspirations for his union, Gibbons was lumped into the same category. Faced with a threat from a gangster, he was nothing better than a goon. The protection he needed was not going to come from the state. The fact that he and others like him had to look elsewhere for help was part of the reason why labor racketeering proliferated in this era in the pockets of urban America where organized crime had come to wield influence.

3

THE WORKINGS OF RACKETEERING:
BLOOD AND PROFIT

With offices at the very heart of the Garment District's so-called Chinatown, Rosebelle Frocks was located on the ninth floor of a loft building at 261 West Thirty-Fifth Street—just down the street from the site of William Lurye's attack. From cluttered work spaces in the buildings that lined this street, jobbers such as Rosebelle sent out pre-cut fabric pieces to non-union contractors, whose workers assembled the low-price dresses, while mob-connected trucking firms facilitated the process. On May 9, 1949, Rosebelle's managing partner, Leo Greenberg, was out of town dealing with a contractor in Philadelphia. On the fifth floor of the same building, the proprietor of another non-union dress shop and Greenberg's associate, Joseph Ross, recalled seeing an ambulance make its way down the crowded street that day, followed by a "cop's car [that] was trying to get through and they made a lot of noise." [1] One of Ross's employees came up and told everyone about seeing where Lurye had fallen on the sidewalk and how "there was a lot of blood in front of 224 [West Thirty-Fifth Street]."

Neither Greenberg nor Ross had taken part in the attack on Lurye, but just the same they were involved in the crime. Both men had been running their shops as non-union operations and had been targeted by Garment Workers' Union organizers, including Lurye. Both had turned to the same mob-affiliated garment trucker for protection from the union in return for payments. The trucker had a partner, Benedicto

Macri, a known gangster. In the weeks before the attack, Ross cut a series of checks to the trucker, and Rosebelle's Greenberg made Macri a partner in his firm, offering 25 percent of the business's profits in exchange for protection from the union. When Lurye increased pressure on Rosebelle by slashing a roomful of the firm's dresses, destroying inventory and delivering a painful economic wound to the firm, this partnership arrangement made it Macri's job to respond. A couple of days later, he did. Macri was one of the two men who stabbed Lurye to death in the phone booth that afternoon of May 9.[2]

Both Ross and Greenberg were small businessmen operating in the Garment District, cutting corners and making deals with shady characters that would give their shops an edge in this brutally competitive industry. In doing so they were adhering to pragmatic norms that were shared by their fellow dressmakers, and in a larger sense by most businessmen. That gap between how people operating within a particular setting understood what is appropriate—what they needed to do to succeed—and the more abstract notions of right and wrong has been described by legal scholar W. Michael Reisman as a conflict between "operational codes" and "mythic norms." Corruption proliferates not because individuals stop caring about the difference between right and wrong, but because they observe a different, real-world standard of behavior for people in their situation. In Reisman's terminology, they are adhering to an "operational code" understood, and adhered to, by the other business people in their sector.[3] Corruption in the form of labor racketeering involved businessmen who partnered with organized crime figures to gain a competitive advantage that would help their businesses succeed. They did so because, as they looked around, they saw many other businessmen adopting the same tactics.

This is the often-forgotten reality of many of the industrial sectors that existed across urban America in this period. Relatively small-scale businesses serving local markets frequently colluded to control competition by fixing prices or assigning customers; the latter practice involved illegal agreements barring one business from taking on customers who "belonged" to another business. Organized crime groups often helped to coordinate and enforce such arrangements. Businessmen in industries that interacted with municipal and state government, either through public contracts or regulation, made their way in a climate of endemic corruption. Construction, local trucking, produce, and sanitation sectors were prominent examples of this pattern. In these business sectors, bribery, kickbacks, and pay-to-play arrangements were accepted elements in the commercial landscape. Successful entrepreneurs learned how to navigate their way through this corrupt topography, or they found another way to make a living. All too often, violence and intimidation were part and parcel of doing business. What has survived in the popular memory is the labor movement's association with the mob, but this was simply one part of a much larger picture in this era.

In the Garment District, organized crime figures were businessmen and—sometimes—union officials who were entrenched in the economic, political, and even cultural landscape of this particular business sector. As gangsters they had a reputation for violence, or for being able to call on others to commit violence for them. But in most other ways, they didn't stand out. They came from the same neighborhoods, shared the same bonds of ethnicity as the businessmen who operated in the garment industry. Even the most notorious of them tended to operate out of business offices, located in the heart of the district, and they frequented the same neighborhood hangouts. They were not a strange and alien presence within the District. Rather, they were Garment District fixtures with deeply embedded functions within this world, and labor racketeering was one of those functions. Reformers and investigators would later depict labor racketeering as an insidious invasion, invoking the same tropes used to depict communist infiltration, the other great Cold War scourge. In fact, it was anything but—and that is what made racketeering such an intractable problem.

The garment industry of the 1940s and 1950s was an industry of small shops operated by immigrant businessmen and their grown children, all of them scrambling to keep their businesses afloat. The business attracted immigrants because a relatively small initial investment might bring big returns. The *New York Herald Tribune* reported in 1958 that an initial investment of $50,000 and a winning dress style could earn a dressmaker as much as $2 million in sales.[4] It was an industry where competition was so keen that every year about 15 percent of the firms failed.[5] Leonard Bernstein entered this industry in the 1950s, working in his family's business; later, he published short stories based on his experiences. He recalled the excitement and the potential for success that drew entrepreneurs. But, as Bernstein knew from personal experience, the Garment District was also a "place of struggle and worry. For each manufacturer who guesses the season's hot style, there are a hundred who guess it too early or too late."[6]

Getting started was relatively easy, partly because the garment industry divided up the dress manufacturing process. Jobbers designed dresses, created the requisite patterns, and arranged to have fabric pieces cut to match those patterns. But the actual dress construction took place in small manufacturing plants, operated by contractors. Thus to open his business, a jobber needed only a dress design and enough credit to buy some fabric that could be cut into pieces, then shipped to a contractor who would assemble the dresses, press them, and ship them back to the jobber on hangers, ready to be sold to a retailer. The jobber's overhead and staffing needs were therefore quite limited. Such a firm, Young Tempo, opened in 1951 and secured a loft space on the eleventh floor of a building at 1375 Broadway, eventually becoming one of the most successful jobbers operating in New York. The three managing partners had worked in the garment industry for years and they divided up the tasks three ways: sales, design and production, shipping and purchasing. Their staff consisted of a dressmaker who put together the sample dresses, a couple of cutters, two or three clerical workers, and four shipping clerks.[7]

The contractors who put these dresses together might buy forty or fifty sewing machines and some presses on credit, then set up their shop in an industrial loft space on one of the side streets in the Garment District, or out in Brooklyn, Queens, or the Bronx. Or they would move farther out, to small towns in Pennsylvania or Connecticut, where they would locate in vacant storefronts or even garages. Jack Needelman put up $12,000 in the early 1950s to open a contracting plant in a loft on West Thirty-Seventh Street with some forty-five machines. An immigrant from Romania, Needelman had worked for years as a garment presser, then tried a contracting partnership that failed before he found success on West Thirty-Seventh Street. By 1958 he employed 120 people, including 76 sewing machine operators. From a crowded office in a corner of the loft, Needelman kept a constant eye on his bottom line. "Rock-bottom I ship out 1,000 dresses a week," he explained to a newspaper reporter. "Just to cover my expenses, I got to ship 3,000 a week. After that I start making money." The goal was to keep a steady supply of work coming into the shop, and in the slack season that meant Needelman hustled to find orders. "When things are slow with my jobber, I look around outside my jobber. My girls don't come in to play. They come in to make money and they're my responsibility." [8]

This was a small-scale version of clear-cut capitalism. The contractor was a fixture in the life of the shop, maintaining a personal relationship with his workers and constituting a physical presence on the factory floor for at least part of every day. He was keenly aware of each step of the production process, stepping in to kibitz on details as mundane as how the dress lapels were pressed or whether the biased seams hung well. An anthropologist studying a Garment District dress shop in 1947 compared the contractor in some ways to the old-style padrone. But he also remarked on the contractor's "constant preoccupation with business conditions," as he fretted over keeping his costs down and bringing in enough business to maintain his shop. Most days, the contractor's lunch hour and part of the afternoon involved touching base with his jobber and networking with other jobbers in a constant search for possible work. [9]

Bill Cherkes remembered running such a shop in Pennsylvania and how he and his fellow contractors saved money by taking on as many roles as they could. Speaking of the contractor, Cherkes explained, "He was the personnel man, he was the bookkeeper, he was the equipment buyer, he was everything. . . . When you're a plant owner like myself [it means] that you're everything." A contractor stuck around after his staff left and saved money by doing his own sorting and packing, or he operated the blind stitching machine himself rather than hire someone else to do it. He functioned as his own personnel manager, taking on the role of a confidant for the women who labored at his sewing machines. "And so when Susie wants to talk to you about getting beat up last night because her husband got drunk, you have to listen to her, you know. Or, when Susie wants to talk to you about her kid not having good grades in school, you listen to it because that's part of being a personnel manager." You did it because if it was a "plant employing fifty, sixty people, there's no money for all these different individual jobs." And so, they "become your job." [10]

Cherkes had been brought into the business by his father, a Russian Jewish immigrant, who had been a union official, then set up shop as a contractor in the 1940s. As Cherkes recalled it, his fellow businessmen were almost uniformly immigrants, Italians or east European Jews. "I know when I came into the industry as a young kid to learn the industry you had to speak either Jewish [Yiddish] or Italian." When these men spoke English, they did so with an accent. From Cherkes's perspective that accent, and the shared ethnic identity that it signified, established mutual bonds of trust among these businessmen. "They understood that if you had an accent, you came from someplace and you were looking for the same the same thing they were looking for." Having grown up in the United States and served a brief stint in the military, Cherkes found himself an outsider in this world. "When I got here in the 1950s, I had a problem because I had no accent. I was suspect because I had no accent." And so, to fit in, he consciously developed an accent. [11]

Garment manufacturing was a world of hard bargaining, where businessmen found themselves adopting practices that violated society's standard notions of right and wrong—the "mythic norms." In one of Bernstein's short stories, a garment industry insider explains this tension to a relative who is considering getting into the family business. "Our position," the narrator asserts, is "to make a buck in the fastest way and within the boundaries of the law, as much as possible." Later, the narrator refers to the gap between society's established norms and the practical approach he has to take in business. "There are a whole lot of principles that I believe in, and some of them don't get practiced all the time." The reason they didn't was because the garment industry was "a jungle." "Everything is a fight. We fight for orders, we fight for prices from our suppliers. We cheat, we lie, we handel [a Yiddish term for hard bargaining]." [12] In other stories

Bernstein describes the mechanics of how jobbers produced cheaper knockoff versions of other firms' dress designs, surreptitiously buying dresses at nearby department stores in order to copy them, then using cheaper materials and scaling down the details. Some firms found ways to save fabric—and money—by slightly shrinking the garment's pattern, producing dresses that were just a bit smaller than their stated size. This was called "shrinking the marker." "There isn't a cutter in the United States who doesn't know about shrinking a marker and some of them know too much about it." [13]

Bernstein's point was not that every garment shop resorted to such tactics all the time, but that many found themselves having to cut these kinds of corners when they felt that the survival of their business depended on it. In more academic terms, this was an "operational code," a standard of behavior that was accepted within the garment industry, although it contradicted standard notions of right and wrong. The *New York Herald Tribune* expressed the same idea in the form of a headline in 1958, "Dress Trade Is 'The Jungle' Ethically: Industry Here Is Economically Prosperous and Morally Bankrupt." [14]

The relationship between these businessmen and the union was shaped by informal understandings that belied the strict, formal language of the collective bargaining contracts. These understandings informed a similar kind of operational code of right and wrong that shaped businessmen's behavior. Hoping to stabilize the industry, the International Ladies' Garment Workers' Union had developed contract language that linked each jobber to a specific set of contractors. Contractors were registered to a jobber, who could not send work to other contractors unless he could demonstrate to the union that his existing contractors were overwhelmed, or demonstrably incompetent. This ostensibly guaranteed a contractor a steady supply of orders, allowing him to keep his workers (the union members) steadily employed. Competition between these contractors was further limited because the union set up a standard formula regulating how much jobbers had to pay their contractors. By the late 1930s, the union had developed a system for calculating the labor cost of every new dress design according to a preset schedule of the time and skill involved in each possible dress feature. Every time a jobber came up with a new dress design, he would submit it to a union price-adjusting process, which would determine the cost of making the dress. This price-adjustment procedure also took into account the price of the dress the jobber was selling to the stores that were his customers. Higher-priced dresses were assigned higher labor costs. The union required jobbers to pay their contractors a fixed rate of 30 percent above the labor cost of making a dress, ensuring that 30 percent as a standard dependable profit. This price-setting procedure was part of a broader system of contractual rules designed to bring order to the garment industry and to provide union members with a stable and fair working environment.[15]

On paper these union contracts supposedly created a collective bargaining rule of law, but in practice an informal, arbitrary system held sway. Jobbers could and did find ways to manipulate the union's price-setting procedures. Certain aspects of labor costs were by their very nature debatable. As one jobber told the FBI in 1959, "the settling of prices" included "haggling and discussion over what the particular price a [specific] factor in the manufacturing of a garment should be."[16] Some jobbers did better in these negotiations than others, and some union officials were more accommodating than others. Jobbers sometimes also provided the union with a selling price for their dresses that was lower than what they actually sold for, claiming they sold a dress for nine dollars, for instance, when in fact it sold for eleven dollars. This manipulation reduced the union's determination of its labor costs, and thus lowered what the jobber had to pay his contractors. The union had accountants assigned to check the jobbers' books to make sure they didn't do this, but some jobbers kept two different sets of books to avoid getting caught. For their part, contractors who hoped to get steady work from a jobber learned to take less than the 30 percent above cost that the union contract required. A contractor who insisted on the full 30 percent would find that his jobber would start sending the bulk of his work to his other contractors.[17]

When, later in the 1950s, the FBI conducted an anti-racketeering investigation in the garment industry, both contractors and jobbers depicted the union's system of regulation as inherently arbitrary. The union's contracts regulated so many features of the production process

and were so stiff in their requirements that as a practical matter garment makers found themselves routinely in violation and thus subject
to a range of punishing fines. As one jobber put it, "The I.L.G. contracts were written so that they must be violated." [18] This gave the union
a hammer to wield over every employer. "The union can put anyone
out of business if they so desire," one employer explained. "They can
do this merely by insisting on enforcement of the contract which everyone is required to sign." A congressional investigator's report from
1958 recounted one jobber's explanation of the arbitrary system that
resulted. He said that "historically the International Ladies Garment
Workers' Union had insisted on a stiff contract with employers, but
they had made oral 'adjustments' in the actual enforcement of these
contracts. It was a very confusing process since these adjustments varied from one company to another and in fact from one [union] official
to another so that actually there was no contract at all." [19] The union
itself acknowledged the vast discretionary power its officials wielded
when it contested an effort begun in 1959 by union business agents
seeking to form their own union. Top ILG officials described how
business agents charged with enforcing the contract had the choice
of following either a "hard policy" of "invoking the union contract
at every opportunity" or a "soft policy" of accommodation. The ILG
argued that because these local union business agents had authority to
make or break the businesses they dealt with, they were clearly super-
visory employees and thus ineligible for union representation. [20]

Arbitrary power fostered corruption. Officially, employers questioned by the FBI denied making any payments to any union officials,
carefully distancing themselves from possible legal violations. Off the
record, however, and assured that they would not be required to testify
on the matter, some garment makers were more forthright. One contractor located outside Philadelphia described how he started out giving dresses two or three times a year to the ILG business agent he dealt
with. Then he began making a cash payment of $100 to $150 a year
around Christmas time, the equivalent today of roughly $1,200. This
contractor portrayed such payments as common. They were, he told
an FBI agent, a "general thing in the dress business and he takes the attitude [that] 'when in Rome, do as the Romans do.'" The money wasn't

intended as a payoff for a particular violation, but rather as incentive for the union business agent to use his discretionary power in ways that would help the contractor prosper and "avoid causing the employer a lot of trouble." From his point of view, although the payment might be illegal, it fit well within the actual standards of behavior that guided businessmen like him. According to the FBI's report, he compared this payment to another type commonly made by employers. It was "similar to a businessman giving a gift to a policeman for certain privileges [that] the officer is able to grant." [21]

For the businessmen in the Garment District, operating non-union brought several advantages, including an escape from the sometimes arbitrary power of the union officials. For jobbers, it gave them the freedom to use whatever contractors they wanted, to switch them at will, and to negotiate their own deals with these contractors. Contractors gained stronger control over their workforce, and the freedom to make managerial decisions. Employers operating non-union might choose to save money by offering their workers lower wages; or, in the interest of keeping good workers, they might not. But they would definitely save money by avoiding having to contribute to the union's pension and welfare funds, which added another 10 percent to a firm's payroll on top of wages. In the tightly competitive business of producing lower-priced dresses, where cost mattered far more than design, this kind of labor cost advantage could prove pivotal. [22]

In order to operate non-union, dress firms had to overcome certain obstacles. They had to avoid detection by the union, or if that failed, they had to get deliveries of dresses past the union's picket lines. Doing so meant keeping a relatively low profile, so as to avoid union organizers who would be on the lookout for firms sending out cut garments or, for the small factories, sewing those pieces into finished dresses. But jobbers and contractors also needed ways to connect with each other. Jobbers needed to locate non-union contractors willing to make their dresses and, especially during the busy season of the first half of the year, a jobber might be quite desperate to get enough contractors to complete a big order. A government wiretap in 1948 caught a jobber telling someone on the phone about this kind of dilemma as he searched for contractors. "You know I'm cutting a lot of stuff [fabric] and I want to get it out before July 4th. I don't want to get stuck with it." For their part, contractors needed work, and they especially hoped for steady work to keep their machines busy during the second half of the year, the garment industry's slack period.[23]

This is where the labor racketeer came into the picture, although the actual point of contact was often anything but dramatic or ominous. Contractors were frequently approached by garment truckers, whose daily routes gave them a sense of the jobbers with unfinished work and the contractors with idle machines. A contractor in Union City, New Jersey, told the FBI how, after he opened his business in 1949, he was looking for orders and one day a driver for Roxy Trucking stopped by and offered to give him a batch of cut garments from a jobber in New York that he could finish. If he agreed to take the order then all he had to do was sign the trucker's business card, which, as the FBI report put it, signaled that "from that point on Roxy would be his trucker." The freight charges paid by the contractor became, in effect, commission payments for the trucker's role in connecting him up with jobbers. A trucker would also take a commission from the jobber. These fees in total would range from three to fifteen cents per dress. This kind of business was so lucrative that sometimes trucking companies provided contractors with their initial financing and then sent enough work their way to keep their machines occupied. In such cases, inflated freight charges would also cover the initial financing provided by the trucker. The trucking firms engaged in this kind of activity had mob connections; typically an organized crime figure had some form of ownership stake in the trucking company. This had been the case, for instance, with the trucker who serviced Rosebelle Frocks, the company that Lurye had been trying to organize for the ILG.[24]

At other times, contractors might take on a mobster as an additional partner and gain immunity from union organizing, as well as a steady stream of work from mob-connected jobbers. One contractor described to the FBI the way the arrangement was framed: he was "offered continuing contracts with no union organizing [in return] for a piece of the business."[25] William Failla of Scranton Frocks, a small contracting shop in Pennsylvania, told the FBI that he had brought

Joseph Riccobono, Gambino crime family. *New York State Archives*

Joseph Riccobono in as a partner in 1954. "Riccobono's job was to get work" for Failla's firm, the FBI report explained. Over the next twenty-seven months, Failla paid Riccobono $22,350 of his company's profits—the contractor assured the FBI that he was well satisfied with the arrangement. "According to Failla, Riccobono put him on his feet when he was on the verge of going out of business."[26] It turned out that Riccobono was also a high-ranking member of the Gambino crime family; his arrest at the Apalachin Mafia conference in November 1957 brought him a measure of notoriety.[27]

We can discount Failla's claims to the FBI that "he did not know Riccobono's background." But it is also true Failla might well have perceived the tall, slightly built, sixty-two-year-old Riccobono as something quite different from the stereotypical depiction of a gangster. Beyond the shared bonds of Italian ethnicity, both Failla and Riccobono were garment industry insiders. Riccobono had been working in the Garment District as far back as the early 1930s. In 1937 he was indicted for acting as a bagman for more prominent garment mobsters, but the charge resulted in a suspended sentence. Besides a 1930 arrest for carrying a concealed weapon, it was Riccobono's only criminal record. Investigators looking into his activities in the mid-1950s found him operating two dress-contracting shops in Brooklyn and living in a modest, 1,900-square-foot, ranch-style house in suburban Staten Island.[28]

At other times, businessmen dealt with lower-level go-betweens, drawing on contacts that were no more nefarious than knowing someone who knew someone who could help you out with a problem. Leo Kleinman and Joseph Mishkin operated Judy Lee Dance Frocks as a non-union jobber and for several years their trucker, Sid Zucker, had set them up with a steady supply of contractors. They paid him a commission of five cents a dress, and they understood that on the other end the contractors paid a three cent per dress commission. Sid the trucker also provided them with protection from the union. When this trucker retired, they were put in touch with a Kevin Morrison, who promised to provide similar services for a straight-up fifty dollars a week fee. Another jobber, Manny Mittman, told the District Attorney's Office that he learned about Morrison's services from a previous partnership Mittman had had in the Garment District. His partner in that business had introduced Morrison to him as someone who could help him operate non-union. These businessmen were told that if the union did show up at their shop, they should say they were being taken care of by Morrison. And it worked. When a union official visited Mittman's shop and threatened to call a strike, Mittman mentioned Morrison's name and the union official left him alone.[29]

Neither jobber knew exactly who Morrison was, or how his connections worked, nor does it seem likely that they really wanted to know. But even if they did want to know, as one businessman told the FBI, "you don't ask questions of fellows like that."[30] Instead, each week they took fifty dollars out of their firms' "travelling expenses" account and handed it to Morrison when he showed up, satisfied with the results they were getting.[31] Both Morrison and his predecessor, Zucker, were basically nobodies; neither man's name appears in thousands of pages of FBI files on garment industry rackets, or in any of the many organized crime compendiums. They were the low-level collectors that a businessman dealt with in what was a fairly prosaic transaction. There were several individuals in the Garment District who played roles similar to Morrison, collecting money from garment firms on behalf of more prominent gangsters and thus insulating those mob figures from possible prosecution.[32]

Bigger firms, it appears, made direct connections with one of the more prominent gangsters in the Garment District. Young Tempo, for instance, had an arrangement with John Dioguardi, better known by his nickname, Johnny Dio. One of the firm's partners told the FBI how at their initial meetings in 1951, when they were planning to launch the firm, the other two partners "had pointed out the possibilities of labor arrangements at the beginning of Young Tempo, Inc., and indicated that they could arrange to operate non-union if they paid off the right people."[33] The Justice Department later charged that the firm had paid Dioguardi $10,000 annually to operate non-union, funneling the money out of the company through a variety of mechanisms.[34]

These payments gave mobsters such as Dioguardi a kind of ownership stake in the companies that used their connections. To take one detailed example, after pickets showed up outside Quality Fashions' production plant in 1954, the company began making monthly payments to Dioguardi in return for his help in allowing the business to continue to operate non-union. The bookkeeper later described to the FBI how these payments were based on a "definite percentage of the prior month's net sales" and then charged out on the company's books as entertainment expenses. Each month when she wrote the check for this protection, she would "attach to the checks statements of the prior month's net sales and the computation made to arrive at the face amounts of the checks." The company's owner cashed these checks and then handed over the money along with a copy of the statement to a man who worked for Dioguardi. The bookkeeper recalled that she had warned the company's owner about possible legal repercussions from getting involved with gangsters like Dioguardi. "Things work differently now," the owner responded. "They have perfected operations." An FBI report explains, "She interpreted this to mean that racketeers' activities are harder to discern than they had been since they now operate under apparently legitimate fronts."[35]

By the time the owners of Quality Fashions had reached out to him, Dioguardi was a well-established Garment District insider who had been a part of the scene since the early 1930s. Although he had not been directly involved in the attack on the ILG organizer Lurye, the extensive police investigation of Lurye's murder had uncovered that one of the attackers had previously worked for Dioguardi, guarding a craps game that the gangster ran out on the New Jersey–Pennsylvania border. Not the most powerful of the Garment District's mob figures, Dioguardi was nevertheless one the most notorious gangsters of his era. He embodied the combination of polished, manly good looks with a reputation for rage and brutality that has come to exemplify our ideas of the typical organized crime figure. This was not simply a coincidence. When Lee J. Cobb played the notorious gangster Johnny Friendly in the iconic 1954 movie *On the Waterfront*, he helped to cement a lasting gangster stereotype. Cobb based his depiction of that character on Dioguardi, who had received a great deal of news coverage for his labor racketeering activities in the early 1950s.

Dioguardi's parents were Italian immigrants who had settled in New York's Lower East Side on Forsyth Street. John was the oldest of their three sons. After attending a local grammar school, he spent a year and a half at Stuyvesant High School before he dropped out to help his father, who drove a yeast delivery truck. By the age of seventeen he was working with his uncle, James Plumeri. It was at this point that he became involved in the Garment District rackets.[36]

Plumeri and another man, Dominick Didato, had taken over the Five Boroughs Truckmen's Association in lower Manhattan. They located their organization in the same office building as a powerful and corrupt Tammany district leader, Albert Marinelli. Their ties to that leader apparently gave them a measure of immunity from arrest or prosecution as they set about pressuring local trucking companies into joining their organization. The association functioned as a trucking cartel, assigning customers to particular firms and, in return for the group's membership fees, controlling competition by regulating hauling rates. The teenaged Dioguardi was one of the group's enforcers, pushing reluctant operators into the association and policing the cartel's allocation of customers. In 1933, for instance, when the Dependable Transport Company refused to give up a new customer the firm had acquired, the owner's brother was beaten by thugs wielding ax handles. In other cases, recalcitrant trucking operators found

James Plumeri (top) and John Dioguardi. *New York City Municipal Archives*

emery placed in their truck engines or had stink bombs tossed into their business offices.[37]

According to court testimony, in 1932 a forthright, still-teenaged Dioguardi simply told one trucker, "If you don't give up the account, we'll wreck your trucks and put you out of business." When police arrested Dioguardi the next day outside this same trucker's offices, they found a beer bottle filled with emery in his car. Despite such apparently damning evidence, he won an acquittal when the case came to trial, suggesting that the case was fixed. And in fact when one trucker threatened to call the police, Dioguardi's uncle, Plumeri, had bragged that he had already fixed dozens of such previous complaints because of his political connections. Thanks to Dioguardi's acquittal, when Plumeri was severely wounded in a shootout at their trucking association's offices in 1933, the young nephew was essentially left in charge of the operation.[38]

By 1934, Dioguardi and his uncle had expanded their operation by having themselves placed on the payrolls of two other previously independent trucking associations. Dioguardi became the labor manager of the Garment Center Truck Owners Association. The directors of that association would later be key prosecution witnesses, testifying on the stand that they had paid money to Dioguardi and his uncle out of fear. But, despite their prominent roles, it seemed evident that Plumeri and Dioguardi were not acting on their own. When New York's racket-busting district attorney, Thomas Dewey, prosecuted them for extortion in 1937, he concluded that the two men were part of a larger gang structure that wielded influence in New York's garment industry. Dewey was convinced that the two were being sponsored by two leading crime figures in the garment industry at that time, Louis "Lepke" Buchalter and Jacob "Gurrah" Shapiro. Or as Dewey later put it in his memoir, "These two thugs were not important gangsters and we were absolutely convinced that they had important racket sponsorship." He never proved the connection but, Dewey explained, "logically" it had to have been "Lepke and Gurrah." [39]

And in fact Dioguardi and Plumeri's activities coincided with a larger process of organizing in the Garment District. At the same time that they were corralling garment trucking companies into employers' associations that functioned as cartels, the garment unions organized the drivers who worked for these trucking companies. In the International Ladies' Garment Workers' Union, these drivers were put into their own local union, Local 102, which was formed in early 1933. [40] Undoubtedly the two organizing campaigns were interrelated, although no record survives of the specific arrangements involved. The mob-dominated trucking cartels would have helped shepherd the garment drivers into Local 102; and the founding leaders of Local 102, as a result, would have been beholden to the mobsters who controlled those trucking cartels. Those ties meant that Local 102 could, in turn, force a new trucking firm to join a mob-dominated cartel by threating job actions against a company that tried to operate independently. Such symbiotic ties between local unions and business cartels had existed as far back as the 1890s in various urban sectors. In the years that followed the union's founding, Dioguardi maintained very close ties to the leadership of Local 102 and to the trucking associations that worked with it. These ties were a source of his influence in the Garment District.

Abe Chait occupied a similar role in the industry, one based on his ties to the garment truckers' union and the trucking associations. Like so many others in the Garment District, he was an immigrant, arriving from Kiev, Ukraine, with his parents when he was about seven years old. He grew up in the Bronx and never went beyond a grammar school education. By the age of eighteen he had been arrested twice and received a six- to eleven-year jail sentence in 1918 for grand larceny. He went into the trucking business in 1924, when records show he incorporated his own company, Faultless Trucking. Chait entered the business of garment trucking just as this segment of the industry was assuming a growing role in the manufacturing process. Previously, most dresses were produced by manufacturers in their own factories, but in the interwar years the trend was for jobbers to send out cut goods to widely dispersed contracting shops, creating a more flexible system of production. Pivotal to this mode of production were a couple hundred small trucking companies, most of them one- or two-truck operations, that hauled the cut goods out to the contractors, brought back the finished garments, and then later carried them to long-haul distribution points or retail stores.[41]

The truckers who did this work operated in an incredibly congested setting that left them exposed to a variety of pressures. Each block of the Garment District contained some 475 separate firms, and the only available parking was curbside; the buildings' elevator facilities were similarly limited. Truckmen jockeyed for parking spaces and waited in line for their turn to use a building's elevator. Unloading from the truck's side door because there was no room to use the tailgate, a typical delivery of 1,800 pounds of cut goods took one or two hours, and three-fourths of that time involved waiting for the elevator. The man driving the truck was often the truck company owner, who employed a helper to carry the goods on handcarts or garment racks along the crowded sidewalks, to the elevator and up to their final destination. This was a very public kind of labor, where the street functioned as the truckers' depot and loading dock. It was also comparatively small

The Garment District in the 1940s. *Associated Press*

scale. To take one example, Ideal Trucking serviced some forty accounts with two trucks and a few handcarts. In the garment trucking industry, one's business, including the identity of one's customers,
would be impossible to keep secret. The loss of a few of those accounts
could prove fatal to a small business.[42] This was the kind of setting
that was ideal for the cartel-style organizing in which Plumeri and
Dioguardi were engaged in the early 1930s.

Like trucking in general, garment trucking was a business that
attracted tough customers. One of the early leaders of the truckers'
Local 102 told another Garment Workers' Union official, "50 percent
of our members are graduates of Sing Sing [the New York State peni-
tentiary] and the other 50 percent are candidates for Sing Sing." As an
ex-con himself, Chait would have fit in easily. And his business apparently prospered. By the 1930s, his firm, Champion Trucking, was one
of the most prominent in the Garment District.[43]

At some point Chait became involved with the leading Jewish racketeers in this period, Louis Buchalter and Jacob Shapiro, aka Lepke and
Gurrah. In 1933, he was arrested again, this time for aiding a federal

fugitive. The case involved the notorious Verne Miller, a professional hitman who had ties to Buchalter and who had been involved in the Kansas City Massacre, a botched effort to free a federal prisoner that left two FBI agents dead in June 1933. Miller's role in the massacre made him one of the Bureau's most wanted fugitives. After a shootout with agents in Chicago, the FBI traced a set of car license plates Miller had used back to Chait. The case fizzled after Chait's alleged co-conspirator in supplying the plates turned up as a stripped, mutilated corpse on the side of a Connecticut roadway. After that the charges against Chait were dropped, apparently for lack of evidence. That was his last arrest. In the years that followed, Chait gained in prominence as law enforcement efforts curtailed the careers of Buchalter and Shapiro. Buchalter was executed on a murder charge in 1944 and Shapiro died in prison three years later. In their absence, Chait became the dominant Jewish gangster in the Garment District.[44]

Informants within the industry explained to the FBI that the men who served as directors of the various Garment District truck owners associations acted at Chait's behest. Barney Shapiro, for instance, who served as a director of the Garment Truckmen's Association, was described as "an associate of Abe Chait and followed instructions given to him by Chait." In turn, the association policed a cartel arrangement among the district's truckers. To operate within the district a trucker had to belong to the relevant association, but once he did so he could register all of his stops with the group and they would make sure no other firm took away his business. These associations ensured that a basic hauling rate structure stayed in place and these small trucking firms were provided with a secure and stable business environment.[45]

During an FBI probe in the 1970s, garment manufacturers invoked a particular metaphor to describe the resulting arrangement: the manufacturer was "married" to his trucker and could not switch from one to another. Nor could the manufacturer effectively bargain to get lower hauling rates. The businessmen did not like the situation, but they also admitted to the FBI that trucking charges were a very small part of their overall costs, and so the situation was not a major source of frustration.[46] For the truckmen, the cost of this beneficial situation was the membership dues to belong in the association and an initiation fee that could be quite high, as much as $1,500 for a new member. Also, the association received a percentage of the sales price any time one truckmen sold an account or his whole business to someone else. The FBI's informant assumed that Chait had ways to siphon the association's revenue into his own hands.[47] But there were other benefits that Chait would have accrued from his influence over these organizations. It provided him with influence in the entire garment industry, since it would allow him a way to track who was doing business with whom.

Chait exerted a similar form of influence through the truck drivers' union, ILG Local 102. The head of that local was Sam Berger, described by one FBI informant as someone who "is completely controlled by Chait." The informant went on to explain how the gangster could use Berger to "bring union pressure to bear on any member and also call strikes when it is to the interest of Chait and his associates."[48] A lengthy investigative report by the District Attorney's Office in 1948 drew on a wiretap of Local 102's phones that had been in place for eight months in 1946. The report emphasized the close ties that existed between Berger, Chait, and Chait's associates, the brothers John and Thomas Dioguardi. The District Attorney's wiretap recorded the mobsters asking Berger to intercede and help out firms facing a union picket line. They also recorded the gangsters using Berger and Local 102 to track down information on dress manufacturers who were attempting to work with non-union contractors on their own, discarding the services of their mob-connected truckers. To take one example, in September 1946, John Dioguardi called Berger to ask, "I want you to find out where Seigel and Lenikoff have been sending their work to—what I mean is, find out who the contractors are and if the work goes to N.Y. or N.J. shops." These transcripts demonstrate how Chait and his associates used their influence in Local 102 to police the existing arrangements between dress manufacturers and the gangsters who provided them with contacts and protection from the union. Through Local 102, the mob could limit the businessmen's ability to dodge the union without paying a fee to them.[49]

In the post–World War II era, providing garment manufacturers with access to non-union contractors, or making it possible for contractors to operate on a non-union basis, was a lucrative source of revenue for gangsters. A particular case of one of the more prominent mobsters engaged in this activity illustrates the kind of money involved in this activity. In 1959, investigators looking into the finances of Thomas Lucchese, reputed to be the head of the Lucchese crime family, explored his ties to the Budget Dress Company, a jobber. Lucchese allegedly had a secret ownership share in this firm, and as a result it sent its work out to a string of contractors with links to the Mafia leader. Those contractors in turn split their profits with Lucchese. In the case of just one firm, State Fabrics, a contractor located in the Bronx, congressional investigators alleged that Lucchese's share of the profits amounted to $20,000 in 1957 and $15,000 in 1958. This would be roughly equivalent to a quarter-million dollars today.[50]

There were other benefits besides the money. A mobster with a role in the garment industry had a source of income he could legitimately declare on his taxes. This was something of real value in the face of a possible tax investigation by the IRS, which would require organized crime figures to document the source of their wealth. Dioguardi declared income from a contractor in 1950 and 1951 as earnings for his role as the firm's production manager. This was a common tactic. Asked to explain what being a production manager entailed, mobsters told investigators that they located dress contractors, especially in the busy season, ensuring that these contractors could get the work done in a rush and to the standards of workmanship required. The explanation left out their role in keeping the union at bay, but it did accurately convey the other aspects of their involvement in these firms and so offered them a kind of legitimacy that had strategic value. Joseph Valachi, a Genovese crime family member, described how he received "a couple of hundred [dollars] a week" from a Bronx-based contractor with whom he had partnered. It was a good situation, since his partner actually ran the operation and, as he put it, "I got something for the tax people if they start nosing around."[51]

In the 1940s, much of this racketeering centered on northeastern Pennsylvania, where mob-connected contractors linked to mob-connected trucking firms proliferated. Two large garment truck-ing firms monopolized the routes to this region, and Chait allegedly had an ownership interest in both of them. He also had a stake in sev-eral garment factories in the region. His mob associates had interests in about forty other similar shops.[52] Chait also allegedly controlled the leadership of the Pennsylvania Garment Manufacturers Association. The head of the association, Barney Fishgold, was a business partner of Chait's wife and the group's "Price Setter and Expediter." Fishgold was a convicted murderer and, according to an FBI informant, "in the direct employ of Abe Chait."[53] In addition to these commercial ven-tures, FBI reports indicate that Chait took a share of the money made by loan sharks and bookies in the Garment District.[54]

These activities had made Chait a wealthy man and earned him the title of the Garment District's leading racketeer. By the 1950s he and his wife kept a five-room rent-controlled apartment up in Washington Heights, where he was known as a good tipper. During the week, he rode a chauffeur-driven car down to his office in the Garment District. On the weekends, the couple could be found at their country estate, the twenty-four-acre Good News Farm, which had a pool and horse

Abe Chait, the Garment District's boss trucker. *Herald Tribune*

stables and was located outside Peekskill, New York. Like so many of his contemporaries in the Garment District, Chait was an avid fan of horse racing. The couple ran a professional stable, with his wife and son listed as the official owners, since Chait's criminal record barred him from being licensed by the Racing Commission. A similar maneuver made him a part owner of the Yonkers Raceway. Eventually the Racing Commission put a stop to all of this, concluding that his wife and son were merely fronting for Chait. But before that happened, he had a taste of real success at the track with a thoroughbred grandson of the great Man o' War, named Combat Boots. Chait's stable bought the colt for $3,600 in 1949, and by 1953 it had won over $125,000 in prizes at the tracks, making it one of the top-earning horses of that era.[55]

A 1958 profile in the *New York Herald Tribune* described Chait as "one of the toughest, and perhaps the biggest" of the "racketeers who infest the chaotic Seventh Avenue garment center."[56] The term "racketeer," however, obscured the complex nature of his role in the industry. Although he had served time in prison himself and had ties to men with violent criminal pasts, Chait's relationship to the garment manufacturers did not fit any simple model of extortion through fear. Instead he was someone who sold a service to businessmen who expected to reap a tangible economic benefit from this arrangement. The character of this relationship comes through in a wiretapped conversation from 1948 between Chait and a dress manufacturer. In the tape transcript, Chait warned the businessman, Willie Schwartz, that there was likely to be a union picket line placed on his business. Schwartz responded, "You take care of that—that's your job to look after me."[57] This was not the voice of a terrorized victim.

In 1973, when the FBI analyzed why previous law enforcement efforts to curb mob influence in the Garment District had failed, one of the chief reasons they cited was that the legitimate businessmen had in effect protected the "hoodlum element" by refusing to cooperate with reform efforts. The businessmen acted this way, the Bureau concluded, "due to the need of these businessmen of the services offered by the LCN [La Cosa Nostra, i.e., Mafia], such as quick ECT [extortionate credit transactions, i.e., loan shark] loans, protection from union problems, and in many cases, the elimination of competition from industry-wide controls."[58]

A loose structure apparently governed these mobsters, and limited competition between the racketeers who were involved in the garment industry. Individual gangsters collected their own payments for protection from the firms that dealt with them; they would be expected not to poach another gangster's firm, and so would leave a company alone if it was already paying off another organized crime figure. A portion of this protection money was turned over to a mob-managed pool of funds that was shared out generally and used to aid garment center gangsters doing time in prison. The pool was reportedly managed by Joseph Stracci and Ben Kutlow, two crime figures who had earlier belonged to Buchalter's gang.[59] Chait was the overall arbiter who settled disputes when they arose. As one informant explained it, Chait was "the official judge in settling disputes between unions and manufacturers and various others associated in the garment area."[60] His partner in managing these arrangements was Thomas Lucchese, who apparently inherited an alliance between this Mafia group and the Jewish gangsters that had first been established by Buchalter.[61]

This was a group of insiders whose role in the industry and place in the Garment District were firmly established. As Italians and eastern European Jews, their ethnicity matched that of the businessmen who predominated in the dress industry. They had been involved in this industry for decades, and in the post–World War II era they continued to be a daily presence in Garment District. If Chait wasn't at the office of his trucking company at 217 West Thirty-Sixth Street, then you might have found him hanging out at Jack and Charlie's cigar shop at 233 West Thirty-Fifth Street, the same block where Lurye was murdered.[62] Joseph Stracci showed up every day at 8:45 a.m. at his office on the twelfth floor of 500 Seventh Avenue, where he was the general manager of a garment manufacturing firm, D. Zimet. But if you needed his intervention in some Garment District business, you probably would sit down with him at Dunhall's Restaurant on Broadway, a block and a half from his office.[63] In 1949, Dioguardi spent most of his time at Rosemary Fashions, at 1270 Broadway on the southeastern edge of the Garment District, where he was listed as the firm's production manager.[64] His uncle, James Plumeri, was based at his trucking company, Ell-Gee Carriers, whose office was at 254 West Thirty-Fifth Street, a block away from Chait's.[65] When this group met to hash out issues, they often did it at well-known locales right in the Garment District. A New York City Crime Commission report from 1951 described one such meeting, which included Chait, Stracci, Dioguardi, and Plumeri, taking place one evening at a semi-private table at the Cavalier Restaurant at Fortieth Street and Seventh Avenue.[66]

To say that they were a familiar presence does not mean that they lacked menacing characteristics, or that their activities were perceived as benign. Dioguardi had a reputation for having a dangerously violent temper, but by all accounts his uncle Plumeri was the more menacing and the more highly placed gangster. At his 1937 extortion trial, one of the witnesses, a trucker who had balked at Plumeri's organizing efforts, described how the gangster had threatened to "lop off my ears and cut off my tongue." Later, after his release from prison, Plumeri took over Ell-Gee Carriers after its previous owner, a business associate of Plumeri's, was shot and killed. When they arrived at the scene of the murder, the police found Plumeri in a neighboring apartment. His presence there seemed to be much more than a coincidence, but no charges were ever filed.[67] For his part, Chait's associates included Salvatore "Blackie" Graffagnino, an individual who had a string of sixteen arrests on charges that ranged from extortion and felonious assault to robbery. Graffagnino hung out at the offices of Chait's trucking company and was reputed to be his "muscleman."[68]

There is no record of Chait committing murder to gain control of a trucking company, but investigators did come across an episode that had occurred in 1945 illustrating how he straddled the worlds of organized crime and business in ways that epitomized the complex nature of racketeering. At that time, two trucking firms monopolized the garment-hauling business from northeast Pennsylvania to New York City. Then the owner of one of those firms, Ehrlich-Newmark, died in 1944. Chait allegedly offered to buy the firm from the remaining partner, but was refused. So instead, Chait arranged to be brought in as a 50 percent partner by another trucking firm, Friedman's Express,

which had Interstate Commerce Commission authorization to operate in this region. Then Chait and several of his mobster associates
visited Ehrlich-Newmark's customers and convinced them to switch
their freight hauling to Chait's company, Friedman's Express.

Thus far this reads like the scenario of a classic mob movie, in which
the gangster uses force to muscle aside some legitimate business. But
in the months that followed, Chait assumed his other role, that of the
veteran garment trucker. He helped Friedman's Express pick a location for a new freight terminal in northeast Pennsylvania. According
to FBI reports, the company had no experience in garment trucking
and so FBI reports describe how Chait spent considerable time at this
new location, talking to Friedman's employees "about how to handle
dresses, ship & pack dress pieces and finished dresses." Thereafter he
visited the new terminal for a couple of days every month "to make
sure that things were running smoothly." [69] In other words, he acted as
a garment trucking businessman, one with decades of expertise in this
field, taking a personal role in managing a new phase of his operation.

The racketeers in the Garment District combined two identities:
they were criminals who belonged to criminal gangs that wielded influence at least partly by committing acts of violence; and they were
also businessmen with experience and expertise in the industry, who
provided their fellow businessmen with services. Dressmakers used
those services in hopes of acquiring an edge, which is why two dress
manufacturers, Leo Greenberg and Joseph Ross, had given money to
Benedicto Macri, the gangster who had taken part in the murder of
the ILG's William Lurye in May 1949. Greenberg, Ross, and other Garment District employers who turned to the mob would have known
the possible implications of what they were doing. But they also would
have seen these arrangements as fitting within the industry norms.
There was a common understanding that businessmen struggling to
make it would sometimes resort to tactics—copying a competitor's
dress style, shrinking the marker, hiring a mobster as your production
man—that society at large might find reprehensible.

That sensibility, or operational code, underlay the role that racketeers played in the Garment District. To the extent that racketeers
had a role in similar industries in New York, such as the waterfront

shipping industry, the produce and seafood markets, or waste hauling, that role reflected a similar reality. This pattern of racketeering reflected the presence of two key factors: the insiders' acceptance that the rules sometimes had to be bent, and the presence of mobsters, who were very much insiders themselves, and who helped the businessmen bend those rules.

4

AN ORGANIZER'S FIGHT FOR
JUSTICE: RAGE AND DIGNITY

The ambulance that worked its way through the truck-clogged Thirty-Fifth Street on the afternoon of May 9 brought Will Lurye to St. Vincent's Hospital, where his family members waited as surgeons worked to save him from the deep lacerations to his chest and lungs. Several dozen pressers from Will's local union crowded the hospital's hallway as they lined up to give blood. Over thirteen hours later, just as dawn approached, Will died. The people who remained throughout the night included Will's wife, his sister Min Matheson, and Sasha Zimmerman—the union leader Will had been trying to call from the phone booth when he was attacked.[1]

Sasha Zimmerman was a friend and mentor to Will's sister Min, herself a dedicated official in the International Ladies' Garment Workers' Union. She and Will grew up in a fiercely progressive household with a defiant, union activist father. In a family of seven children, Min and Will had been especially close. "He was next to me," she remembered, "fifteen months difference in our age, so we used to hang together."[2] Now she sat at his bedside and watched him succumb to his wounds. The experience would haunt her for years afterward and shape her attitude toward the garment industry mobsters she later encountered. A year after his death, she wrote to Sasha, "I go to sleep nights and I live over from beginning to end the long corridors of

St. Vincent Hospital, and I see Will over and over again, fighting to breathe and live. I cannot forget the last breath he took."[3]

Like her father Max Lurye, Matheson was an activist, an avocation she had adopted as a teenager in Chicago, and which she now drew upon in pursuit of justice in her brother's case. Pressuring law enforcement to apprehend her brother's killers, she also demanded that the union take action against the fellow members of Lurye's picket crew, whom she believed had betrayed him. In March 1950, as the first year anniversary of the killing approached with no arrests, she requested a meeting between her family and the district attorney, writing, "They would like to hear from you directly on what has been done and what is being done to apprehend the murderers of my brother."[4]

The year had been a hard one for the family—Max Lurye died just days after Will's murder, and the family was reeling. They fully believed Will's murder was the cause of Max's death, provoked by grief over the circumstances of the murder. Vowing justice, the family doggedly pursued their own leads in the investigation with a hired investigator. On the actual anniversary of the killing, Matheson's family had a one-hour meeting with the DA in which they persisted with their demands to apprehend the still-at-loose murderers, but also pressured the DA to go after the employers who were involved. "We feel," Matheson told the press later, "that in a certain sense the dress company owners are as much guilty as those who actually killed my brother."[5] Writing to the ILG's leadership, she also demanded a chance to confront the other members of Lurye's picket crew. The union discouraged her, yet she later described challenging one of the crew, who she suspected had worked as an informer for the mob. The encounter took place at the ILG's Organizing Department, on the anniversary of Will's death, around the same time that the family met with the DA.[6] Matheson had nothing solid to support her charges, so the belligerent organizer, Cal Yagid, shrugged off her accusations. Matheson recalled, "I said, 'You know, Cal, I'm going to push you right out of that window, I swear!' And my mother, God bless her, she went and opened up the window!"[7]

The emotional conviction and righteous outrage that made her formidable on the picket line intensified as she grieved for her brother and

The Lurye family, from left Sie Lurye (brother), Min Matheson (sister), Maxine Lurye (sister), Bernice Lurye (widow), leave district attorney's office. *Queens Public Library Archives*

fumed over the lack of justice. Matheson believed that some members of the union's six-man picket squad were on the payroll of Garment District mobsters and they had set her brother up to be murdered that day. Her suspicions centered on Yagid and another man, Tony Miletti. Witnesses had told the police that Will called out for a "Tony" as he lay mortally wounded on the curb of Thirty-Fifth Street.[8] Matheson had apparently concluded that Will was calling for Miletti, who was supposed to be protecting his fellow union picket, but instead had managed to disappear just as the knife-wielding attackers closed in on Lurye. In the ILG's archives there is a postcard addressed to Miletti; though unsigned, the Wilkes-Barre, Pennsylvania, postmark strongly indicates that it came from Matheson. The postcard's author writes in the voice of the murdered Will Lurye, reminding Tony that he sent Will into the telephone booth where he was murdered and that, as the fatally wounded victim staggered out of the building's lobby, he called Tony's name. "I trusted you Tony . . . Did you hear me calling you Tony? Calling you again and again, Tony . . . Tony . . . Tony . . . but you never came did you Tony? . . . Tell me why, Tony," the letter asks. And then the writer suggests it was because "you could not look at my red blood flowing because of your treachery." The letter concludes on a threatening note: "Its cold and terribly quiet in the grave Tony. Your grave will be even more so Tony . . . soon . . . soon . . . do you hear me calling you Tony? This time you will answer . . . soon . . . soon."[9]

At the time the postcard was written, Matheson was in the midst of efforts to organize women garment workers in northeast Pennsylvania, in the region known as the Wyoming Valley—a collection of small towns anchored by two medium-sized cities, Wilkes-Barre and Scranton. The three ILG locals she helped organize came to include about ten thousand members.[10] Despite stiff resistance, she built a vibrant union movement in that valley. For the members of these local labor organizations, the union meant better wages but also a meaningful change in their status. In oral histories, these women remembered Matheson as an ideal union official, one who understood their situation firsthand and whose commitment to their cause had no apparent limits. They also remembered her courage. In those years, organizing in northeast Pennsylvania meant confronting the same kinds of individuals who were responsible for her brother's death.

Matheson was strongly influenced by her father—a revolutionary who had fled Tsarist Russia in 1904. Matheson remembered him as "an extremist in many ways," a "no-compromise person in all his actions."[11] These traits made him a lifelong radical, but also affected his ability to earn a decent living for his family, and his hard-line positions got him kicked out of union leadership roles more than once. Unlike her father, however, Matheson balanced outrage with a pragmatic realism, and this would shape her response to corruption and criminal influence within the union and the industry. She drew on both tendencies to support her enduring commitment to the union as a force for social good.

Min Matheson's parents were Jewish immigrants, childhood sweethearts who married upon reaching America, and raised seven children in the crowded working-class neighborhoods on the West Side of Chicago. Max Lurye moved from job to job, sometimes helping to put out a radical Jewish newspaper, at other times picking up employment where he could. Eventually, in the 1920s he found work as a junk peddler. Here, as everywhere in his employment, he took up organizing. "Dad wouldn't work at anything, I don't care what it was," Matheson remembered, "without getting others who were also doing the same thing together." He helped put together an organization of junk peddlers, occasionally taking one of Matheson's older brothers along to the meetings.[12] Max Lurye was no stranger to the brutal violence that marked Chicago's labor environment of the 1920s and 1930s, and his activities made him the direct target of such violence several times.

Relentlessly committed to the cause of workers, he stayed active in radical circles throughout his life, setting an example for his daughter, who remembered being "totally immersed in my father's doings."[13] As a seven-year-old, she accompanied him to Socialist Party rallies to hear the presidential campaign speeches of Eugene Debs. During World War I, the Lurye children, like all committed Socialists, refused to participate in the school war bond drives. As a result, she later recalled, "the kids and the teachers isolated us and the abuse we took was something to be remembered."[14] On Sundays, Matheson and her siblings went to Socialist Sunday School, an alternative education movement created in the early 1900s and dedicated to providing students with a curriculum that would prepare them to challenge the status quo. As one of the founders of the movement put it, "The kids [at these schools] are learning to be good rebels."[15] Matheson encountered radicalism at home as well. The Lurye house was, according to Matheson, "sort of a haven." It was a place in Chicago that radicals turned to "if the police were looking for somebody or if somebody had to hide out or if there had to be a secret meeting or you had to hide the literature." Among the radicals who stayed at their home was the anarchist firebrand Emma Goldman.[16]

It was a youth filled with moments of real drama, often involving confrontations with authority. Matheson watched the police search her home during the Red Scare of 1919. They were hunting for radical literature, which was in fact stored in the Lurye household, but the police didn't find it. Her mother had hidden it on the top shelf in the pantry, behind the jelly jars. In high school, she joined the Young Workers' Communist League. She organized rallies to support striking workers and helped to distribute the Communist Party's newspaper, the *Daily Worker*. Looking back, she remembered, "We were so busy that there weren't enough hours in the day for all the things that there were to do to make the movement grow." [17]

By that time Min had made many of the decisions that would shape the rest of her life. She had joined the Communist Party. And then, frustrated by its top-down command structure and the way it subordinated the needs of American workers to Soviet priorities, she withdrew. The breaking point came when the party ordered its activists to organize workers into separate communist-controlled unions. Min believed that the result would be a divided and a weakened labor movement. "That I couldn't stomach," she remembered. "As strong as I was for the Party, I was nurtured and brought up on it, to me it was a major tragedy when I had to break with the Party. But I did, purely on the question of 'What's good for Russia isn't good for every country.'" [18]

The break was all the more significant because her social world revolved around the Party. All her friends were members. She met the man with whom she would spend the rest of her life through the Party. But by 1931 she was out of it and working as an itinerant union organizer, going where she was needed, helping with a strike or a particular organizing effort, and then moving on. She drifted over to New York City, where she ended up serving as the private secretary for Jay Lovestone, who led a breakaway group of former Communist Party members. One of Lovestone's adherents was Sasha Zimmerman, the head of Local 22 of the International Ladies' Garment Workers' Union. Zimmerman needed volunteers for the ILG's upcoming organizing campaign and Matheson signed up. She worked in the resulting strike, joined the union, and devoted the rest of her career to the ILG. [19]

Doing so meant she spent the next seven years working in a dress shop as a sewing machine operator. The ILG had a rule at the time:

Women working in a garment factory, 1940s. *Kheel Center, Cornell University*

"To be an officer [in the union], you had to work in a shop." Matheson worked at a shop of one of the larger contractors, putting together dresses that sold for $3.75, the low end of the women's dress line at the time.[20] She came to know the quotidian reality of the women who made up some 75 percent of the union's membership.

The bulk of the women in these shops worked as Matheson did; they were sewing machine operators, seated at rows of tables, thirty, forty, fifty, or more women in a loft, each woman bent over a machine with a bin of cut garment pieces at their side, sewing them into the finished dresses. The women were paid piece-rate wages, calculated according to the union's formula, with the goal of providing the operators with the union's negotiated weekly rate. To reach that wage they had to make a certain number of dresses each day. It was a wage system designed to ensure that they maintained their level of productivity. Walking into these shops, observers made note of the constant noise, the "incessant z-i-i-ipp of the Singer machines," and the focused intensity of the operators.[21]

The women were more than machine operators. The jobber provided the contractor's shop with a completed model of the dress, but it was the operator's job to figure out how to put the pieces together so that they came out exactly replicating the model. It took time to learn a new style, and often a woman would turn to her fellow operators for advice on particularly tricky details. Supervisors would assess the final product, judging whether or not the operator had done it correctly, or needed to redo it. Every time the contractor took on an order for a new style of dress, or got a batch of cut garments from a different jobber, it required the operators to start all over again, figuring out how to put together the new set of dresses. These style changes slowed down their productivity and cut into their earnings, which were typically on the low end of the scale, despite the pressure from the union. In 1956, garment workers averaged $55.60 a week, significantly less than the $74.76 weekly average for manufacturing workers as a whole.[22]

The pace of the work, and the concentration it required, was exhausting. In the small workshops, the boss, in the form of the contractor or his supervisor, was often right there behind the operators and, faced with his own pressures to keep costs low, he often pushed the operators relentlessly. Minnie Caputo, who worked in a shop in this era, remembered, "Girls couldn't pick up their heads. If they talked to the girl next to them, if he [the boss] saw them, [he would ask], 'What in the hell is going on.'" "We worked hard," she remembered.[23] The ILG had won the seven-hour day by 1934, but since these women combined domestic duties with their factory jobs, the actual workday was significantly longer. A dressmaker from Brooklyn told a journalist in 1958 that she reported to the contractor's shop at 9 a.m., but her workday started at 6:30 in the morning, when she got up before the rest of her family and got started on her day. "This is the time when I have to get all my things done." She caught up on the household chores, made her family breakfast, and got her kids ready for school. Finishing work by 5 p.m., she came home and took up where she left off, with whatever energy she had left.[24]

There was limited room for advancement. Faster operators, with more skill, could make more money as they completed more dresses. They might find work at shops that specialized in more expensive dresses, which required more skill, and paid better wages. A few could move up to more-skilled positions, working as the forelady who oversaw the other women, or as model makers, who took the dress design and produced the first dress for the operators to work from. But most skilled positions that paid better wages were reserved for men. The pressers worked large power steam presses and earned more money. They had their own local union within the ILG and it was divided into component sections that represented Jewish and Italian pressers, all of them men. Cutters also had their own local, earned significantly more money, and were always men.[25]

By the 1940s and 1950s this hierarchy had racial components too. African Americans and Puerto Ricans made up an increasing proportion of the workforce and they were relegated to the lowest-wage sectors of the industry. The black and Puerto Rican sewing machine operators were less likely to make it into the better-paying occupations, or to gain the skills needed to move into the better-paying dress shops. The men found themselves confined to laborers' jobs, such as pushing the handcarts of dresses. These minority workers were the first to be fired when the rush season passed and work routinely became more scarce; as a result, their annual earnings were lower than their white counterparts.[26]

The union's leadership ranks reflected these occupational hierarchies: for the most part its officials were white males. Though women made up over 75 percent of the ILG's membership, they were limited to a token presence among the national officers. For decades there was only one woman on the union's General Executive Board. Few of them held office at the local or the regional level. The union's president, David Dubinsky, told an interviewer that "women cannot serve . . . as business agents and organizers, particularly outside the metropolitan areas where you have to travel at night and be away from home." The pattern of office-holding in the union also reflected the implicit racism that belied the official stance of the ILG, which had long championed civil rights for African Americans. In New York City, no black or Puerto Rican served as a local union manager or assistant manager, despite the fact that by 1958 these groups made up about one-quarter of the union's membership.[27]

The gap between the leadership and its rank-and-file members who labored as sewing machine operators mattered because the union played a pivotal role in the working lives of these women and minorities. The piece rates for each dress style resulted from a give-and-take negotiation between the employers and the union's representatives. The bargain they reached determined how hard a woman had to work just to make the union's minimum wage. A bad bargain left the operator endlessly scrambling to meet a production goal that was always out of reach. The operator's only option in such a case was to appeal to the union to correct the negotiated piece rate. This powerful role was apparent to an anthropologist who spent months studying a dress contractor's shop in 1948. He wrote, "The researcher felt that the union existed for the workers largely in the form of a distant favorable god upon which they depended and to which they paid tribute." Few of the women in this shop had ever met their local union's business agent, and they avoided going to union meetings.[28]

For them the face of the union was the chairlady, the position in which union organizer Min Matheson began her ILG career. The chairlady was the shop's union representative, an elected post in the ILG, and the person that the other operators first looked to when they wanted something addressed by their union. The shop's chairlady was also the eyes and ears of the local union within the factory, the person who determined whether or not contract violations were occurring, or if those violations merited a response from the union.[29]

Matheson moved up from that position in 1937 to hold office at the local union level, serving as a chairlady of Local 22, the second-largest union in the ILG. She won this office as part of a slate of candidates run by the Progressive Group within the local. This was a group led by ex–Communist Party members who gathered around Sasha Zimmerman, the head of Local 22 and over the years one of Matheson's closest colleagues in the union. Zimmerman was born in Russian Ukraine, near the city of Kiev, a community that was the target of periodic pogroms throughout his childhood. He remembered how the family hid in their cellar when these attacks occurred, his grandmother quietly reading to them from the Hebrew Book of Psalms.

Immigrating to America at the age of sixteen, Zimmerman was

trained as a sewing machine operator by his sister and soon became active in the ILG. He joined the Communist Party and for many years led the party's faction within the garment union, a role that made him the target of anti-communists such as David Dubinsky, who helped engineer Zimmerman's expulsion from the union in 1926. But like Matheson, Zimmerman had become increasingly frustrated with the Party's leadership. By 1929, he was among the faction of Communist Party leaders, including Jay Lovestone, who were expelled from the organization. They formed a dedicated left-wing clique of anti-Stalinist progressives and established a working alliance with the Socialist faction in the ILG that was led by Dubinsky. The alliance opened the way for Zimmerman to return to union office. He won election as the secretary-manager of Local 22 in 1933 and helped lead the ILG's great organizing strike of that year in New York, recruiting activists such as Min Matheson to help him.[30]

Under Zimmerman and his Progressive Group, Local 22 became a model of social unionism, extending a labor organization's goals and activities beyond the realm of wages and benefits. The ILG had grown fivefold as a result of the 1933 strike, but Zimmerman and his fellow Progressives believed that in order to maintain that membership they had to transform these newfound union recruits, most of whom had no background in organized labor, into steadfast members. They planned to do this by building an ambitious union educational program that would prepare members to become union activists. Taught about the history and goals of their movement, and engaged in a range of union activities, these new members would establish a potent connection to the union. Such an emotional tie was critical to the growing strength of the ILG. The new members had to be willing to risk their jobs and to strike to enforce the union's agreement; otherwise, the ILG's explosive growth in 1933 would be just a short-lived interlude followed by a slide back to the union's previous marginal state. As the head of Local 22's Education Department explained, "The strength of a union lies fundamentally in the solidarity, consciousness and militancy of its members."[31] Without militant members, the union would be vulnerable to the inevitable employer counteroffensive.

This was a broad vision of labor education. It included classes on such subjects as the principles of unionism, economics, American history, and American literature. But the ILG's vision of labor education also incorporated a range of cultural and athletic activities, from union-produced theatricals, choruses, and an orchestra, to team athletics such as basketball and swimming. Members learned to jitterbug at union dances and they took hiking trips together at Camp Unity in the Pocono Mountains. The goal was to help members understand their role in a larger labor movement and to make the union an important part of its members' social world. As Min Matheson later told an interviewer, "We didn't consider a union just a place to pay dues and to worry about your piece-rate or your earnings in the shop. We considered it a way of life and we made it a way of life."[32] Local 22's educational program created a broad sense of community within the union and it also fostered the development of a cadre of rank-and-file leaders, such as Min Matheson, who emerged from the ranks.[33]

But after winning a local union office in 1937, Matheson took a step in 1941 that jeopardized her leadership role. She decided to have a baby. She had been living with Bill Matheson since 1929, their careers following a parallel track. They had met as Communist Party activists in Chicago, and both had relocated to New York, left the Communist Party, and become officials in the ILG. In 1940 they made their relationship official by marrying at City Hall, and a year later Matheson gave birth to a baby girl. It was a breech birth and—ever the dedicated unionist—while in labor Matheson told the doctor, "This is more exciting than the picket line!"[34] But within the union leadership, as a mother and an elected officer, she was an anomaly. Her old friend, Sasha Zimmerman, wrote to congratulate her and noted, "You do not realize that you established a record and a precedent. You are the first chairlady of the Executive Board to give birth to a child! It is making history."[35] This was a bittersweet achievement for Matheson, who was forced to apply for a leave of absence from her position so that she could care for her baby. In the months that followed, the temporary leave became permanent, as she followed her husband out to northeast Pennsylvania, where he had been sent by the ILG to work as an organizer. They had a second daughter in 1942, and Matheson was asked to take out an official withdrawal card that formally ended her membership in the union.[36]

It was a bitter pill. She shared in a letter to a friend that she hated having to leave the union. Keeping the membership had been a last "hope that I may at any time get back into things."[37] As it was, she felt cut off from her career and the activism that had been a part of her life since she was a girl growing up in Chicago. In another letter from this period she wrote to Zimmerman: "You ask me how I have been? Not good. After all I've been in the movement since childhood—a good many years—and its most difficult to settle down to a pure + simple domesticated existence at this day + age. I miss the union, its activity and everything that goes with it—<u>very much</u>."[38]

However, she found her way back into the movement not long afterward. The ILG was starting a drive to organize the increasing number of runaway garment shops setting up operations in northeast Pennsylvania. The official leading the drive knew Matheson from her days as a Local 22 chairlady in New York City and asked her to sign on to help, hiring her as a business agent in October 1944. She found a housekeeper willing to take care of the children, and eagerly went back to her life as a union activist.[39] In November 1944, she wrote to Sasha Zimmerman, "Excuse the hurried note. It's like the good old days + almost no time for personal business. Swell group of union people down here."[40] Within two years, she became the manager of the ILG Local 249, based in Pittston, Pennsylvania.[41]

Dress contracting shops had been moving out to this area since the 1930s, taking advantage of the improved truck transportation that facilitated the shipping of cut goods and finished dresses. Well outside the New York City Garment District, contractors hoped to exploit the distance in order to evade the union. Doing so allowed them to pay lower wages, but it also gave them the chance to restructure the dress manufacturing process, assigning a sewing machine operator to just one stage of the dress, such as sewing sleeves, rather than having an operator complete each dress. Section work, as this was called, allowed the contractor to hire less-skilled seamstresses and, contractors argued, it also increased the pace of production. In New York the ILG had opposed section work, and the move to Pennsylvania shops of-fered a chance to sidestep that opposition.[42]

At the same time, contractors also were drawn by a plentiful supply of labor. Coal mining had been the primary employer in this region, but as more and more homes and businesses had shifted to other heat-ing sources, such as oil, the mining industry had declined. There were few other sources of employment in the area. For the wives of unem-ployed miners, the dressmaking shops opened an economic lifeline for their families' survival.[43] Minnie Caputo, an operator in the "out-of-town" factories, later recalled, "You know there was nothing here for the men. There were just the mines and when that went, it was just the women working."[44] The economic changes also affected family dy-namics. It was a shift that Bill Cherkes noticed. A dress contractor who moved into the area in the 1940s, he recalled the change: "Because the man, the miner, had no jobs . . . the women were the providers. They paid the college bill, they paid for the mortgage payments, they paid for the six-pack of beer the guy would drink."[45]

A region of small towns and mining villages, northeast Pennsyl-vania was different from New York City's Garment District, but as Matheson would discover there were underlying similarities. Instead of the Jewish and Italian immigrants who had formed the bulk of the workforce in New York City, the women working in the Pennsylvania factories tended to come from second-generation American families; eastern European surnames were common, but so too were English and Irish names. In New York, the union had been shaped by decades of labor strife in the Garment District, reaching back to the days of the Triangle shirtwaist factory fire in 1911. Northeast Pennsylvania lacked that history, but it had its own powerful legacy of labor conflict in the region's coal industry. Union identification was strong in these rural valleys. As one woman wrote to an ILG leader in this era, "Our family have been coal miners and our people have struck many times." And as a result she understood the ideal of labor unity: "Coal miners help coal miners everywhere. I know blouse sewers help blouse sewers."[46]

These women understood the benefits that a union could bring, and they had real grievances that needed to be addressed. Since the 1930s, when garment factories first began opening in the region, contractors had forced new employees to initially work for less, or even no wages, on the premise that they were learning the trade. As Matheson explained, "They would bring women in and they would say, 'We'll teach you.' These [women] were natural sewers, and sometimes they'd work for a month for nothing."[47] There were also issues with how they were paid. The employer arbitrarily set the piece rates that determined their wages, and often imposed a grueling, if not impossible, pace of work on the women. Minnie Caputo compared the environment to the classic feature of New York's Garment District: "They were like sweat shops. They stood behind you with the stop watch and timed you and if one girl did eight operations, he would, you know, [say] why not you." There was a pervasive climate of fear in these shops, so if the women felt that their paycheck shorted them, they had to swallow their anger. "You couldn't complain," Caputo remembered.[48] Wages were low in these shops, set at the state's minimum wage rate. "But by that time," Min Matheson explained, "people were fed up with a lot of other things. . . . It wasn't so much the wage rate as it was generally the atmosphere and the conditions in the shop."[49]

As a result, "the people wanted the union." Matheson remembered one of her fellow ILG officials exclaiming, "It's an organizer's dream."[50] Matheson saw the women's willingness to sign up as part of a larger process of female empowerment. "There was really an awakening amongst the women throughout the area," she said. It stemmed from their new status as primary wage earners in their families. "See there was a big change in the relationship within the family which reflected itself in town, which affected what we were doing." All of this was producing a new assertiveness. "The women were really coming into their own."[51]

Tapping into this latent militancy, Matheson enjoyed some initial successes, particularly in Wilkes-Barre, one of the larger towns in the area. But she stumbled into a hornets' nest of opposition when she tried to organize in nearby Pittston, a town where dress contracting shops had cropped up throughout the downtown, taking over vacant storefronts. Mobsters owned these shops, or contractors with mob connections owned them. Local Mafia figures dominated the town, including its political leaders and its police force. It made for a very different kind of organizing experience. "In Pittston, when we came down the first time, I don't know how they knew we were coming," Matheson remembered. "But the police met us at the [railroad] station." It was not a hospitality committee. "They just took us by the shoulders and put us back on the train and told us we weren't welcome in Pittston."[52] She switched to driving into Pittston with a crew of organizers, but then once there she had the daunting task of maintaining a picket line. Sometimes the women faced police harassment. Other times, they encountered mob thugs, "like in the moving pictures, real tough guys." The women would form a picket line outside a storefront factory on one side of the street, and a group of these men would be lined up on the other side. "We were scared."[53]

It was a situation that she hadn't been expecting. She hadn't known about the prominent role of the Mafia in this region, but she would learn that it had deep roots.[54] The Pittston area Mafia traced its origins back to the early 1900s and included immigrants coming from the Sicilian village of Montedoro, in the heart of the island's violence-prone sulfur mining region. In northeast Pennsylvania these immigrants encountered a coal mining industry that was also wracked by violence. The conflicts centered on subcontractors that the coal companies hired to increase miners' output by evading union-imposed restrictions. Efforts to curb those contractors, and to more strictly enforce the union's rules, came to involve violence on both sides. Subcontractors who defied the miners' efforts to end this practice were sometimes victims of dynamite bombs. Some of the union's vocal critics of subcontracting, or of the union's apparent tolerance for the practice, were assassinated. In one case a shootout occurred in the district headquarters of the United Mine Workers union (UMW), leading to the death of a local union president. From 1916 to the early 1930s at least thirty homicides were linked to this struggle.[55]

This climate of disorder and violence offered an opportunity for organized crime. Mafia figures became prominent subcontractors, and the murder of local UMW officials marked the mob's successful effort to subordinate the union's local leadership. The last of these killings occurred in 1951, a few years after Matheson had begun organizing for the ILG in this area. The president of UMW Local 8005, Charles Mecadon, was driving through a residential district in Wilkes-Barre on his way to visit his son when a bomb went off in his car. The blast shook houses in a quarter-mile radius, sent debris flying as far as one hundred yards in all directions, and injured three little girls playing on a neighborhood sidewalk. Mecadon died in a hospital seven hours later and the local Mafia tightened its hold on his local.[56]

The FBI suspected that Angelo Sciandra had engineered this killing, though he was never arrested for it. Angelo was the son of a famous local Mafia leader, John Sciandra. The way Matheson later heard about it, John Sciandra oversaw Pittston in the 1930s in the style of the old-time Mafia don, holding court, resolving disputes brought to him, including "even family problems, separations between man and wife." "He was very fair in his decisions," she was told, so much so that people went to him with their problems. After Sciandra's death he was succeeded not by his son, but instead by his brother-in-law, Russell Bufalino, who by the 1950s became the dominant Mafia figure in northeast Pennsylvania until his death in 1994.[57]

In appearance, Bufalino was unassuming. He stood five feet, eight inches tall, weighed about 140 pounds, with dark hair and gray eyes. His left eyelid drooped, a muscle irregularity, and that was the only distinctive feature of his face. Like several other Italian mobsters of that era, he inexplicably had an Irish nickname; friends called him McGee. He lived with his wife in a modest house, in a suburb outside of Wilkes-Barre. A Teamster official, Frank Sheeran, who came to know him quite well, once told an interviewer that "of all the crime bosses he ever met, the mannerisms and style of the Marlon Brando portrayal in *The Godfather* most nearly resembled Russell Bufalino." It was a quiet kind of authority that drew on a ferocity that only rarely surfaced. But when it did, one got a glimpse of the man's real character and the source of his authority. Sheeran recalled Bufalino rebuking a drunken Frank Sinatra one night at an Atlantic City casino, "Sit down or I'll rip your tongue out and stick it up your ass." Even when Bufalino was in his seventies, an FBI bug recorded him collecting a debt by telling the borrower that if he didn't pay up, "I'm going to kill you—I'll do it myself."[58]

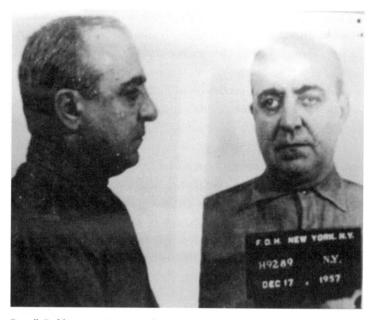

Russell Bufalino, prominent northeast Pennsylvania Mafia figure. *New York State Archives*

His parents had immigrated from Sicily in 1904, and he came over with them as an infant, so young that for much of his life he believed he had been born after they arrived in the United States. He was the nephew of a prominent local Mafia leader and, though in his youth he worked for a while as an auto mechanic, by his twenties he had apparently adopted a career in organized crime. He had a string of thirteen arrests in Buffalo, where his family had moved when he was a teenager. The Buffalo police listed him as a safecracker and burglary suspect, but the charges never stuck; he was only convicted of a disorderly conduct charge, for which he was ordered to pay a ten dollar fine.[59] In 1940, he returned to Pennsylvania and set up his base of operations in downtown Pittston, where he was listed as an auto mechanic at the City Auto Service Center. According to a state police report from that era, "The garage appears to be another front for the Pittston, Italian underworld." The agency described Bufalino as "an important part of just about every Italian underworld racket in this area." He banked loan sharks and local big-stakes poker games. He was the man behind the large-scale floating crap games that the state police occasionally stumbled upon. Through associates like Angelo Sciandra, he had influence in the local Mine Workers Union and probably had a piece of mining subcontractors, such as the Knox Coal Company.[60]

He was also very active in the area's dress contracting businesses. He had an ownership share in several of the shops located in Pittston, and he also earned money as a production man for prominent New York City–based jobbers looking for non-union shops to sew their dresses. As part of this business he traveled each week to New York's Garment District, staying at a hotel on Forty-Ninth Street between Seventh and Eighth Avenue, and dining at Vesuvio's Restaurant, a favorite mob meeting place in the Theater District. At either location, he was likely to be found meeting with other prominent mob figures in the garment industry, including James Plumeri, Plumeri's nephew, Johnny Dio, and Harry Stromberg, a Jewish mobster who operated out of Philadelphia and New York. As Matheson's organizing activities began to make an impact, one of Bufalino's associates, Nick Benfonte, created a rival labor organization, the Northeastern Pennsylvania Needleworkers' Association. Mob-connected dress factories in Pennsylvania signed collective bargaining agreements with Benfonte's union as a way to keep Matheson and the ILG at bay.[61]

It soon became apparent to Min Matheson that Bufalino was her main obstacle in Pittston. The men lined up across the street from her organizers were part of Bufalino's crew, and they included people like Angelo Sciandra, the man who had allegedly engineered the killing of the UMW leader Mecadon. Another suspect in that killing was Dominick Alaimo, Sciandra's cousin.[62] He too stood among the group of men who faced Matheson's organizing squads in downtown Pittston. A trumpet player, Alaimo would sometimes sit on the hood of his car and play a mournful version of "Taps" as the union women showed up to walk their picket line. They were a scary bunch of guys. One of the pickets remembered a time when the local police showed up during a picket line encounter and Bufalino's hoods chased them away too.[63]

By all accounts, in the face of this intimidation Matheson was fearless. If there was a picket line to be walked, she was on it, showing up at

6 a.m., or even more likely driving a group of women to the site in her own car. On one occasion, she was ferrying a carload of women pickets to an early morning picket line when they saw a crew of Bufalino's men waiting for them. They were outnumbered and it looked like the men were poised to assault them. One of Matheson's companions suggested turning around and leaving. Matheson remembered, "I said, 'Helen, no matter what happens today, we have to stop. Because if we don't turn up today, this may hurt our chances to really get this town organized. We have to just put up a very brave front.'" She suggested they think of doing "something spectacular to worry them like they think they are worrying us." With little time to talk it over they settled on a surprise strategy. "The minute we stopped, as we got out of the car, we were all screaming. I got out of the car and I said, 'You rotten hoodlums! What are you doing in this town? You don't live here. We live here. This our town, not yours!'"[64]

She was defiant. On one occasion a hood across the street yelled that Matheson should get her "weakling husband" over to the picket line and see if he was tough enough to take it. Matheson stormed across the street and confronted Bufalino himself, sticking a finger in his face and shouting, "I don't need to bring Bill up here, Russ, because I'm twice the man you'll ever be." Another time, someone yelled across the picket line that Matheson was a "slut." She called up her housekeeper, had her bring over her two preschool daughters, dressed in brightly colored, starched pinafores for the occasion. Matheson gave each girl her own picket sign and put them on the picket line to show she was no "slut," nor would she be cowed.[65]

Even her opponents seemed to have been impressed by her courage. Dorothy Ney, who served as picket captain alongside Matheson in these years, recalled, "Even that gang up there [in Pittston], they had a lot of respect for Min, you know. They knew she was doing her job. They didn't want her there, but they had a lot of respect for her."[66]

Her union members respected her even more, and she developed a devoted following among these women. Minnie Caputo summed up her view of Matheson by saying simply, "She had guts. But let me tell you, she believed in it [the union], you know."[67] "Fiery, very fiery," was how Dorothy Ney remembered Matheson. "She made the

Min Matheson and David Dubinsky at a 1972 testimonial in her honor. *Kheel Center, Cornell University*

best speeches. She could convince anybody to join the movement."[68] These women knew that Matheson had worked in a garment factory just like them and understood the problems that they faced. She was "down to earth," and she gave these members a sense that she put their interests first. "She really catered to the members," Ney recalled, "and they knew that." If "they had any problem they knew they could walk into her office and talk to her." No appointment was required. "You just went over to see her, that's all."[69] And according to Caputo, if a member brought a complaint, Matheson "made sure she took care of it. . . . The girls were not afraid because they knew she would be behind them."[70] And as a result, these members stood ready to back her up, to help her organize or to walk a picket line. "Min could always get pickets," Ney said.[71]

Matheson drew on this broad base of member activism in her organizing campaigns. She focused on organizing a shop from within, winning over the women sewing operators by addressing their concerns and working with the natural shop floor leaders.[72] While Pittston remained a distinct problem, in other towns she eschewed the confrontation of a picket line in favor of sending in teams of her members to pay visits to the homes of the women working in shops that the ILG hoped to organize. At the same time, the district office of the ILG bought time at a local radio station so that Matheson could speak directly to the women and to the community at large.[73] She and her members touted the economic benefits that union membership offered, promising sewing machine operators a higher guaranteed minimum rate and time-and-a-half overtime pay for working over eight hours a day, or for working on a Saturday. They also promoted the union's benefit funds that would provide for a paid vacation, health insurance, and maternity benefits. But other issues had to do with non-economic concerns. The union would provide someone to represent their interests right in the shop, "a chairlady and a shop committee to speak for you," as one flier put it. The union would give the worker a say in how her piece rates were set, and protect her against favoritism in setting these rates, or in other workplace decisions.[74] Caputo, who would have been one of the women conducting these visits, described the union's benefits in terms of a different working environment. "It was a different thing when you went to work in the morning," she explained. If there were problems with someone's piece rate, or if their sewing machine didn't work properly and this kept their earnings down, they could raise these issues without fear of being fired for it. "You could complain, you felt relaxed you know." "You knew you had somebody" to represent you.[75]

As she built up the union in this area, Matheson sought to recreate the kind of union she had known back in New York City, when she had been active in Sasha Zimmerman's local. "When I came to Pennsylvania," she told an interviewer, "I continued what I had learned in Local 22, just amplified on a Pennsylvania base, because it was something we needed in order to carry on our work."[76] Her husband Bill became the Wyoming District's educational director and put forward a range of programs to involve the local union members. Voting rights classes began as a way to address a pattern Matheson had noticed soon after she arrived in the region—women were discouraged from voting with the refrain that their husbands would cast their votes for them. By the 1950s, this initiative had morphed into political education programs designed to educate members on the key issues of the day and mobilize their political engagement in support of organized labor. Wilkes College agreed to set up a curriculum of college credit courses in the humanities and social sciences for rank-and-file union members. The union also ran Educational Institutes, which were more episodic but also more focused. They featured daylong seminars led by experts invited to speak about particular issues relevant to organized labor, such as proposed labor legislation or changes in the garment industry. Other programs appealed to the members' interests, offering them classes on photography or dancing, and drawing them into activities where they encountered their fellow members outside the workplace, thus building a sense of community within the union's ranks, an approach that followed the playbook of Local 22 in New York.[77]

For the women involved in these experiences, the effects could be transformative. One of the organizers recalled, "People who were not politically motivated became active because of what we did. They became active in the Democratic Party and in local politics. We had active committees in the shops."[78] Matheson believed that the union's capacity to spark change stemmed from the fact that in this region where mines were closing, the wives and mothers had already taken the first step toward change by assuming the new role of family breadwinner. Now the union's message of empowerment encouraged more change. "We were like the yeast in the dough when we came in," she explained, "and we were into everything, like monkeys."[79]

Her goal, as she explained it years later to an interviewer, was to create a meaningful democracy for these women. Real democracy wasn't achieved simply by having the right to vote in elections. "You've got to have a say in your working conditions because that's where you spend most of your life. And if you can't determine your own life in the sense that you have some say in your working conditions . . . you don't have a democracy." For Matheson, this was why a real union that championed its members was so critical. "If you don't have a labor union, or you don't have an organization to represent you on the job, you're really being denied your rights, your democratic rights."[80]

She called this "my little speech about democracy." And as she recounted it for an interview in 1988, she remembered how she had given it to one of Russell Bufalino's subordinates, Dominick Alaimo, back when she was trying to organize in Pittston and arguing against his effort to keep his dress contracting shop running as a non-union operation. "As a matter of fact, just as I explained it to you, I explained it to him. [I said to him], 'I can't afford to have any shop [run] non-union, because you guys are gonna get ideas and we're going to go back to the olden days and we're not going back to that. The women don't want to go back to that. It's not me saying it, it's them. They work hard and they deserve to have protection on the job.'"[81]

5

A PATTERN OF ACCOMMODATION:
ALLIES AND ENEMIES

In May 1949 the New York Police mounted what the department described as "one of the most extensive manhunts in the city's history," searching for the men who had murdered William Lurye. Over one hundred "hand-picked" detectives were assigned to the case, with an additional force of fifty uniformed officers helping to canvass the surrounding area for any witnesses. According to news accounts, the cops questioned every person on every floor of the surrounding buildings, and they checked the records of every known labor racketeer active in the Garment District. The result was an imposing amount of paper. The reports piled up, got filed, and quickly filled several filing cabinets.[1] The impressive police response reflected the union's ability to mobilize public concern over the murder, which it achieved by staging a one-day strike of dressmakers in the Garment District and bringing over a hundred thousand people out into the streets to rally against racketeering. But the scale of the police response also reflected the fact that they had something to prove. The ILG publicly blamed them for Lurye's murder, claiming that the authorities had failed to respond to previous mob attacks on union officials. This time around the police intended to leave no one in doubt about their commitment to fight racketeering.

The energy displayed by the police contrasted with the muted reaction from people working on Thirty-Fifth Street, the Garment

District's so-called Chinatown, a warren of mob-protected non-union shops. The murder had taken place "in one of the most congested areas of the city," the district attorney noted. And yet, he told the press, "not a single witness came forward."[2] In Chinatown, people were wary of getting involved. Eventually, detectives located witnesses, including the two bookies who had been taking bets from the building lobby where Lurye was murdered. Those two and a couple other bystanders were brought into custody as material witnesses, and then put before a grand jury to answer questions about the attack. Here the witnesses faced potential contempt charges if they didn't cooperate, and perjury charges if they tried to lie about what they saw. These were hardball tactics for compelling the reluctant to cooperate. They also gave the prosecutors a chance to nail down the witnesses' testimony, just in case they might later—for some reason—change their minds about what they had seen.[3]

On June 21, 1949, the District Attorney's Office announced that it was indicting two men, Benedicto Macri and John Giusto, for Lurye's murder. Macri had ties to Albert Anastasia, the underboss of one of the city's Mafia families. Macri had previously fronted for Anastasia in a Brooklyn stevedoring business, and one of his older brothers was Anastasia's bodyguard and trusted lieutenant. Investigators also announced that they had uncovered the apparent motive for the attack. Two non-union garment manufacturers on Thirty-Fifth Street admitted giving Macri money to keep away union organizers, including Lurye.[4] The other attacker, Giusto, was apparently a hired hand. He had an arrest record that included armed robbery charges, and he had done strong-arm work for other mobsters.[5] Macri and Giusto had been seen on that stretch of Thirty-Fifth Street several times in the days before the attack on Lurye.[6]

By the time the indictment against them was announced, both men had fled. Apparently they had been warned. Macri and his family had abandoned their Brooklyn home just a few days before the police announced they were looking for him. With much fanfare the police mounted a nationwide manhunt, posting officers at the railroad stations and the airports, alerting the guards at the nation's borders, and printing out 250,000 wanted fliers, but neither suspect was caught

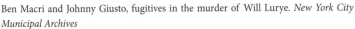

Ben Macri and Johnny Giusto, fugitives in the murder of Will Lurye. *New York City Municipal Archives*

in this ostentatious net. At one point, the authorities announced that they were focusing their search on the Southern states, having reason to believe the suspects had fled there. In fact, Macri had taken his family south, just not that far. They had moved into a beach bungalow on Staten Island where they managed somehow to evade the NYPD's well-publicized nationwide search. Giusto was never caught.[7] As a result, the crime was officially solved, but the perpetrators remained at large.

In celebration of the indictments, the authorities held a triumphant awards ceremony at City Hall on June 22 to provide commendations for the ten detectives who had led the investigation. New York mayor William O'Dwyer spoke at the event. In his speech, he made a claim that demonstrated the problematic role of local government in this era. According to the *New York Times*, O'Dwyer told the assembled crowd that the success of the police in this case "was proof to industry and labor that 'they do not need goons and gorillas' to supplement the protection provided by established law enforcement agencies." It all boiled down to a simple claim, which Americans in a later era might take for granted. The mayor asserted, "I want to take this opportunity to send word to labor and employers that the Police Department is willing and able to do its job."[8]

Even as he made the claim, O'Dwyer knew it wasn't true. Within less than a year, his police commissioner would resign as New York City was rocked by one of the largest police corruption scandals in its history. Testimony at the subsequent trials revealed systematic payoffs from a gambling syndicate to every level of command structure in the force, from precinct officers to division-level commanders, and even the police commissioner's squad. The chief of detectives who had overseen the Lurye investigation was one of those named as taking payoffs. Desperate to block these corruption prosecutions, elements within the police leadership made a bargain with organized crime figures, who persuaded the key witness involved to sabotage the prosecution's case.[9] A similar arrangement unfolded in the murder trial of Lurye's case—a witness was tampered with and no murder convictions occurred. These developments would have made it even more clear to the leaders of the International Ladies' Garment Workers' Union that despite Mayor O'Dwyer's claims, they could not depend on law enforcement. They would have to turn elsewhere, and in doing so the union's leadership chose to make an accommodation with organized crime.

Labor opponents labeled this kind of accommodation racketeering, and the arrangements in New York's Garment District were part of a pattern in which organized crime and corruption played a larger role in America's labor relations than in any of its industrialized counterparts. One of the most influential explanations of why that was the case emerged from Sydney Lens, a working-class intellectual with firsthand experience in this environment.[10]

The child of Russian Jewish immigrants, Sydney Lens was raised on the Lower East Side of New York by his widowed mother, who put in long hours toiling in the Garment District. He graduated from high school on the eve of the Great Depression and spent a couple of years scrambling for employment wherever he could find it. He was working as a waiter at Saratoga Springs resort in 1932 when he organized his first strike, a walkout by a group of fellow waitstaff. "[My] first adventure as a labor leader came to an abrupt end," he remembered. "Along about midnight . . . the county sheriff unceremoniously shook me out of bed, took me for a thirty mile ride into a wooded area, slapped me around a bit, and left me miles from nowhere with my suitcase for company." "I should have felt pained and angry," he recalled, "and I did to an extent, but I also felt exalted—I had joined a great fraternity."[11] After that experience, labor organizing became part of his life's work. In the 1930s he organized retail workers in New York City. He took part in the United Auto Workers' sit-down strikes in Michigan. By the 1940s he was organizing grocery store clerks in Chicago, where he found himself faced with an entrenched, mob-connected local union leadership in the AFL's Retail Clerks Union. In a series of hard-fought organizing campaigns he brought his clerks into another union, and continued to lead his local for years. At the same time, he maintained a second career as a prolific journalist, writing twenty-three books and producing a stream of articles for left-wing journals such as *Dissent* and *The Progressive*.[12]

In his 1959 book *The Crisis of American Labor*, Lens sought to account for the apparent proliferation of labor racketeering, exhaustively exposed by the Senate's McClellan Committee hearings, a high profile congressional probe that stretched from 1957 to 1959. "The mass of revelations [regarding racketeering] was so great," Lens noted, "and its publicity so constant, that in many minds the whole labor movement became suspect."[13] Meanwhile, in Europe, according to Lens, "bribes, pay-offs by employers, 'sweetheart' contracts, and other vices that exist in some American unions are unknown."[14]

Lens asserted that the reason for this phenomenon was the decline of social unionism in the United States. Since the 1930s, the CIO had followed a "wide road toward institutionalization," with CIO leaders becoming what Lens labeled "un-radicals," in effect entrenched bureaucrats who resembled their slightly more conservative business unionist counterparts.[15] Many of the most committed progressives were gone from the labor movement, because in response to Cold War concerns the CIO had ousted Communist Party members from its ranks. When certain affiliated unions resisted this push, the CIO expelled them, purging eleven left-wing unions from the federation. In 1955, the gap between the CIO and AFL essentially disappeared when the two labor federations merged to create the AFL-CIO. The resulting malaise, Lens argued, undercut organized labor's ability to organize, or to respond to the growing trend of mechanization; it also, he asserted, had set the stage for the proliferation of racketeering.[16]

This is the standard explanation for why labor racketeering has been an enduring problem for the American labor movement. Crass business unionism displaced the more idealistic social unionism that existed elsewhere, creating a climate in which some union leaders felt free to indulge in abuse of their positions and to make the accommodations with organized crime groups that led to labor racketeering.

It's an explanation that does not really fit what happened in the International Ladies' Garment Workers' Union. This was an organization founded by socialists, and which had from the very beginning organized immigrant women laboring in low-wage sweatshop conditions—the opposite model of the typical AFL craft union. The ILG's leadership had helped to found the CIO. In the years that followed Lurye's murder, the ILG officials who reached out to the mob included union idealists, whose dedication to labor's cause had been established by a lifetime of activism. Among them was Lurye's sister, Min Matheson. Her role demonstrates this complicated history. Given the options available in that time and that place, choosing to work with mobsters amounted to a pragmatic choice, one that a labor leader with the best of intentions might pick out of necessity.

It was a choice ILG leaders made as they monitored the progress of efforts to bring Lurye's killers to justice. Those efforts had stalled in the wake of the indictment of Macri and Giusto, since both of them had fled shortly before the police had begun looking for them. Giusto was never caught, and the district attorney's case file suggests that he relocated to Quebec.[17] But Ben Macri turned himself in to the authorities a year after he was indicted, using Walter Winchell, the famous newspaper columnist and radio personality, to serve as his intermediary.

Winchell had played a similar role a decade earlier when the notorious labor racketeer, Lepke Buchalter, had surrendered to him.

Bringing in Macri offered Winchell a chance to reenact the glory of that episode and to shore up his fading celebrity status. Winchell also planned to claim the $25,000 reward offered by the ILG and turn the money over to a charity he had created to honor his friend Damon Runyon. The columnist got his shot at the limelight after the actor Robert Montgomery, the first choice of Macri's representatives, turned them away. Montgomery was apparently unwilling to abide by their conditions, a concern that Winchell didn't share. In return for giving Winchell the chance to boost his profile, they asked the columnist to promote a more positive image of Macri. They wanted him to publicize the fact that Macri had a wife and children and had never been arrested before.[18] In a series of radio broadcasts that preceded Macri's surrender, Winchell did just that. The front-page article in Winchell's home newspaper, the *Daily Mirror*, continued this theme, referring to Macri's "attractive young wife and three small children." It quoted Winchell's radio broadcast, reminding readers that Macri "was never in trouble before and had led a good clean life as a father and a citizen." Finally, the *Mirror*'s article cited an unnamed law enforcement source who explained that Macri had never intended to kill Lurye. "They just planned to beat him up a little bit."[19]

While news coverage made Macri look better, Lurye's image plummeted. Stories surfaced in the wake of his death of his involvement with a crew of union pickets that had roughed up a non-union cutter. As one newspaper headline summed up the story, "Garment Area War Vet Says Lurye Beat Him Up." The *New York Journal American* began referring to Lurye as a "union strong arm man."[20] And the *New York Sun* reported to its readers that "it was learned at the District Attorney's Office that the fatal stabbing of William Lurye . . . likely was the result of his use of strong arm tactics in forcing non-union garment workers to join the union."[21] Testimony at Macri's trial further emphasized this negative depiction of Lurye. In his opening statements, the prosecutor told the jury that a few days before he was stabbed to death, Lurye had broken into Rosebelle's shop while it was closed and slashed a batch of dresses. The prosecutor linked the destructive vandalism to Lurye's murder. Rosebelle was the same firm that had brought Macri in as a partner in return for the mobster's promise to keep them non-union. Lurye had openly boasted to his fellow union organizers about what he had done, and it was one of these colleagues, in turn, who helped Macri set up his ambush in the building lobby on Thirty-Fifth Street.[22]

Despite laying out a clear motive for the attack, the trial did not go well for the prosecution. Testifying in his own defense, Macri depicted himself as the victim. Wearing a suit and horn-rimmed glasses, and described as "thin faced" by the *New York Times*, Macri said that he was on Thirty-Fifth Street that day for his trucking business. He had gone into the lobby at No. 224 to use a payphone just as Lurye was being attacked by some other individuals. Those same men attacked Macri and, as he testified, "I ran out scared. I ducked and I ran like hell." He had noticed a union organizer involved in the fray and so, afraid of being targeted by "union strong arm men," he fled to Ohio, where he had lived for a year until he turned himself in.[23]

It's unclear whether or not the jury bought Macri's story, but in the end that didn't matter much. The prosecution's case had already disintegrated after the testimony of the state's two key witnesses: the cigar stand operator and one of the bookies who operated out of the lobby at No. 224. The cigar stand operator, Morris Weinberg, had testified that he saw the two men attacking Lurye that day, a pivotal point for the DA. Next, the prosecutor asked him if one of the two attackers he had seen was in the courtroom, and if so, he requested that Weinberg walk over and point him out to the jury. This was when things went awry. Getting up from the stand, Weinberg walked past the seated Macri and instead picked out the assistant defense counsel. Without saying a word, without contradicting his previous statements to the grand jury, Weinberg found a way to undo his testimony. The bookie, Samuel Blumenthal, also proved to be a problematic witness. In his testimony before the grand jury he had described seeing Giusto and Macri attacking Lurye in the phone booth. But at the trial he could only clearly recall seeing Giusto engaged in the attack. He claimed an unclear memory in regard to Macri's actions. The prosecutor's efforts to pin him down brought only equivocation, as Blumenthal asserted that "he did not know what Macri was doing."[24] He was blatantly contradicting his sworn testimony before the grand jury, and as a result, at the trial's end, the judge cited him for perjury. But the damage was done; Macri was acquitted.[25]

Macri's trial coincided with another high-profile case: a police corruption scandal that grew out of a probe into organized gambling by the Brooklyn prosecutor, the Kings County District Attorney's Office. In 1950, Brooklyn investigators had arrested the head of a gambling syndicate, Harry Gross, and when he agreed to cooperate, they uncovered a massive system of protection payments that went up and down the NYPD's command structure.

A short, pugnacious, middle school dropout, Gross had expensive tastes in clothing that clashed with personal mannerisms that remained firmly rooted in the working-class Brooklyn where he had grown up. The *New York Times* described him as someone who "looks like Broadway and talks like Brooklyn." He combined a math wizard's gift for numbers with a gambler's sense of nerve and an uncanny ability to cultivate useful connections. By the mid-1940s his operation included a string of illegal horse-betting rooms and close to two hundred so-called runners, men who took bets from customers, at locations throughout Brooklyn, the Bronx, and Manhattan. This included the building lobby at 224 West Thirty-Fifth Street where Martin "Chink" Sherman and Samuel Blumenthal took bets from employees working in the shops up and down the Garment District's Chinatown. Gross's operation brought in $20 million a year in illegal bets and paid out a million dollars of "ice," the preferred term in that era for payoffs to the police. He brought in well-placed members of the force as his partners and in turn the NYPD sponsored the expansion of his syndicate, pushing formerly independent bookies, like Sherman and Blumenthal, to become part of Gross's organization.[26]

In effect, the police and Gross were in business together, and it was a partnership that elements within the NYPD's leadership ranks valued highly. This became apparent in 1949, the same year Lurye was murdered. That fall, Gross took too many layoff bets from other gambling syndicates on the World Series and lost $40,000. Unable to pay his debts, he fled to Los Angeles. His friends in the police were desperate to get him back and restore the system of protection payments Gross had established. They reached out to the Mafia, contacting Joe Adonis, who arranged for another Mafia figure, Willie Moretti, to front Gross $100,000 to pay off his debts and reestablish his syndicate.[27]

After Gross was arrested by the Brooklyn prosecutor's office in 1950, these same NYPD officers reached out again to their contacts in the Mafia, hoping to sabotage the DA's effort to convict some thirty members of the force on corruption charges. This police corruption trial was scheduled for October 1951, the same month as Macri's case. In return for $200,000, Gross agreed to testify in such a way that the case against the thirty policemen would have to be dismissed. Macri's brother, James, was one of the guarantor's of this agreement and so too was Willie Moretti, both of them prominent members of what was known as the Mangano crime family.

Standing behind James Macri and Moretti was Albert Anastasia, who had moved up in 1951 from underboss of the Mangano crime family to boss of the family, after the disappearance of the former boss, Vincent Mangano. It was assumed Anastasia had him killed and then disposed of the body. Technically, according to Mafia rules, the heads of the city's other Mafia families were not supposed to allow another boss to be killed by one of his underlings. But in this case they let it go. As the Mafia historian John Davis has noted, by the late 1930s Anastasia already "had become perhaps the most feared member of La Cosa Nostra [aka the Mafia]." The FBI believed that he was responsible for over sixty murders during his career and often his role in these killings was quite direct. In one case, he stabbed his victim to death with an ice pick. "He especially enjoyed killing with his bare hands," wrote Davis. Born in southern Italy in 1902, Anastasia had come over to the United States as a child and grown into a "robust, barrel-chested, hirsute man of medium height with a dark complexion and curly black hair." He had an "intimidating stare" and he spoke in what one author described as a "rapid-fire, Cagneyesque" style.[28]

In 1931, he had been tasked with putting together a squad of professional killers who would take on assignments given to them by the New York Mafia's leadership. He assembled a group of young Jewish and Italian gangsters from Brooklyn who were later dubbed "Murder

Albert Anastasia, brutal leader of the Mangano crime family. *New York City Municipal Archives*

Inc." He shared leadership of this group with Lepke Buchalter and Joe Adonis, but most accounts depict Anastasia as the central figure and for this reason he was often referred to as "The Lord High Executioner."[29]

His base of operations had originally been the Brooklyn waterfront, but by the 1940s he had also established ventures in the Garment District; Ben Macri's activities were one element of Anastasia's move into this area. In New York's Mafia circles, Anastasia was close to Adonis, who was the mob's most adept political fixer. After Mangano disappeared and Anastasia became the boss of the family, he made Adonis his underboss.[30] When the NYPD turned to Adonis to help them out, they were in effect turning to Anastasia, the most brutal face of the mob. The same was true two years later, when they used James Macri and Moretti as intermediaries; both were close associates of Anastasia and turning to individuals like him to help fix a criminal case demonstrated the character of these NYPD officials.

In September 1949, Gross slipped away from the district attorney's police squad that was guarding him and met with mob figures including Moretti, who paid him part of the agreed-upon sum. Returning to

custody, Gross led the DA to believe that he still intended to cooperate, waiting until after the trial was well underway, and he was called
to testify, before he balked. As a result, the DA was forced to ask the
judge to dismiss his case. Under the rule of double jeopardy, none of
the police defendants could ever be tried again on these charges. As
he watched his case collapse before his eyes, the district attorney, who
was prosecuting the case himself, broke down and cried in front of
the entire courtroom.[31] He later told the press that he doubted that
"anything could be salvaged from the case."[32]

Ben Macri's trial for Lurye's murder case was sabotaged through a
similar method. A few months before the trial began, a mob-connected
official in the Jewelry Workers Union, George "Muscles" Futterman,
approached the bookie Blumenthal, who had witnessed Lurye's murder. Blumenthal described what happened when he later testified at
Futterman's obstruction of justice trial. The Jewelry Union official told
him that Macri was backed by important people, including Albert
Anastasia. Futterman warned Blumenthal "to straighten himself out
with these people" and "do what he could not to hurt Macri." "You're
on the spot," Blumenthal remembered being warned. "You're as good
as dead if you don't do what you're told." Futterman gave Blumenthal
$100 "on account" and promised him "big money" when the trial was
over. For his part, the bookie was frightened, but not too frightened to
name his price and he admitted saying that for $5,000 he would com-
mit perjury. At Futterman's suggestion, Blumenthal met with Macri's
attorneys, who coached him on how to testify, advising the bookie
that he should say that his grand jury testimony had occurred so long
ago that he no longer could remember details about the attack. It was
exactly what Blumenthal did at Macri's trial.[33]

We don't know if a similar approach was used on the other key
prosecution witness at that trial, the cigar store stand operator who
somehow confused a defense counsel with Macri. But it seems likely
that someone explained to him that this would be an effective way
to avoid hurting Macri, and thus avoid Anastasia's wrath, while also
skirting any conflict with his previous grand jury testimony.

All in all, the outcome of these trials did nothing to inspire faith in the NYPD or the proper functioning of the legal system, despite what the mayor had said at his press conference in June 1949. In fact, the NYPD, or at least a significant part of its plainclothes units, bore a strong resemblance to a criminal organization. It had formed a partnership with the head of a gambling syndicate and worked with him to regularize protection payments from bookies. When the Mafia did this, it was labeled a street tax, a kind of organized extortion of illegal entrepreneurs. Relations between the police and organized crime figures, such as Joe Adonis and Willie Moretti, were more in the tenor of one group of gangsters dealing with another group of gangsters, arranging for favors and loans, using other mobsters as intermediaries.

Moreover, when these deals went awry, it appeared that the police responded like an aggrieved gang. This became evident after Willie Moretti shortchanged Gross on his payoff for sabotaging the police corruption trial, giving the head of the gambling syndicate only a fraction of the agreed amount. Apparently Moretti tried to make even more money from the situation. FBI reports indicate that in the weeks after that payoff, Moretti and Anastasia were squeezing the police for another $100,000 payment. "As a result of the 'shake-down,'" according to one of these reports, "a certain group of plainclothesmen [NYPD] made an agreement to talk the matter over with Moretti." He was gunned down on October 5, 1951, while sitting at a streetside restaurant table with four men who had been waiting to meet him there. The FBI's report indicated that "two representatives of the [NYPD plainclothesmen's] group were supposed to meet with Moretti and Anastasia at the restaurant the morning Moretti was shot." The remaining text of the report is blacked out, but it seems likely the Bureau reached the obvious conclusion that the NYPD had been involved in Moretti's murder.[34] There were also a couple of attempts to kill Anastasia in this same period. One of them took place while he was attending a party to celebrate Ben Macri's acquittal in the case of Lurye's murder.[35]

The history of this police corruption scandal, along with the outcome of Macri's trial, meant that union leaders seeking protection from racketeers had good reason to be dubious about the NYPD. Nor did the local DAs look much better. The prosecutors may have been less corrupt, but they appeared largely impotent when poised against organized crime.

At the same time, union records indicate that the ILG's leadership believed it had friends among the racketeers; in effect there were mobsters it could deal with in order to pursue the union's goals. These arrangements belied the public perception of the ILG's leadership, including its president, David Dubinsky, whose reputation for honesty and rectitude were often contrasted with other segments of the labor movement, such as the Teamsters Union. Because Dubinsky and his fellow Garment Workers' Union leaders clearly cherished that image, the union's records tend to make only cryptic references to these arrangements with gangsters.[36] Moreover, there has been a consistent effort to obscure this history. When the subject of racketeering came up during oral history interviews with Dubinsky and his top aides in the early 1970s, the transcript indicates several breaks in the conversation, as the microphone was turned off and the conversation continued off the record.[37] Files with the words "racketeering" on their label have been removed from the union records, which are stored at Cornell University's labor archives. The current union's leadership has requested that they not be made available to researchers.

The union-sponsored biography of Dubinsky, published in 1957, sums up the preferred official version of the ILG's encounter with racketeering: it was a problem in the 1930s that subsided after the conviction and execution of Lepke Buchalter. The book refers to Lurye's murder as one of the "minor strong-arm incidents [that] from time to time have marred the garment industrial scene." But, according to this text, after the arrest and unsuccessful prosecution of the man who killed Lurye, the problem of racketeering faded away in the garment industry. "Little . . . has been heard since of hoodlum activity on the sprawling ILG map the country over."[38] The ILG, according to this version of its history, was a union exceptionally free from problems with racketeering, a fact made possible by Dubinsky's leadership and the strong stand he had always taken to keep corruption out of the labor movement. Dubinsky's co-authored autobiography described him as the "conscience and goad for all labor in a no-surrender battle against corruption in union ranks."[39]

This version of events has largely been accepted.[40] The actual history is a bit muddier, although one has to piece it together by sifting carefully through the union's voluminous collections and drawing on other accounts, such as FBI records. One pivotal document was tucked away in an otherwise innocuous set of records belonging to the ILG's executive secretary, Frederick Umhey. Among his boxes of routine correspondence between various executive committees was a file folder marked "Lurye." Its contents included paperwork on a union fund created to support Lurye's widow, along with negotiations with a producer considering a movie production about the murder. Between those papers was a memo with no date and no author, titled "Possible and perhaps probable motive for the stabbing of William Lurye." It offers a very different perspective on the most prominent racketeer in the Garment District: Abe Chait. The memo reviews Chait's prominent place in the trucking rackets that provided protection for non-union shops. It notes that his firm, Champion Trucking, provided these services "for possibly some 135 non-union shops" and that it was rumored that he was a partner with Thomas Lucchese, the head of the Lucchese crime family. But then the memo describes Chait as a potential ally for the union. The document asserts that having achieved wealth in this industry, Chait was now interested in distancing himself from the gangster element, or at least the most violent part of it. He was disturbed by the attacks on the ILG that had occurred in the fall of 1948, "the recent assaults in union offices and the action taken against the [white caps] marine pickets employed by the ILGWU."[41]

Chait wanted to make an alliance with the union. "He was . . . willing to aid the union in their effort to organize various shops." To that end, about six weeks before Lurye was murdered, Chait had met with "some executives of the ILGWU" and afterward had "shown his good faith by putting a number of shops in the union." Other racketeers in the Garment District opposed Chait's move to help the union, seeing it as a threat to their incomes, which would be "depreciated with shops being unionized." The memo asserts that the attack on Lurye was intended "to show the [ILG] organization that in spite of what Chait may have promised, they [these other racketeers] do not have to follow him and release their hold on the non-union shops." The memo concludes with a positive assessment of Chait, who apparently had been unable to forestall the assault on Lurye by these other racketeers. "From information [gathered] Chait feels very bad about this killing. He is not afraid of the gangster element. He is sincerely interested in aiding the union to organize shops."[42]

From the point of view of the union's leadership, this kind of alliance was a necessary evil, given the lack of alternatives. A 1957 report to the ILG's Dress Joint Board by its manager, Julius Hochman, provided an account of the leadership's perspective on its situation in this period. Since the late 1930s the union had seen more and more firms turn to mob-connected truckers such as Chait to avoid the union. Hochman explained, "This new non-union production, organized and backed by gangsterism, put us under tremendous pressure. The development of a group of non-union jobbers created havoc in the market." Firms that continued to adhere to the union contract "complained justifiably that they couldn't compete with non-union production," but "at the time we had no way of bringing these non-union jobbers back under our agreement." Evidently, at some point in the early 1940s, a deal was made with some of the gangsters involved. "A department of our International [Hochman never specifies exactly who, and this kind of cryptic language is typical] was permitted to make certain compromise agreements," which were called "International Agreements." It was supposed to be a temporary arrangement. The plan was that "gradually the [gangster-affiliated] jobbers would be brought back under our regular agreement or the equivalent of it. It seemed a logical, a reasonable expectation."[43]

But it didn't work that way. Once these firms had their competitive advantage they were not willing to give it up. "On the other hand, their success in winning competitive advantages encouraged other jobbers to follow their example," Hochman wrote. He was alluding to a pattern in which other firms found themselves forced to compete with these mob-connected jobbers by reaching out to organized crime figures and making their own arrangements with them. This was what the dressmaker Rosebelle had done in 1949, bringing Macri in as a partner in hopes that he could gain for his firm one of these so-called International Agreements. "We decided ultimately that it did no good to allow a department of the International to set up another group of jobbers, and that it would be better if we organized the runaways ourselves."[44] The result was the ILG's Dress Joint Board's organizing campaign, which began in the fall of 1948 and culminated with Lurye's murder.

In the wake of that violence, the ILG's leadership realized that it could not prevail. As Hochman later summarized the result, "The runaway jobbers and the people who protected them—I'm speaking of the gangsters, the truckers and [ILG] Local 102, the whole combination—created a set of circumstances in which it was impossible for us to insist on full acceptance of our Joint Board Agreement." Like the International Union, the Dress Joint Board found itself making arrangements with gangsters to bring their shops into the union. "We, too, had to compromise, to grant certain exemptions; and we, too, did this with the notion that it would be temporary."[45]

Here again the records of the ILG do not offer many specifics. But there are suggestive references in the daily journal kept by David Gingold, manager of the Northeast Department of the ILG, who in the spring of 1950 began referring to meetings between him, Min Matheson, and Abe Chait. Those meetings were followed closely by stormy encounters between Gingold and key leaders from the ILG, Dubinsky and Sasha Zimmerman. One of Gingold's diary entries from this period reads, "Had another meeting with Minnie Lurye [Matheson] and Sasha Zimmerman again about the Wilkes-Barre Pittston situation. And again meeting broke up in violent disagreement."[46]

An entry two days later seems to refer to the decision to make special accommodations with the gangster element based in northeast Pennsylvania, and it also indicates that this decision came straight from the top of the union. "Met with Chas. [Sasha] Zimmerman in Pres. Dubinsky's office where we again rehash the plaguing problem of the Wilkes-Barre Pittston area. After a long discussion a plan was worked out whereby Chas. [Sasha] Zimmerman, [Jacob] Halpern [field supervisor for the ILGWU's Northeast Department] and [Dress

Joint Board official] Sol Greene will go into Wilkes-Barre and attempt to carry through a satisfactory working arrangement that may bring about the organization of the Pittston District."[47] Gingold's diary referred to other meetings he had involving Chait, as well as the official head of the Pennsylvania Garment Manufacturers Association (PGMA), Matheson, and Halpern.[48] Through these arrangements the ILG created a functioning contract with the PGMA, but in doing so it was forming a working relationship with a group it knew was dominated by organized crime figures like Chait.

One might ask, what was in it for Chait? Why had he offered to aid the ILG in 1949, when he and other racketeers had for years made their living by helping employers circumvent the union's controls? Chait and other mobsters involved in the industry had an oddly symbiotic relationship with organized labor; the mob's self-interest led it to support a strong, progressive union. Because wages were the most significant production cost in garment manufacturing, the union's success in organizing the city, and setting up a stable uniform wage standard, created an economic opportunity for a limited number of shops operating outside the city that could undercut those standards. The mob's ability to keep those shops non-union, or receive favorable union contracts, provided Chait and other gangsters with a way to profit from the situation, but only so long as the union continued to play a dominant role in the industry. In a way, this made Chait and his associates allies of the union. Indeed, FBI informants used the term "union mob" to refer to Chait and his associates. The term invoked the importance of the connections Chait and his group had with individuals inside the ILG's leadership.[49] As one informant put it, they had "union connections and were in a position to either operate non-union shops, furnish protection for non-union shops, or operate under special contract with the International Union."[50]

The perspective of informants working with the FBI and New York City's Anti-Crime Commission was that Chait had made a strategic alliance with the ILG in the early 1950s. He had agreed to use his influence to help the union organize the non-union shops in northeastern Pennsylvania because he hoped the union would strengthen his position relative to other organized crime factions that had emerged to challenge his position. This challenge may have come from Anastasia, who was a fairly new presence in the Garment District. An FBI wiretap intercepted a conversation in 1963 in which a Mafia leader, John Masiello, described an agreement reached about ten years earlier between Chait and ILG president David Dubinsky. According to Masiello, the deal went this way: "We [the Mob] will produce [for organizing] all the non-union shops, but we want so many [nonunion] shops for ourselves. Dubinsky said, 'Fine.' Thirty three guys would be allowed to have nonunion shops." [51]

These accounts also depict the key ILG organizer in Pennsylvania, Min Matheson, actively engaged in bolstering Chait's influence with local contractors. Referring to the Pennsylvania Garment Manufacturers Association, which Chait dominated, an informant asserted, "The men in charge of the organization are able to put the squeeze on various manufacturers through the union local which is headed by a sister of William Lurye [Min Matheson]." By making a demand for higher wages or raising some other grievance, the informant explained, Matheson could force the contractor to turn to the PGMA, and by extension to Chait, for assistance. [52]

Such allegations need to be viewed with a measure of skepticism, but it is clear that in the early 1950s, the ILG did come to an understanding with Chait. That understanding allowed the union to get contracts signed with a number of non-union garment firms in northeast Pennsylvania.

It also meant that union officials, like Min Matheson, developed working relationships with Chait and with other mobsters who were allied with him. She referred to this obliquely in one of her oral histories, when she told her interviewer that over the course of her career she had "met and sat with and negotiated and fought with" a long list of racketeers, including John Dioguardi, Thomas Lucchese, and the Strombergs. The list also included "the guy who was really boss of the garment center for many years," Chait, with whom she had "an extraordinary, most interesting relationship." She had great respect for him, she told the interviewer, and she described one encounter in which she told him so, suggesting he could have achieved great success in a legitimate field, such as the law. "I said to him one day, 'You know, Mr. Chait, you have a judicial mind and you wasted your life.' " He was, she recalled, "pleased as punch," by the compliment and asked her why she said it. "I said, 'You're always able to see through a problem.' And he said, 'Sure, you think I have a judicial mind because I rule in your favor.' "[53]

It was an extraordinary reminiscence that indicated a mutual working relationship between Matheson and Chait, but the interviewer never followed up on it. This is very typical. So too is the notation on the oral history transcript in the midst of Matheson's account of this episode: "There is a long pause on the tape."[54] The oral history then shifts back to the subject of Matheson's youth in Chicago. The interviewer never comes back to the issue of Matheson's relationship with the Garment District's most powerful gangster.

Despite this type of obfuscation, we can still trace some outlines of this history. The nature of the ILG's arrangements with organized crime was complex and unstable. There was pushing and pulling on both sides. While Chait had formed an alliance in 1950, other mobsters resisted the union's organizing efforts until 1953. For their part, union officials such as Min Matheson fought hard to build on these arrangements in ways that extended genuine union benefits to workers in mob-controlled shops. She was far from being cowed or controlled by the mobsters that she dealt with, and for their part they pushed back too.

The remaining conflicts surfaced in the summer of 1952, when the ILG's cloak division launched an organizing drive. The union sent three thousand pickets into the Garment District carrying signs and distributing fliers that announced, "We strike to wipe out the deadly cancer of racketeering."[55] The union's leaders explained to the press that they were targeting a group of about fifty-five jobber manufacturers of women's cheaper, untrimmed coats that were sending their work to out-of-town non-union contractors. These "non-union shops were operating under racketeer protection," asserted an ILG official. At the same time this group of jobbers formed their own employers' group, the Independent Association of Women's Apparel Manufacturers.[56] Internal union reports identified two long-term mob figures,

Joseph Stracci and Gabriel Klar, as the guiding force behind the new association.[57] Publicly, Dubinsky denounced it as "an underworld association." According to the *New York Times*, "He charged that 'underworld characters' were active in these concerns as partners and salesmen." This association demanded that the union negotiate a separate contract with them. When the ILG refused, the association chose an imaginative response, deploying its own pickets to demonstrate in front of union headquarters and filing an anti-trust suit against the union.[58]

By September 1952, the conflict had been resolved. The union proclaimed victory, announcing that it had organized the majority of shops it had targeted, including most of the jobbers who belonged to the Independent Association.[59] For its part, the Association withdrew its anti-trust suit against the union. Thirty-two of its member firms signed contracts with the ILG, but as the group's legal counsel explained to the *Times*, the union agreed to negotiate "independent contracts with them that did not require them to join one of the major employers' associations and that did not exact extraordinary conditions which the members would have found onerous."[60] In effect these were the softer contracts that the mob-protected firms had been angling for all along. "We couldn't get them to sign otherwise," one ILG official acknowledged to a journalist.[61]

More trouble broke out a year later in northeast Pennsylvania. The ILG called a strike against the Pennsylvania Garment Manufacturers Association, the group dominated by Chait and other mobsters, asking for a thirty-five-hour week (the standard in New York City garment factories since the 1930s) and a 6 percent raise in wages.[62] At about the same time, the Northeastern Pennsylvania Needleworkers' Association, a racket union led by mobster associates of Russell Bufalino, began actively organizing workers in the area's garment factories. In a speech broadcast over local radio stations in August 1953, the Needleworkers' Association leader, Nick Benfonte, denounced ILG leaders, including "Princess Matheson," as communists who represented New York interests and were bent on destroying the growing garment industry in Pennsylvania.[63] An informant described in a state police report as "reliable" and "in a position to know" told the Pennsylvania State Police that Bufalino and his close associates, Dominick Alaimo and Angelo Sciandra, "met with the heads of the ILG in New York City late in 1953. Dave Dubinsky, the head of the ILG, was present and the proposition was made to him by the Pittston men that they would permit him to take over the charter of the Needleworkers' Association for a sum said to be $2 million. Dubinsky is supposed to have offered them a large amount of money, but not anywhere near what they asked." According to the report, during the "ensuing argument Dubinsky was alleged to have been threatened by the subject [Bufalino] whereupon Dubinsky got up and walked out of the meeting and has refused to negotiate with them since that time."[64]

None of the surviving records indicate how the conflict was finally resolved, but subsequent developments suggest that it was. After 1953, the Needleworkers' Association ceased its efforts to organize garment workers, though it continued to operate in other area industries, corralling employees into union contracts that protected the company's interests, not the workers.[65] Evidently the ILG had reached some kind of understanding with Bufalino that led the Needleworkers' Association to respect the ILG's jurisdiction. Whether that arrangement involved a payment by the ILG, or some other form of quid pro quo, remains unclear. The Garment Workers' Union had earlier settled its 1953 strike against the Pennsylvania Garment Manufacturers Association, having gained both of its main goals—shorter hours and a 6 percent wage increase.[66]

Min Matheson's correspondence from these years offers glimpses of the balancing act she maintained as a progressive unionist protecting her members' interests while working within a system of brokered understandings. In one letter to her mentor, Sasha Zimmerman, she wrote about an issue involving a local mob-connected firm: "It seems that somewhere, some place, someone made an understanding with this firm not to settle prices." In other words, the company didn't have to negotiate its piece rates with the union, a standard requirement in the ILG contracts. She had raised the issue with officials at the union's Dress Joint Board in New York, "and it seems, whoever made the agreement, the agreement must stand." Another mob-connected

firm, Smart Sue, had an arrangement that allowed it to avoid paying into the union's Health and Welfare Fund. Matheson faced the
looming issue of what to do now that the workers' vacations were ap-
proaching, but there were no payments in the fund to support them. "I
cannot discuss it at length in a letter," she wrote to Zimmerman, "but
you know the problem and I am wondering if anything can possibly
be done to bring a settlement?" [67]

The constant theme in these letters is the need to work within the
understandings that had been reached and still push to achieve the
union's goals. In late 1952, in the wake of the ILG's measured organizing victory against the non-union jobbers who had formed their
own Independent Association, Matheson wrote to Zimmerman. She
was trying to find a way to get the New York jobbers to pay their
Pennsylvania-based contractors more money so that, in turn, she
could get these contractors to raise their piece rate wages to their
workers. "The entire relationship between the newly signed jobbers,
the contractors, and our organization is not good and we must find
some ways and means of getting the contractor-jobber relationship
straightened out, so that we can get a little extra for our people," she
wrote. [68]

To achieve this goal, she met with and bargained with the various Bufalino-associated mobsters whose menacing presence had
made her early organizing efforts in Pittston so frightening. Angelo
Sciandra was one of those men. Law enforcement authorities believed
he had arranged the car bomb murder of the Mine Worker Union
leader Charles Mecadon in 1951. Two years later, Matheson wrote
Zimmerman about her ongoing campaign to get Sciandra to raise his
workers' piece rate wages. Sciandra was putting her off, complaining
that he wasn't getting enough from his jobbers to pay higher wages.
Undaunted by the mobster's reputation or his arguments, Matheson
wrote, "I intend to spend some time with him this week and try to
work out some type of increase in spite of what he says." [69]

She was not intimidated by these men, and her correspondence indicates a willingness to challenge them when she felt they had back-
tracked on the understandings that underlay their relationship with
the ILG. In late 1952, she wrote a letter rebuking Sciandra for his

apparent violation of one of these arrangements and his prevarication over what he was doing. He and Dominick Alaimo, another Bufalino mobster, were helping to support the Northeastern Pennsylvania Needleworkers' Association, despite previous assurances to her they had no ties to it, and that the Association would not organize garment workers. "Knowing me quite well, you know of course that one thing I hate more than anything else is double dealing and double talk," she wrote. She issued them an ultimatum, whose language says volumes about the nature of her relationship with these men. "Needless to say, this situation cannot continue," she warned Sciandra. "I must have an immediate and straight answer from you and Nick as to where we stand on this whole question."[70]

She took a similar stand with Chait, when she felt the situation required it. In her oral history, she recalled pulling the workers from one of his plants after the supervisor had removed the doors from the toilet stalls in the women's restroom. She warned the plant's local manager that the doors had to be reinstalled or she would stage a walkout, taking the women working on the sewing machines out of the plant. "I'm coming down to the factory," she remembered telling the manager, "and we're going to be sitting in the beer joint across the street. You're going to get no production at all." The manager warned her that Chait would not like it. "You know, Mr. Chait this and Mr. Chait that . . . I said, 'I'm not interested. If you want to call him, you call him. I'm not wasting our union money calling New York." Minutes later she was at the factory, arguing toe-to-toe with the manager, who only relented after she made good on her threat and had taken the sewing operators out of the factory and over to a nearby beer joint.[71]

The record indicates that although the ILG had reached an accommodation with organized crime figures, such as Chait, those arrangements did not amount to an abnegation of the union's role. Instead, in an environment where racketeering could not be eliminated, only curbed, union officials like Matheson and her mentor Zimmerman did the best they could in difficult circumstances. Neither person fits Lens's model of a crass business unionist suffering from a lack of ethical backbone. Just the opposite was the case.

To what extent did other unions in this era face a situation similar to the ILG's? Probably there were many, although little has been written on this issue.[72] Those studies that do exist suggest that other unions encountered similar dilemmas when they tried to operate in industries where organized crime had established a significant role. Local trucking was one example; the construction trades were another. For these unions, organizing and working with employers involved making pragmatic arrangements with organized crime figures, or with individuals who had ties to organized crime. The best the union's leadership could hope for in such setting was to limit organized crime's influence, while acknowledging the impossibility of completely eliminating it.

Steven Fraser's book on Sidney Hillman, the progressive leader of the Amalgamated Clothing Workers of America (ACWA), suggests this kind of situation prevailed in the men's clothing industry in New York. Evidence indicates that in the 1930s, payments went from the ACWA to individuals associated with Garment Center racketeer Lepke Buchalter. Fraser concludes that Hillman either agreed to such payments or allowed officials loyal to him to make these arrangements in his stead.[73] Some sort of similar arrangement existed in the Amalgamated Meat Cutters. That union's longtime leader, Max Block, described his decision to work with Mafia figure Carlo Gambino when the Amalgamated organized the meat industry in New York City. As Block explained the situation in his 1981 memoir, "You got to do something. You got to work out some sort of arrangements. . . . You have got to have some sort of understanding with these people."[74] Block's assertion was true only for that portion of the labor movement facing the dilemma of organizing in an industry where patterns of corruption and organized crime influence antedated the union, but for those unions he described a real issue.

The particular nature of these arrangements would have varied from union to union, and from union official to union official; they would have ranged across a spectrum of conduct, from pragmatic but principled officials to those who were nothing more than sellouts. For the union movement as a whole, this situation complicated its response to the issue of union corruption. Unlike the political figures in Congress during this era, who could make dramatic calls for a labor movement completely free from corruption, union leaders faced a more complex situation. A history of pragmatic policies left responsible leaders open to charges of hypocrisy or complicity, making them wary about revealing the details of these accommodations to journalists and investigators at the time, and by extension to historians in the years that followed. It also gave union officials such as Min Matheson valid reasons to be wary of the anti-corruption probes that proliferated in the post–World War II era.

6:

THE USES OF FEAR:
AMBITION AND MANIPULATION

In a column that appeared on May 14, 1949, in hundreds of newspapers throughout the country, Victor Riesel warned that the attack
on William Lurye signaled a new effort by organized crime to "muscle
in on the unions." Writing before the terms "Mafia" or "La Cosa Nostra" had gained currency, Riesel referred to a "combine" or "syndicate,"
or more dramatically, "the ever-present, mysterious national syndicate." It functioned, in Riesel's depiction, as a kind of invisible government that oversaw a nationwide confederation of gangs, with each
gang having jurisdiction over particular rackets in particular territo-
ries. Since the end of Prohibition, these mobsters had gained wealth
and increasing respectability by infiltrating a range of industries. Or,
as Riesel put it, "the 'respectable' racket combines . . . have cut up the
dress trade, the hotel and restaurant fields, the trucking industry and
other operations into special bailiwicks." Now mobsters operated out
of "exquisitely appointed offices," used "prominent attorneys, good
publicity men and certified accountants," and contracted whatever violence they needed to "young thugs" who lacked their connections or
experience. With no more gang wars, and a controlled use of violence,
the public had "forgotten the gangs are still there—in every big town,
operating practically right out in the open."

This public complacency, Riesel asserted, had convinced the syndicate that it could expand its reach. "Many inside labor believe that

the first sign of the mob's new toughness was the assault which almost cut Walter Reuther in half." Next came the attacks on the International Ladies' Garment Workers' Union (ILG) organizers in the fall of 1948, followed six months later by Lurye's murder. Riesel depicted Lurye's attack in his typical melodramatic prose style, one that evoked Mickey Spillane. "A few days ago, a longtime idealist, young in years, old in crusades, husband of a tubercular wife, father of four kids being brought up in the heart of a New York district where life gets rough at times, was slashed to death by three goons." The attackers were "men of strange faces, the torpedoes-to-let," whose brazen attack signaled the syndicate's new aggressiveness. "They were three little men with big knives who could step up to a phone booth in a daylit Manhattan and knock off the representative of a union with $50,000,000 and 400,000 members; a union whose leader has helped to make presidents and shape world affairs." Riesel warned that more attacks were likely, unless the public dropped its complacency and pushed the police to respond to this new threat.[1]

Riesel was one of many voices in the post–World War II era raising an alarm about the menace that racketeering presented to the country. In this early Cold War era, these warnings often took on the tropes of anti-communism, depicting racketeering and communism as domestic threats that bore a striking resemblance to each other. The similarity had little to do with the nature of communism and organized crime. Instead it reflected the fact that many of the individuals voicing concern about racketeering had already established themselves as ardent anti-communists, and as they turned their attention to this new domestic threat they adopted the language and the techniques that had already proven effective for them in gaining an audience. This was the case for Riesel, a labor beat journalist who had initially built his reputation on his crusade to curb communist influence in organized labor.

The labor beat had emerged as a distinct group of journalists in the 1930s alongside the rise of organized labor, which grew dramatically in the New Deal era. Newspapers and news magazines scrambled to provide meaningful coverage of the strike waves that were transforming the industrial landscape, and this meant assigning a corps of reporters who could over time develop expertise on labor and its concerns. Part of developing that expertise involved reaching out to union leaders and union members to understand their concerns. Publishers also hoped to draw more working-class readers by providing sympathetic news coverage that included issues and events that mattered to them. A band of reporters emerged writing for *Time*, *Newsweek*, the major metropolitan newspapers, and the wire services.

Many of them, like Louis Stark of the *New York Times*, were imbued with a sense of mission, hoping to build support for the labor movement by educating the public about unions. A good labor beat reporter, Stark asserted, "must be able to grasp the drama of the more or less everyday business of the unions and in their relations to management, industry, and the nation." Stark hoped that his model of reporting would build support for the labor movement by offering the general public a better understanding of what unions actually did. For this reason, he urged his fellow labor beat reporters to pursue a model of reporting that went beyond covering simply the most flamboyant events, such as strikes or racketeering. They should also explain the "background of these controversies." The reporter should write about the quotidian issues of American workers and their organizations "vividly enough to enlist the attention of the newspaper reader," in ways that could merit "sympathetic consideration and understanding."[2] It was this model of the labor beat that his successor at the *New York Times*, A.H. Raskin, identified with when he later described his aspirations as a reporter during his own career. "I always considered a vibrant principled union movement a hallmark of American democracy," he wrote. "My mission was to bring together organized labor, employers, the workers, and government. My most valuable tool, I thought, was making sense of the turmoil."[3]

Not everyone who covered labor shared this mission, or followed Stark's model of reporting. In the early 1940s, Stark's most important rival was Westbrook Pegler, a conservative columnist who wrote extensively about union abuses, and in particular the problem of labor racketeering, which he depicted as pervasive. Pegler won a Pulitzer Prize in 1941 for his exposés on corruption in the Building Service Employees International Union and the International Alliance of

Theatrical Stage Employees. Those cases were just the tip of the iceberg, he argued, describing the labor movement in general as "rotten with extortion and racketeering."[4] He made attacking this issue his personal crusade, one which was tied to a larger political effort to curb the power of organized labor.[5]

Pegler's rise did not completely eclipse Stark, who won a Pulitzer Prize of his own in 1942. But Pegler's success, especially the popularity of his syndicated column, had made an impact. *Business Week* noted that Pegler "has left his mark on the field . . . by demonstrating to many editors that there is considerable reader interest in union corruption." He also demonstrated the appeal of a labor beat style that eschewed Stark's moderation and balance in reporting. Pegler's "prose style, which frequently gets as close to being as scatological as a newspaper can print," *Business Week* asserted, "plus his crusading spirit, makes him just the opposite of Stark."[6]

Pegler eventually moved on to other issues, writing less frequently about labor as the 1940s came to a close. But like Stark, he had a number of successors.[7] One of them was Nelson Frank, who covered the labor beat in New York City for the Scripps-Howard Newspaper chain and had a daily column on labor matters in the *New York World-Telegram*. Frank specialized in exposing communist influence inside the labor movement. In pursuing this avenue he had a useful background in military intelligence work and ties to staff members at the House Un-American Activities Committee and the Senate Subcommittee on Internal Security, as well as agents in the Federal Bureau of Investigation.

Like Stark, and like Pegler, Frank depicted his labor beat reporting as part of a larger campaign. In Frank's case it was an effort to purge the labor movement of radical communist influence. A letter he wrote in 1953 referred to "a consistent stand that I have taken in my stories in the *World-Telegram* for the past nine years." This stand involved denouncing communist influence in unions, but also bolstering the position of union leaders who turned against the party. "I have blasted Communists wherever and whenever the occasion offered," Frank explained, "and I have endeavored to assist those who wanted to break with the party by giving them such aid as I could when they needed it most." He believed his efforts had contributed to a rightward shift in a number of unions. "I have been fortunate in having had the support of my paper in assisting the backslid Commies in the Transport Workers Union, the National Maritime Union, the United Furniture Workers Union, the United Shoe Workers, among others."[8]

Pegler's most prominent successor, however, was Victor Riesel. The liberal *New York Post* had first hired Riesel to write a column on labor matters in 1943, promoting him as an antidote to Pegler's steady anti-union tirades. Over time, however, Riesel moved to the right. By 1947, his liberal editors at the *Post* had begun to express displeasure with the increasingly conservative tone of his column, warning that it "has created among some of our readers the impression that you have become hostile to labor." Soon afterward he shifted his base of operations to William Randolph Hearst's *Daily Mirror*, where his new conservative, anti-union publisher suffered little anxiety about his drift to the right.[9] Riesel's career became intertwined with a new group of associates, evidenced by his engagements as invited speaker at gatherings of the National Association of Manufacturers.[10] Additionally, internal FBI records from this period described Riesel as "a good friend both of the Bureau and of the NYO [New York Office of the FBI]," one who was reliably willing "to cooperate with the FBI." He had close ties to sources within the labor movement who were actively engaged in waging a campaign against communist influence. And like Frank, Riesel cultivated connections with staff members on congressional committees, including both those focused on domestic communism and labor racketeering.[11]

These sources helped shape his reporting, which came to run along lines similar to Pegler's crusading perspective. In effect, Riesel became the new Pegler. As the *Business Week* article explained it, "Riesel has turned more and more to the 'exposé' story and is today bracketed with Pegler by the *Post* and by some unions."[12]

By the 1950s, Victor Riesel was the most influential member of this exposé wing of the labor beat. He presented a voice that claimed the long-term engagement with the union movement that was a hallmark of the labor beat, but paired it with the aggressive style that Pegler had first popularized. Riesel's personal connection with the labor movement included family ties. His father had been a local union leader in New York's Garment District, and he could write in his column how "I can still recall the day in the early thirties when I walked into the shabby day room of my father's needle trades union."[13] Like Stark, Riesel had spent years accumulating contacts with various union leaders. He claimed to have been covering labor since 1930 and touted his "established and cordial relations with labor leaders from Major Clement Attlee down to local business agents in AFL and CIO."[14] Advertising sent out to promote Riesel's syndicated column referred to his sources as "the big brass at the labor offices in Washington and the local union headquarters around the country"; but this same flier also assured these newspaper publishers that he was "no labor coddler." "He plays no favorites and pulls no punches," they were promised.[15]

And indeed his published writings appeared to show no such restraint. His syndicated column, "Inside Labor," which went out to two hundred newspapers across the country, portrayed a labor movement under siege from intertwined threats of communism and organized crime. In often-hyperbolic prose, Riesel warned that this "underworld-Communist combine" sought control of strategic unions, thus endangering the nation's security.[16] To take one example, in 1952, a column by Riesel focused on the possibility of a "ghoulish combination of crooks and communists" coming together to "move in and take control of one of our most strategic areas—the [East Coast] waterfront." The communists planned to seize the opportunity provided by law enforcement's campaign against established corrupt union leaders on the docks. "In a year," Riesel predicted, "the reds will be working with the thugs as they do throughout the world."[17]

This version of the labor beat had great impact. For many American newspaper readers, particularly those living in cities and towns outside the major metropolitan areas, Riesel's perspective on the union movement had signal importance. As *Business Week* explained, "In some cities the only coverage labor news gets—beyond the big national stories that come from the wire services—is through Riesel's column."[18]

Riesel's columns formed part of a larger stream of news coverage in the postwar era in which investigative exposés spurred hearings, which in turn generated more stories on labor racketeering. In 1948, the *New York Sun*'s conservative publishers sent investigative reporter Malcolm Johnson out to develop a hard-hitting series on labor racketeering on the New York waterfront. The resulting articles won Johnson a Pulitzer Prize and led to a set of widely publicized hearings by the New York State Crime Commission.[19] Those hearings, in turn, formed the basis for the 1954 blockbuster film *On the Waterfront*, which created a powerful image of a labor movement mired in corruption. Scenes that dramatically reenacted an investigative hearing resonated with moviegoers, who had become familiar with the pattern of recalcitrant witnesses and heroic victims featured in news coverage at the time. While later critics of the movie have viewed those scenes in the context of more general hearings on domestic communism, contemporaries would likely have understood the film in more literal terms—as a dramatization of scenarios all too familiar to them.[20] Hearings on communism from this era are well remembered today, but in that same period hearings on labor racketeering proliferated. Beginning in 1947 and stretching through the early 1960s, over a dozen congressional probes threw a spotlight on the issue of labor racketeering, ensuring its place in the public discourse.

Journalists often played crucial behind-the-scenes roles in those congressional probes. An investigative reporter such as Clark Mollenhoff, who wrote for the Cowles Publications that included *Look* magazine and a string of newspapers, was an example of the type of reporter who developed symbiotic relationships with these congressional investigations. A Washington, DC, based reporter, Mollenhoff had been dispatched by his editors to Minneapolis in 1953 to investigate the activities of a local Teamster leader who was closely allied to James R. "Jimmy" Hoffa. Mollenhoff spoke with a group of local union dissidents and met with businessmen who described the shady practices of the local Teamster leadership. The reporter saw the outlines of a significant story, but he came to the conclusion that it could best be developed through the promotion of a congressional probe of the Minneapolis Teamsters. He later recalled the benefits of this strategy, noting that although he was gathering some useful evidence of wrongdoing by Teamster leaders, "we could still be subject to losing a few million dollars in libel suits." This could happen if his sources buck-led to pressure and changed their stories after his articles were pub-lished. "In fact, I wouldn't even be sure that all our employer-witnesses would remain firm on their stories unless we had them under oath." A more secure way to get the story, he argued, was to "pull the story out through a Congressional committee." The resulting testimony would lock the witnesses to their stories and, by law, any allegations pro-duced by a congressional hearing are immune to libel suits.[21]

If he came to the subject of labor racketeering in response to an editorial assignment, Mollenhoff soon adopted it as a professional and personal crusade. He centered his writing on the Teamsters Union, is-suing a steady stream of warnings about the dangerous power wielded by Dave Beck and especially Jimmy Hoffa. He wrote a note accompa-nying a series of articles in 1955 in which he suggested to his editors at Cowles that they include "a map of the United States to run with the series on Jimmy Hoffa. This map would have the Central States, Southeastern States and Southwestern States [Teamster conference ju-risdictions] shaded and the word 'Hoffa Land' printed across it."[22] But Mollenhoff asserted that the problem of racketeering extended well beyond the Teamsters, and he warned of a nationwide pattern of cor-rupt labor leaders operating with impunity. He used his articles to call for more congressional hearings and for legislation that would curb the power of such corrupt union bosses.[23]

At the same time, Mollenhoff developed a network of fellow inves-tigative journalists working on related stories about corruption in the Teamsters Union. In 1954, he reached out to Ed Guthman and Paul Staples, two reporters with the *Seattle Times* who were conducting an investigation of Dave Beck. In Portland, his peers Wallace Turner and William Lambert reported for the *Oregonian*, pursuing stories that involved local Teamsters leaders in that city.[24] Mollenhoff's papers in-dicate similar relationships with reporters in other cities, including Detroit, Hoffa's base of operations.[25]

This network meant that there was a steady stream of investiga-tive journalism on labor racketeering, especially on the Teamsters. Mollenhoff's network would later provide the basis for a potent part-nership between these journalists and the era's largest congressional investigation, the McClellan Committee hearings, which came to focus on the Teamsters beginning in 1956. These groups promoted each other's efforts with a steady exchange of tips and publicity, which resulted in a series of newspaper exposés and headline-grabbing hearings on racketeering in the Teamsters Union in the first half of 1957. It in fact was a journalist who helped launch the McClellan Committee hearings.

In the early morning hours of April 5, 1956, as Victor Riesel was leaving Lindy's restaurant in Manhattan, a hired thug approached him and threw a vial of concentrated sulfuric acid into his face. The liquid splashed directly into Riesel's eyes, searing them. "After a kind of momentary, very momentary, surprise and shock," he later recalled, "there came the sharpest, most painful burning I have felt." [26] The acid concentration was so strong that the runoff disintegrated Riesel's tie. And even later, when law enforcement arrived at the scene, a drop that fell from the columnist's face burned a hole through one policeman's coat. Hospitalized for weeks, enduring terrible pain, Riesel was left permanently blind.[27]

Newspaper reports immediately linked the attack to Riesel's crusading efforts to curb communist infiltration and racketeering in the labor movement. "In the fourteen years that he has been hammering away at Communists and racketeers in labor's ranks," a front-page article in the *New York Times* asserted, Riesel "has received scores of threatening letters and telephone calls." But the "pint-sized," "voluble" columnist with a "writing style that resembles Mickey Spillane's" had shrugged off these threats, the *Times* reported, and had "refused to be deterred from his anti-racket activities." [28]

The attack appeared to vindicate his claims by demonstrating that the targets of his crusade had come after him. The *National Review* touted Riesel's courage by noting that he had been "engaged in exposing two elements which he *knew* to be capable of retaliation. He knew that the labor racketeers against whom he inveighed, and the Communists whose plans he was so constantly frustrating, were uninhibited enemies." The magazine's editor acknowledged, "It is possible that the assailant was not a hired mercenary of Communists or racketeers, but it is unlikely." [29]

Attention soon focused on organized crime's role in the attack, and Riesel's plight became a frightening sign that confirmed the menacing power of labor racketeers. On the evening before his attack, Riesel had made a radio broadcast in which he denounced corruption in the Operating Engineers Union. Some suspected the attack might have been in response to that broadcast.[30] But the U.S. attorney for Manhattan, Paul Williams, charged that the assault had come in response to Riesel's role in aiding his office's existing grand jury probe into labor racketeering in New York. Williams described the attack as a "black effort to intimidate witnesses," asserting a federal role in the investigation of the assault on Riesel.[31] "This attack is directly attributable to articles written by Mr. Riesel and to very important information which he has given me in my investigation," Williams told reporters. In this way, the assault on Riesel became a challenge to the free press and to an ongoing grand jury investigation. Williams explained that he considered it "a direct attack" on his office.[32]

This interpretation of the event has been reinforced by previous histories of labor racketeering in this era: it was a vicious attack on a crusading journalist that led the country to confront the issue of union corruption and organized crime's influence in the labor movement. Journalists and commentators at the time saw it this way, and so too have writers who have referred to it more recently. It turns out to be a more complicated story.

In the days and weeks that followed the attack, front-page newspaper headlines across the country encapsulated the key dimensions of the story. In the immediate aftermath of the attack, the *Boston Evening American*'s headline proclaimed, "Labor Racket Foe Hit by Acid," and the *Washington Post*'s front page explained, "Assault Linked to Fight on Rackets." "Acid Victim Worsening," the *Los Angeles Times* told readers on the West Coast a week after the incident occurred, and when Riesel's bleak prognosis became clear, the *Chicago Tribune* explained, "Acid Victim Loses Sight in Both Eyes."[33] A year later, the *New York Herald Tribune* would publish a story about the national concern over labor racketeering with a picture of Victor Riesel and the headline "Public Victim No. 1."[34]

The brutality of the attack, and the apparent effort to stifle a valiant

Victor Riesel meeting with the press after acid attack. *Queens Public Library Archives*

reporter, generated widespread outrage. As one magazine editorial as-serted, "Never have we seen our community, which is not unfamiliar with crimes of violence, so stirred by an outrage as it was by this foul attack on the crusading labor columnist."[35] A year later, the *New Re-public* would refer to "the depths of public anger over labor racketeer-ing, especially since the Victor Riesel case."[36]

For his part, Riesel embraced his role as the martyred victim and argued that the attack signaled the need for a major new congressional investigation of labor racketeering. Dressed in a robe with large ban-dages over his eyes, he held a defiant press conference from his hospi-tal room six weeks after the attack. A widely distributed news photo of the event shows him with his arms raised and fists clenched—the caption reads, "Courage."[37] Riesel blamed the attack on "sleazy labor racketeers" who were "trying to frighten the community," and warned that organized crime's power had grown in recent years to such an ex-tent that it now amounted to a "second government—the mobs. . . . I fought them all my life, and being blind will not keep me from turning out my columns as before; they haven't scared me. I can't see, but I can hit back and I'm going after the mob!" The attack against him represented "an act of arrogance against the community, a challenge to the decent elements of the community," he asserted. The response should be a new congressional probe into labor racketeering.[38] It was a point he repeated a couple of weeks later during a televised appearance on *Meet the Press*.[39]

Many people found this argument persuasive, including President Dwight Eisenhower. The president had watched Riesel's appearance on *Meet the Press*, and according to news reports "had been impressed by Riesel's demands for action against union racketeers." A couple of days later, while meeting George Meany during the dedication ceremonies for the AFL-CIO's new headquarters, Eisenhower indicated that he would push for a campaign to combat "underworld infiltration into unions."[40] The president's choice of words, "infiltration," followed Riesel's lead and, similarly, invoked the parallel nature of the two dominant domestic threats. In the 1940s, the trope of "infiltration" had justified a range of efforts to curb left-wing influence into unions including the Taft-Hartley Act.[41] Now a decade later, it was being raised again, as the influence of organized crime presented a new reason to probe unions and to question their powerful role in the country.

The same language appeared again, a month after Eisenhower's statement, when Irving Ives, the moderate Republican senator from New York, proposed a resolution calling for a new congressional investigation into labor racketeering. "I believe, I hope correctly," he said, "that only a small fraction of the nation's labor unions have been *infiltrated* by these evil men." Then he warned, "But the truth is, no one knows the extent to which racketeers have moved in on the labor movement." In support of his resolution, Ives cited the attack on Riesel and noted the columnist's call for a congressional investigation.[42]

Other voices in Congress were making similar calls and they were echoed by newspaper editorials that summer.[43] In an article entitled "Why the New Move to Investigate Racketeering in Labor Unions," the magazine *U.S. News & World Report* gave credit to Riesel's appearance on *Meet the Press*. In addition to the president, the article noted, "several members of Congress, after seeing the program, moved for a new investigation."[44] Not surprisingly, some of the most vociferous supporters of a new probe came from the conservative end of the political spectrum, including long-term opponents of organized labor such as the Michigan congressman Clare Hoffman. In the 1950s, he had chaired a series of House subcommittee investigations into labor racketeering. In the wake of the attack on Riesel, Hoffman claimed that his and other's congressional investigations into labor racketeering had been hamstrung. The shocking attack on Riesel changed the political situation dramatically. "I hope that the house will take cognizance of the present situation because Victor Riesel has certainly paid a price for his opposition to those gangsters and their activities which no individual should be called upon to pay," Hoffman said. "Victor is in a position to call for action and to make it so imperative, so necessary, that we do something, that maybe we will get a real investigation."[45]

That August the *Wall Street Journal* made a similar point on its editorial page, arguing that both political parties should call for a new congressional probe of labor racketeering. Everyone acknowledged "the prevalence of union racketeering," the *Journal* asserted. "Exposing aspects of it cost columnist Victor Riesel his eyesight when a thug threw acid in his face." Riesel's subsequent call for a congressional probe had credibility because the columnist was a "staunch friend of labor" and because the attack on him revealed how the problem had "assumed the dimension of a national scandal." In an allusion to Riesel's injury, the editorial charged that widespread union corruption and racketeering constituted a prominent "black eye" on the face of the labor movement, and closed with a line that reinforced the link between Riesel's blinding and a new political environment: "The disservice, to labor and to all the people, would be for the parties to blind themselves to labor's black eye."[46]

Many other editorials employed the same blinding metaphor. This approach had the benefit of invoking the brutal nature of the attack on Riesel while also implying that organized labor's political influence had blocked previous efforts to deal with the problem of racketeering. The *Reading Eagle* urged congressional leaders to put their political fears to the side and launch a new probe: "The investigation that might be expected to follow would not restore Victor Riesel's sight, but it would open the eyes of many people who are blind to the power that enables some unscrupulous men to levy tribute against legitimate business and sentence those who defy them to blindness and even death." [47]

Then in late August 1956, a new development brought the story of the acid attack on Riesel back to newspaper front pages all across the country. The FBI arrested a group of men that the Bureau alleged had arranged for the acid attack on Victor Riesel. According to the press briefings provided by the Bureau and the U.S. Attorney's Office, these men had accepted a contract for $1,000 to stage the acid attack on Riesel and to point him out to the individual pegged to throw the liquid at the columnist's face. The man who actually threw the acid, Abraham Telvi, was not among those arrested. He had been murdered in late July, killed apparently after he had asked for more money and because he had accidentally scarred his own face during the attack, which made it too easy for the authorities to identify him. About a week after the initial suspects had been brought in, a second round of arrests included John Dioguardi, the Garment District mobster, and some of his close associates. As the New York Times put it, the case now "had the elements of a gangster motion picture," with a classic villain at the center of the story—the villain was Dioguardi, who had allegedly ordered the acid attack. [48]

Dioguardi was often mentioned in New York City news reports, especially throughout 1955 and 1956 when he had become involved in efforts to sway a union election involving the New York Teamsters Joint Council. Those efforts centered on a group of local unions chartered to Dioguardi by a small national union, the United Auto Workers of the American Federation of Labor (UAW-AFL), an organization that had broken away from the much larger United Auto Workers of the CIO. Dioguardi had staffed the officer positions in those unions with a collection of ex-convicts who preyed on both employers and their union membership. When the AFL forced the UAW-AFL to revoke Dioguardi's charters, Jimmy Hoffa had worked to bring them into the New York Teamsters Joint Council. The newly chartered locals provided the crucial votes to swing a Teamsters Joint Council election over to a Hoffa ally. All of this had received widespread coverage in local newspapers, which referred to Dioguardi by his nickname, Johnny Dio, and in the coverage of his arrest for arranging the acid attack on Riesel, the gangster was depicted as both notorious and incredibly powerful. The lead for the *New York Times* article read, "John Dioguardi, alias Johnny Dio, considered to be one of the most powerful labor racketeers in the nation, was accused last night of having arranged the acid attack that took the sight of Victor Riesel." [49]

In the newspaper accounts of the U.S. attorney's explanation of the case, Dioguardi had ordered the acid attack on Riesel to block his testimony before a federal grand jury investigating labor racketeering in Manhattan. The horrific nature of the attack amounted to a kind of terrorism, meant to deter not just Riesel but all others from cooperating as well. It was, according to the *New York Times*, "a premeditated signal from the underworld to any and all witnesses—newspaper men, garment manufacturers, truckers, union officials, et al—that a word to the wise was sufficient and that a word from the unwise would be fatal." [50]

The language became more portentous when efforts to prosecute Dioguardi for the Riesel attack failed, indicating the gangster's apparent ability to defy the U.S. government. In December 1956, the U.S. Attorney's Office won convictions against three of the men who had arranged for Telvi to throw acid into Riesel's face. But the federal case against Dioguardi rested on the cooperation of one of the conspirators, Gandolfo Miranti, whose willingness to testify evaporated as the time of the trial approached. Though he faced an eighteen-and-a-half-year jail sentence for refusing to testify, Miranti still balked, certain he would be killed if he testified. When another co-conspirator made the same decision in May 1957, the U.S. attorney was forced to drop his case against Dioguardi. [51] *Life* magazine labeled the result "a shocking show of underworld power." [52] Others agreed, and a piece in *Time* magazine later noted how the outcome of the case indicated just how "powerful" Dioguardi had grown. [53]

It was against this backdrop that a new congressional investigation into labor racketeering was launched. The Senate's Permanent Subcommittee on Investigation (PSI) had begun a series of preliminary investigations into labor racketeering beginning in late August 1956. These amounted to speculative probes, efforts to determine the feasibility of a larger investigation and a way to assert the committee's claim to what now appeared to be a politically advantageous enquiry. The PSI was a subcommittee of the Senate's Government Affairs Committee; under the leadership of Senator Joseph McCarthy in the early 1950s it had gained prominence by investigating the menace of domestic communism. In 1956, Senator John L. McClellan, a conservative Democrat from Arkansas, chaired the committee and Robert F. Kennedy was the PSI's chief counsel.

The PSI had meandered onto the subject of labor racketeering in the previous year when it began looking into a cartel of garment manufacturers involved in the production of military uniforms. Dioguardi was among the individuals active in that cartel, and soon thereafter the acid attack catapulted him into a new prominence. In the midst of a fairly blasé probe into military procurement practices, the committee had essentially stumbled onto a high-profile target. Meantime, Riesel's call for a major new investigation into labor racketeering had met a positive response from the president and in the halls of Congress. After newspaper headlines linked Dioguardi to the acid attack, the PSI quickly shifted its focus to center on him. It then pursued Dioguardi's ties to a powerful leader in the nation's largest labor union—James R. Hoffa, a vice president in the International Brotherhood of Teamsters.[54] Robert Kennedy received encouragement to follow this path from the Cowles reporter Mollenhoff, who brought together Kennedy's investigators with the network of journalists working on Teamster stories in Seattle, Portland, and elsewhere. The resulting partnerships between the journalists and Kennedy's staff provided a crucial jumpstart to this investigation.[55]

The direction of the PSI's investigative efforts also demonstrated the significant political impact of the acid attack on Riesel: the event helped attract the Senate's premier investigating committee to the subject of labor racketeering. The PSI's move in this direction also reflected Senator McClellan and his chief counsel Kennedy's keen political instincts as they maneuvered their committee toward what

one newspaper predicted was "potentially the most sensational congressional probe in 1957."[56] The *New York Times* reported, "It is generally recognized at the Capitol that a labor investigation, properly
conducted, would yield political 'pay dirt' for two to four years." In
January that year, the Senate resolved competing claims over who
should conduct an investigation into labor racketeering by creating a
new Select Committee on Improper Activities in the Labor or Management Field (usually referred to as the McClellan Committee) and
appointing members of both the PSI and the Senate's Labor Committee. In a nod to the preliminary investigative work they had already
done McClellan was appointed chair and Robert Kennedy was made
chief counsel.[57] The resulting probe would be the largest congressional
investigation of its kind up to that time, dwarfing comparable efforts.
The McClellan Committee's staff numbered over one hundred people, including eighty investigators. Previous investigative committees
featured much smaller staffs. The Senate's Permanent Subcommittee
on Investigation, when it was under the chairmanship of Joseph Mc-
Carthy, had about fifteen investigators, and the House Un-American
Activities Committee included about twenty.[58] By all contemporary
standards, this was an impressive allocation of resources.

The McClellan Committee's investigation occurred at a critical political moment. Conservative elements within the business community had responded to the merger of the AFL and the CIO in 1955 first
with apprehension and then with a rekindled commitment to mount
a counteroffensive against organized labor. As Elizabeth Fones-Wolf
has noted, many conservative business leaders "saw in the merger
the specter of a labor juggernaut."[59] At the National Association of
Manufacturers (NAM), internal memoranda from 1956 document the
leadership's desire to find a way to blunt the growing power of organized labor. A policy memo issued in February that year urged, "The
NAM must conduct a broad public relations program to educate the
public to the abuses and evils of organized labor, the potential threat
represented in the newly merged AFL-CIO, which makes it the largest
organization and most powerful political force in the country today."
The central theme that NAM wanted to emphasize was the dangerous

accretion of power by organized labor. Or, as the group's public relations expert put it, "the program will emphasize . . . [the] vast uncontrolled power of labor unions."[60]

But in those months preceding the acid attack, NAM's internal documents also acknowledged major obstacles blocking its ability to make much headway with this program. Though the employers' association liked to invoke the issue of organized labor's exemption from anti-trust regulations, a confidential internal report in February 1956 noted, "The public appears to be relatively little concerned with the charge of 'labor monopoly' as such." Indeed, although NAM was quite alarmed about the dire consequences of union power, its staff noted that the general public exhibited no similar level of concern about the issue: "Efforts to expose labor unions' harmful activities—no matter how justified and buttressed by facts—appear to make little impact on the public." NAM wanted some way to change that situation, by drawing attention to the prevalence of violence, racketeering, and undemocratic practices in unions. What was needed, NAM's staff decided, was a campaign to shape "public consciousness through the multiplication of case history upon case history in order to focus limelight attention on these practices—and thus arouse the public, which now sits back and accepts injury and violence without serious protest." But the employers' association realized it was ill-equipped to accomplish such a task on its own. "Unfortunately, however, it is difficult to obtain sufficient number of documented case examples."[61]

NAM needed an empowered organization to take on this task. By April 1956, the same month Riesel was attacked, the employers' association began calling for a congressional investigation.[62] That July, NAM mailed out to all members of Congress a complete copy of the article series Riesel had written in the wake of his acid attack, entitled "My War with the Mob." In this series, Riesel asserted that, "Only the spotlight of a properly conducted Congressional investigation can light up the murky corners [of the labor movement]." He criticized the "over-zealous defenders of labor" who worried that such a probe might tarnish the movement. "Unwittingly, these men become, in effect, the secret weapon of the mob."[63]

Riesel's call for a new investigation in the wake of the acid attack had important political ramifications. Although there had been previous congressional probes of union corruption in the post–World War II era, political opposition to these efforts caused them to run short of resources, and often they ended abruptly and inconclusively. A series of hearings by a subcommittee of the House Committee on Government Operations demonstrated this problem. Labeled "quickie" investigations by fellow committee members, these efforts at times were called off mid-hearing.[64] As one historian has noted, in terms of creating the impetus for new legislation, "none of these probes had any national impact."[65] Moreover, such ineffectual efforts had the potential to forestall serious investigations by making it appear that the ground had already been covered and there was little potential for achieving new results.[66]

The outrage that came in response to the acid attack on Riesel, combined with his call for a new probe, echoed by President Eisenhower, changed the political equation. It made a new probe not only possible, but also imperative. This new urgency led the politically powerful Senator McClellan, a leading member of the conservative coalition in Congress, to position himself to head this investigation, in turn guaranteeing that this particular effort would receive a plenitude of resources. McClellan was, as one historian put it, someone who "could pull the wires and levers to sustain an investigation," and it would last for two and a half years.[67]

Once the McClellan Committee began holding its hearings, NAM's leadership offered dramatic praise for their effects. A newsletter sent to members of NAM's National Industrial Council in February 1958 proclaimed, "The Senate Rackets Committee, chairmanned [sic] by Senator McClellan (D.-Ark.) continues to unfold sensational examples of union leaders' betrayal of the trust reposed in them by their members. Each new exposure of corruption, graft and mismanagement by labor bosses points up the desperate need for corrective legislation."[68]

But even if such legislation failed to occur in the short term, employers' groups expressed satisfaction with the results of these hearings. The U.S. Chamber of Commerce's president, Philip M. Talbott, asserted in September 1957, "To my way of thinking the great, overshadowing good that is served by this committee is public education."

The news coverage of the committee's sessions and its revelations had served to "jar public thinking." "A general public, which has—in the main—been largely indifferent to the problems posed by the growth of the labor movement, has been alerted."[69]

At the same time that employers were seizing the opportunity created by the aftermath of the acid attack against Riesel, so too were prominent figures within the Republican Party. By 1956, President Eisenhower's administration was abandoning its earlier efforts to build a political bridge to moderates in the labor movement. The president's political advisors had concluded that the Republican Party's best hope for regaining a majority status lay in an "attempt to separate the leaders of labor politically from the rank and file."[70] The McClellan Committee's revelations offered a chance to do just that, and Eisenhower soon embraced a focus on the problem of labor racketeering.[71] Further to the right, Barry Goldwater staked his 1958 Senate re-election campaign on an attack against the racketeering bosses of big labor, demonstrating the populist appeal this issue held.[72]

The political opportunity being seized by employers and conservatives had first opened up because of public outrage over the horrific attack on Riesel. Everything the public encountered in the news media indicated that the attack was a vicious move to silence a crusading journalist who had hammered away at communist and gangster infiltration of labor unions. It was depicted as retaliation for his testimony before, and assistance to, a federal grand jury investigating labor racketeering in New York. According to U.S. attorney Paul Williams, the assault was an "effort to intimidate witnesses" and "a direct attack" on his office.[73]

In Riesel's series "My War with the Mob," he described the attack as a brutal reprisal for his decision to wage a "fight on terror" by standing up for all the helpless victims of labor racketeering. "Let no one think I wanted to be blinded for life," he wrote." "Let no one think I did not know the risk involved in this kind of fight I've been making." And there were all of the other victims, who turned to him as well, the "ex-GIs" who were union reformers, and the "owner of a small chain of stores." "Can you stand unmoved by such men and women who cry out—literally—for help? I couldn't. So the crime cartel hurled its acid." Editorial commentaries echoed this assertion. Blindness for life was the price Riesel had to pay, the *Des Moines Register* asserted, "for his crusade against gangsters who have succeeded in clamping their greedy hands on a few labor unions in that city."[74]

But Riesel's account of the attack was dishonest. Moreover, the U.S. attorney, the FBI, and eventually the McClellan Committee all knew it to be false, from very early on, and never allowed that information to become public. Their complicity in suborning this deception means that the public reaction to the attack was not just misguided; it was misdirected, and misdirected in a way that suited the interests of a number of key players, including Riesel, the U.S. attorney in New York, and by extension NAM and the Republican Party.

In fact, almost every aspect of what the public had been led to believe about the story behind the acid attack was not true. Riesel had not testified before the federal grand jury impaneled in the spring of 1956 to investigate labor racketeering in New York City. He had never been asked to testify, and had he been asked, as he explained to his assistants, he would have declined to offer testimony. As a journalist, he never considered testifying before a grand jury to be an appropriate role.[75] FBI records obtained through a Freedom of Information Act request make it clear that the Bureau was very aware of the misleading nature of the claims being made by U.S. Attorney Williams. A memorandum written on the day of the attack summarizes a conversation that the special agent in charge of the FBI's New York Office had with Williams. According to the memo, Williams "informed Kelly [the special agent in charge] that he had not subpoenaed Riesel nor intended to use him as a witness."[76] As Williams began issuing very different statements to the press, characterizing the acid attack as "a direct threat to the [grand jury] investigation," FBI director J. Edgar Hoover made clear his opinion of the events. In a handwritten notation, Hoover wrote, "Here we go! Williams couldn't resist the temptation to cash in on this."[77]

The U.S. attorney claimed that Riesel was more than just a grand jury witness: the columnist had provided valuable information to his office, greatly assisting the grand jury investigation. This also was not true. When the FBI questioned Williams's staff about its contact with Riesel, they could point to only one scheduled meeting with Riesel, which was supposed to have been on March 28, 1956. Even this meeting failed to take place, however, as Riesel sent his assistant, Alton Levy, to go in his place. And Levy's goal was to get information, not give it. Riesel explained to the FBI that he sent "his associate [Levy] . . . down to talk to Williams for the purpose of obtaining information from Williams on cases showing racketeering in labor, so that he could use this information in his column." There were more informal contacts. From time to time, according to Riesel, he spoke with Williams over the phone and "Williams would ask him whether or not certain individual labor figures had criminal records." But as the Bureau report noted, "Riesel indicated here that this was sort of 'silly' also inasmuch as Williams had access to all sorts of criminal records." The U.S. attorney did not need a newspaper columnist to find out who had a criminal record. These types of interactions had more of the flavor of a politically ambitious prosecutor indirectly plying an influential journalist with information about his investigation, in hopes of getting his name in the newspapers.[78]

The notion that Riesel had been providing important information to the Justice Department, beyond what was publicly available in his columns, had always been a problematic aspect of the case. It belied the way Riesel functioned as a columnist. His columns usually repackaged information Riesel had gleaned from other publications, or from what the staff of various government agencies or congressional committees provided to him to promote their own agendas. When he wrote about union corruption he used published sources or focused on the complaints of union dissidents, whose opposition to their organization's leadership was already well known. His melodramatic writing style did not give one the sense that he was withholding significant information or sensational details in his columns.

The U.S. Attorney's Office never presented evidence that Riesel had assisted its grand jury investigation. When it prosecuted the men who had conspired to carry out the acid attack for Dioguardi, the government put forward a two-count indictment. One count alleged a conspiracy to obstruct justice, which was based on the claim that Riesel had been assaulted for his work with the grand jury investigating racketeering. The second count involved a conspiracy to aid a fugitive fleeing across state lines to avoid prosecution; this count was based on the fact that the acid thrower had been sent to hide out in Pennsylvania and Ohio for several weeks after the attack, and these men had helped arrange for his travel. At the commencement of the prosecution's phase of the trial, the government promptly announced that it would not seek to prove the first count of the indictment, the obstruction of justice charge linked to Riesel's purported assistance to the grand jury. Prosecutors did call Riesel as a witness, but they questioned him only about the circumstances of his attack and the injuries he had suffered. When the defense sought to ask Riesel if he had testified to the grand jury before his attack, the prosecution objected, and the question was disallowed.[79]

And, in fact, in the weeks before the case came to trial, prosecutors had privately stated their misgivings about taking an obstruction of justice charge to trial. According to an FBI report from October 1956, U.S. Attorney Williams's top assistant informed the FBI, "It would be most difficult to establish that acid was thrown at Riesel to impede and prevent his testimony before the federal grand jury." For his part Williams allegedly told a colleague that "he did not think that enough evidence could ever be gathered to make a strong federal case, but he realized that there was no one on the Federal Bench in the Southern District of New York with enough guts to throw the case out. He stated that in all probability, the case would be reversed in a Circuit Court, but that would be of no consequence." By then, the politically ambitious Williams, who apparently planned to run for governor, would already have gained credit for winning a courtroom victory in a high-profile case.[80]

If the acid attack had not come in response to any contributions Riesel had offered to the federal grand jury, there was also no indication that it stemmed from his work as a crusading journalist. In the years that he had been producing his syndicated column, going back to 1941, he had written about Dioguardi just twice, once in 1953 and again in 1954. The FBI catalogued all of his columns from January 1, 1955, until the month after his attack a year later, and in reviewing the log one is struck by how infrequently Riesel wrote about union corruption. When he did write about it, he rarely offered specifics and he never wrote about corruption in the Garment District, the center of Dioguardi's activities. The only reference to corruption in the garment center came in a column published on April 2, 1956, which referred to the U.S. attorney's investigation and described in general how the trucking cartel worked to control competition in that industry. This column, however, appeared over a week *after* Dioguardi had already approached Miranti about having acid thrown at Riesel.[81]

Moreover, there was nothing new in this column; much more detailed information had appeared elsewhere—for instance, in an article by Lester Velie titled "Gangsters in the Dress Business," which appeared in the *Reader's Digest* in July 1955 and mentioned several specific names, including Dioguardi and his uncle James Plumeri. Riesel's piece mentioned no names and offered little in the way of specifics.[82] If the goal of the attack was to retaliate against a muckraking journalist whose articles spotlighted Dioguardi's activities—a problematic assumption in and of itself—then Riesel was a very unlikely target.

But it does raise the question of why, for years leading up to his attack, Riesel wrote almost nothing about a notorious labor racketeer like Dioguardi. The gangster was widely covered by other journalists, and his racketeering would seem to offer ideal material to a daily news columnist eager to find subjects for his column and ardently crusading against mob infiltration into the labor movement. Riesel's counterparts certainly grasped the appeal of writing about Dioguardi. Murray Kempton, a labor columnist who wrote for the *New York Post*, described Dioguardi's activities frequently in his columns, beginning in the early 1950s. Kempton had been one of the first to expose the criminal backgrounds of the officials Dioguardi had brought into the UAW-AFL.[83] A.H. Raskin, the labor beat reporter for the *New York Times*, also wrote often about Dioguardi. Raskin's coverage chronicled Dioguardi's leadership of the corrupt locals of the UAW-AFL and his controversial role in trying to organize a cab drivers' union.[84] These stories demonstrate that Dioguardi was eminently newsworthy; the lack of similar reporting by Riesel is notable.

There was an explanation for this apparent anomaly, but again it was one that never reached the public. According to the FBI's reports,

two of its informants told them that Riesel avoided writing about
Dioguardi because the columnist was taking money from him. The
gangster allegedly paid Riesel to keep his name out of the column.[85]
The evidence for such payments was circumstantial: neither Dioguardi
nor Riesel ever admitted to it; the FBI apparently never bothered asking them. But another labor leader, Hyman Powell, who led the notoriously corrupt Jewelry Workers Union, told the FBI that he had been
making similar payments to Riesel for years. Powell said that Riesel
demanded gifts and then later flat-out cash payments in return for not
writing about him and his union. The Jewelry Union leader provided
FBI agents with documentation to prove these payments, including
check stubs and canceled checks that went back several years. Powell said that he understood that Riesel had similar arrangements with
other corrupt union officials, including Dioguardi.[86]

There was even an account of the place and time where that arrangement would have been established. The FBI reports include a description of an encounter between Dioguardi and Riesel in 1953, soon
after the columnist had written the first of his two articles about the
gangster. Edward Cheyfitz, a lawyer who worked with Jimmy Hoffa,
and who knew both Dioguardi and Riesel, described the meeting to
FBI agents. It took place at an AFL Convention in St. Louis in 1953,
which Riesel was covering and Dioguardi was attending. According to
Cheyfitz, Dioguardi was seated at the same table as Riesel and complained about his mistreatment by the press. Dioguardi expressed a
desire to achieve a respectable position in the labor movement. He
urged Riesel to be more fair in his coverage. And, soon afterward, he
asked Cheyfitz to see if Riesel would accept either a new color television set (worth about $1,000) or a $1,000 cash "gift" from him as
a gesture of goodwill. Cheyfitz told the FBI he conveyed the offer to
Riesel, but he did not personally pass on any money or other goods.[87]
For his part, Riesel confirmed to FBI agents that he met Dioguardi on
that occasion and that Dioguardi had wanted better press coverage.
But in his account of the episode Riesel made no reference to the offer
of a gift or a payment.[88]

In the years that followed, Riesel occasionally encountered
Dioguardi socially. The columnist's two aides and his mistress each

described having dinners with Riesel at a New York restaurant owned by a notorious garment center racketeer, and during these dinners, Dioguardi and Riesel's parties socialized together.[89] After the acid attack and the charges against Dioguardi became public, the gangster's wife told a neighbor (who passed the information along to the FBI) that "Johnny and Riesel were friends."[90] In January 1956, a few months before the attack took place, Riesel and his mistress were guests at the same hotel in Miami where Dioguardi was staying during the AFL-CIO's annual executive council meetings. They flew back on the same plane. Riesel's mistress also characterized the relationship between the two men as "friendly." According to the FBI reports, she "described DIO [Dioguardi] as a source of information for the victim [Riesel]," with whom "he enjoyed good relations."[91]

There were, the U.S. attorney's staff informed the FBI, clear indications that Riesel was not telling them about the full extent of his relationship with Dioguardi. According to a Bureau teletype, the U.S. attorney's chief assistant told them, "He was of [the] opinion that Riesel was withholding information from [the] government concerning his relationship with John Dio."[92] Indeed Riesel acted like someone who was hiding something. In the summer of 1956, after he had left the hospital and resumed writing his column, FBI agents working on bringing his attackers to justice asked the columnist to come in for a follow-up interview. Riesel was reluctant and insisted on being accompanied by his wife. In a handwritten note on the report describing Riesel's response to this requested follow-up interview, FBI director Hoover expressed growing skepticism about the columnist. "This is certainly a sorry state where in a case where we are trying to locate a man's assailants, he dictates the terms on which he will consent to be interviewed. . . . I am becoming more + more suspicious of Riesel," the director wrote. "No more contacts are to be made with him except with my personal approval."[93]

There were other indications that Riesel was uneasy about what the investigation might turn up. His assistants noted that their boss was wary of testifying before the grand jury that had been called to hear the case being developed against Dioguardi and his co-conspirators. One assistant described how Riesel had him help practice testifying before the grand jury, rehearsing how the columnist would respond to particular questions. According to this assistant, Riesel became "very flustered" when questions approached particular subjects.[94]

Unfortunately we do not know what those subjects were because that section of the FBI report has been blacked out, but it may have had something to do with deals Riesel had brokered using his connections to Dioguardi and other organized crime figures. In one case that did surface, an employer who was facing a union organizing effort by one of Dioguardi's associates turned to Riesel for assistance. The columnist told the employer that in return for a $6,000 payment, he could take care of the problem. Riesel requested the money be paid in the form of a $2,000 invoice for consulting work and a $4,000 cash payment; both payments later became an issue when the IRS audited the employer's taxes in 1957, thus confirming the employer's account.[95] The employer's description of this incident suggests it was not an isolated case on Riesel's part; he seemed matter-of-fact about the arrangements for payment and certain of his ability to solve the problem. And if in fact the columnist had begun profiting on his ties to Dioguardi, it raises the possibility of a dispute between the two stemming from Riesel's failure to share his earnings with the gangster. The acid attack, in that case, would have been a warning and a rebuke to Riesel. In contrast to other possible explanations, this scenario would also explain Riesel's reluctance to speak candidly with authorities about why he believed he was attacked. It would explain why he would find a grand jury appearance alarming.

Riesel's involvement in taking money from employers in order to help them fend off union organizing efforts, an apparent use of Dioguardi's influence, provides one possible explanation for why the acid attack occurred. However, given the silence of both Riesel and Dioguardi, we may never know why the gangster ordered the attack on the columnist. One point, however, is certain: the narrative of the attack encountered in the news media was misleading.

This pattern of misdirection continued as the McClellan Committee took up the issue of labor racketeering in early 1957. The committee focused a great deal of attention on Dioguardi and his activities, but as it did so it followed the lead of the FBI and the Justice Department and never offered information that varied from the narrative of the acid attack already established in the press. Yet in an effort to emphasize Hoffa's ties to the Mafia, and one Mafia figure in particular, the committee devoted an entire set of hearings in August 1957 to Dioguardi's leadership of the UAW-AFL local unions; these were the group of locals that had been brought over to the Teamsters Union apparently at Hoffa's behest. Although the acid attack was the subject of an ongoing series of criminal trials and outside the purview of the committee, the congressmen referred to it several times. Chairman McClellan, for instance, asked Dioguardi if he knew Riesel. The mobster was pleading the Fifth Amendment in response to all the questions asked by the committee, but that did not stop McClellan from going on to ask suggestively: "You wouldn't want to tell us, I suppose, whether you know anything about the incident that resulted in his blindness?"[96] Committee members invoked Riesel's acid attack to demonstrate Dioguardi's notorious ruthlessness and his willingness to defy the conventions of decency and block a federal grand jury investigation; in this way they sought to highlight Hoffa's willingness to work with the worst kind of organized crime figure.

In a later set of hearings, Riesel's name surfaced in a different line of investigation. The committee's staff had tracked down a transaction involving $310,000 paid by the leadership of the Carpenters Union to the publisher of the *Trade Union Courier*, Maxwell Raddock. The publisher was purportedly paid to produce a biography of the union's longtime president, William Hutchinson. The committee found that instead of researching and writing this book, Raddock had plagiarized en masse from a dissertation by Robert Christie.[97] Testifying before the committee, Professor Christie asserted, "As far as I can see the only expense he [Raddock] had in writing this book was a pair of scissors and a pot of glue." Raddock's records for the period from 1954 to 1956, however, appeared to belie Christie's assessment. They indicated that out of the $310,000 he had received, Raddock paid about $28,000 to have five thousand copies of this book printed. His assistant, whom the committee's staff described as Raddock's "ghostwriter" for the book, received $11,000 in salary, and $500 went to a researcher who also produced the book's index. Riesel got some of this money too, about $4,000 (the equivalent today of $32,000), listed on check stubs as payments for research and editorial work.[98]

The committee's staff had concluded that this was no straightforward book deal. Raddock himself was a questionable character. The Federal Trade Commission had issued a decision against Raddock's *Trade Union Courier* in 1955, concluding that the publication falsely identified itself as affiliated with the AFL; it was not. In fact, a spokesman for the AFL labeled the *Trade Union Courier* an "outlaw racket publication," "condemned and repudiated" by the federation's affiliates in New York.[99] The publication engaged in a form of journalistic extortion. In aggressive phone calls, the *Courier's* salesmen urged businessmen to place an ad in the paper as a way to ensure good relations with the labor movement.[100] In regard to the $310,000 Raddock received from the Carpenters Union, the committee's staff traced some of that money to a complex payoff scheme involving state-level criminal charges in Indiana facing the Carpenters Union's president. Essentially it was used to bribe prosecutors in order to shift the criminal charges to a more sympathetic jurisdiction.[101]

Riesel's involvement in this matter would seem worth pursuing; it would, after all, be an anomalous episode for a crusading, antiracketeering journalist. One of the senators on the committee did ask a couple of questions about the purpose of the payments to Riesel, but Chief Counsel Kennedy shut down that line of questioning. "We made an investigation of the book and Mr. Riesel's name has come into it," Kennedy explained. Then he quickly dismissed the issue with a statement that could be described as either brusque obfuscation or simply confusing: "It is a common and ordinary practice in a procedure such as this where payments will be to other people, where newspapermen and otherwise are making this kind of arrangement in their operation." To which Chairman McClellan blandly responded, "All right, proceed." And the issue never surfaced again. Unlike everyone else involved in this affair, Riesel was not called as a witness.[102]

7

THE CONGRESSIONAL HEARINGS:
REVELATION AND RHETORIC

In August 1957, *Life* magazine produced a two-page photo spread of the McClellan Committee's hearings in New York City that provided an iconic portrait of labor racketeering in the Cold War era. The spread captured a moment during the second week in which an impeccably dressed John Dioguardi snarls as a cigarette dangles from his mouth, while another man—the newspaper reporter Dio has just punched—falls out of frame. Entitled "Strong Arm Dio Doing What Comes Naturally," the photo emphasized the contrast of Dio's high-end style and streetwise menace. Or rather, as the short accompanying article put it, "The brutishness he had tried hard to mask" by dressing as a respectable businessman "erupted uncontrollably on the face of gangster Johnny Dio."[1] Versions of the photo had already appeared in the national daily newspaper coverage of the incident. Dioguardi's snarling face became one of the most widely used images from the most extensive investigation into labor racketeering in the 1950s. By 1959, the *Reader's Digest* journalist Lester Velie would note that "Johnny Dio" had "become a household word synonymous with union racketeering."[2]

He embodied a central message promoted by the McClellan Committee hearings: the existence of nefarious ties between notorious gangsters and powerful union leaders that made labor racketeering a national threat. This was a depiction of labor racketeering that

Johnny Dio throws a punch at a press photographer at the McClellan Committee hearings. *Getty Images*

tapped into Cold War era concerns. It emphasized organized crime's expanding influence and the danger presented by unscrupulous union leaders whose growing economic and political power created a new internal danger to America, on par with the threat of communism. But in showcasing that message, the McClellan Committee hearings failed to present the quotidian reality of labor racketeering as it affected the lives of real workers. The voluminous records compiled by the committee's diligent staff make it clear that they had amassed all of the information needed to tell this story. The investigators had encountered the grim reality of union corruption and come to know the victims as individuals with dignity whose stories were compelling and important. But those same committee records indicate that committee leaders chose to focus their hearings on a more politically expedient message, one that would center on Johnny Dio.

Dio assumed the starring role in a set of McClellan Committee proceedings known as the Paper Local Hearings, which exposed a pattern of endemic corruption in certain sectors of the union movement in the New York metropolitan region. The term "paper local" referred to an illegitimate labor organization, one that was a union on paper only, existing solely to provide an income for its officers, who were often shady characters. One example of this corruption involved a group of union officials who were making their way through a Jersey City knit goods factory in 1959. They had formerly been business agents for the Doll and Toy Workers Union. Now they represented Teamsters Local 875—the result, evidently, of a $20,000 payment made by their local union's leadership to Anthony Corallo, an organized crime figure with a history of involvement in the Garment District. They had essentially purchased a union charter. With the charter, the leaders of the Doll and Toy Workers Local Union 238 shifted themselves and their membership over to Teamster Local 875. Those same union leaders let it be known that garment manufacturers looking for an easier union contract could sign up with IBT Local 875. The Jersey City knit goods shop was one of many that had taken the union leaders up on the offer. The company had simply gone out of business one day, ending its existing contract with the International Ladies' Garment Workers' Union (ILG), and then reestablished its business under a different name. The new company promptly signed a union contract with the former Doll and Toy Workers, now operating under a different name as well.[3]

The McClellan Committee hearings in August 1957 had looked at Teamsters Local 875 as one of a group of local unions that had been originally chartered in 1950 by the United Auto Workers-AFL. In addition to Dioguardi's role in these unions, the Committee's interest in them reflected the ongoing proliferation of criminal charges faced by the locals' officers, many of whom were already ex-convicts. The first charter went to a UAW-AFL Local 102 in September 1950. It listed Samuel Zakman as the head of the new union. Zakman was a former Communist Party member, a veteran of the Spanish Civil War, and in the postwar era had worked as a union organizer for a range of local unions. By 1950, he had decided that he wanted to run his own local union and had made arrangements with an official named Sam Berger, the head of the ILG's trucking local, who agreed to help him get the charter from the UAW-AFL. Berger introduced him to Dioguardi, who, Zakman was informed, would help bankroll the new union. Within a couple of years, Dioguardi had supplanted Zakman as the official leader of the local, and Zakman had moved on to another local, this one associated with the Laundry Workers Union. There his attempts to organize messenger service employees resulted in charges that he accepted money from employers and those charges in turn led to an extortion conviction in 1953.[4]

In this same period Dioguardi had become a regional director for the UAW-AFL, and as such oversaw a half-dozen recently chartered locals. When pressure mounted and the UAW-AFL forced him out, the same group of locals took up newly issued charters in the Teamsters Union. In 1955 and early 1956, those locals played a controversial role in a hotly contested election for the leadership of the New York City Teamsters Joint Council. Hoffa's allies in the city apparently intended to use the votes from these locals to defeat the incumbent head of the Joint Council. Their effort raised the possibility that local unions, which existed largely on paper staffed with disreputable officials who had no real ties to the labor movement, could determine who controlled one of the most powerful elements of the city's labor movement. The maneuver drew scrutiny from the press and from law enforcement, prompting investigations by the New York County District Attorney's Office as well as a grand jury probe by the U.S. Attorney's Office. That attention, in turn, had attracted Robert Kennedy's interest as he dispatched his initial teams of investigators in the fall of 1956.[5]

When the McClellan Committee's staff set up the framework for the hearings on the New York paper locals, an internal memo summarized the story line they hoped to tell this way: "During the years 1952 and 1953, there was considerable chartering activities by the UAW in the New York area. This it would seem is the nut of our case. During this time, at the initiation of Dio, the labor movement in New York was invaded by bookmakers, dope peddlers, Communists, and hoodlums with long criminal records." Cementing this Cold War framework of events, the memo continued, "the command post for these activities was centered in Local 102."[6] The memo offered a compelling narrative focused on a notorious criminal and inferring the kind of nefarious underworld alliance of crooks and communists that the columnist Victor Riesel had blamed for the proliferation of labor racketeering. However, it failed to capture the reality of the pattern of endemic corruption in which the paper locals had come to exist.

In fact, the UAW-AFL paper locals were far from unique; nor was the corruption in which they engaged new, or a dramatic aberration. The kind of union organization they embodied, the type of corruption they practiced, the sorts of individuals involved all predated Dio's charters from the UAW-AFL. This type of union corruption thrived in the particular combination of economic, social, and political conditions that existed in post–World War II era New York. For that reason, paper local–style unions continued to exist long after Dioguardi had left the scene.

The reality of this racketeering involved the exploitation of America's most vulnerable workers. Union corruption worsened the exploitation of black and Puerto Rican workers toiling in low-wage sectors of the economy that had little appeal to mainstream organized labor. Employers here operated on narrow margins that offered minimal room for wage increases or benefits payments; the workers could ill afford to pay the kinds of dues that would support the typical union organization. Scattered among a diverse group of small-scale shops, in unrelated industries, and staffed by immigrant and minority workers, this sector received little attention from either the prominent industrial unions of the CIO or the often still craft-oriented organizations of the AFL.

But if mainstream unions passed them by, these workers were not overlooked entirely. In the postwar period that saw a sweeping union resurgence, a few reputable groups—like District 65 of the Retail, Wholesale and Department Store Workers Union—organized in this low-wage sector of New York City, motivated by an idealistic sense of mission.[7]

Other union officials active in this sector, however, had different motives. Often they were unscrupulous operators, in essence the slumlords of the labor movement. They cobbled together diminutive local unions by signing so-called sweetheart contracts with small-scale employers that provided almost no benefits to the workers, but gave the bosses protection against being organized by a more reputable union. These organizations treated their locals like a kind of mom-and-pop business, their revenue based on a collection of small shops and the dues payments generated by the workers employed there. Such income would be supplemented by other sources including problematic benefits plans and various kinds of irregular payments from the employers. Organized crime figures played a limited role in this activity, essentially taxing these marginal operators in the same way they did other forms of illegal activity, such as gambling; or gangsters brokered the deals that brought the employers to these union operators.

These were the paper locals. The term became the title of the August 1957 McClellan Committee hearings, and in those proceedings it applied specifically to the locals controlled by Dioguardi. But many other local unions in New York City exhibited the same characteristics. These were labor organizations that were based on top-down organizing, with a membership gained by essentially selling employers collective bargaining agreements that provided no real protections for their workers. The paper locals were an updated version of a company union. In 1957 the AFL-CIO estimated that it had received complaints involving well over thirty thousand "Puerto Rican, Negro and other minority group workers" in New York City who were "subject to intense exploitation" by these organizations. A spokesman for the Association of Catholic Trade Unionists offered an assessment of the impact of these unions on minority working conditions. Testifying before the McClellan Committee, John McNiff warned that if the existing pattern of paper local union organization was "allowed to continue, we can assure you that over a million workers will be deprived of any bona fide union representation."[8] While the McClellan Committee hearings framed other forms of labor racketeering in more grandiose Cold War rhetoric, paper locals constituted a kind of corruption that victimized real workers in everyday settings.

One such setting that the McClellan Committee investigators profiled was the Newcraft bag factory. In October 1956, one of those investigators visited Newcraft's small plant, which made cellophane bags in Long Island City. The company was part of New York City's industrial sector, which in the 1950s was still a vibrant economic zone of small factories and workshops scattered in an archipelago of gritty neighborhoods that stretched from the Bronx, through the city's Garment District, down Manhattan's West Side, and across the East River to Long Island City, in Queens, and Greenpoint, in Brooklyn.[9] Newcraft employed about thirty-five workers, and had been organized by an affiliate of the Chemical Workers Union-CIO back in 1952.

In this nondescript, small-factory setting, the congressional investigator talked with the Newcraft workers about their experiences as union members. His report includes notes on his conversation with Mary Nettles, an African American woman who had worked at the plant for four years, lived in Harlem, and raised a child on her own with the meager wages she earned. She had nothing good to say about the union. Nettles and the other workers earned a dollar an hour, the legal minimum wage at the time. She had never been to a union meeting, had never voted in a union election, and in fact was not at all sure who the officers of her union were, having only heard reference to an "Artie" and a "Dave." She was so unimpressed with the organization that Nettles had refused to sign her union card. But, despite that fact, each month union dues were deducted from her paycheck. Referring bitterly to her union's leadership, Nettles said, "We pay $4 a month and have nothing from them."[10]

Some of Nettles's confusion about her union's leadership may have stemmed from the local's itinerant habits. In the years since Nettles's shop was organized, the leaders had moved their local from the Chemical Workers to the UAW-AFL, and then in 1956 re-chartered their organization as Teamsters Local 284. Local 284 was one of several notorious paper locals associated with Dioguardi, which was the connection that would be highlighted during the congressional hearings.

But while the McClellan Committee erroneously depicted Dioguardi as the central player in the region's union corruption, he was in fact peripheral. Louis Lasky's career provides a better example of the type of players who typified New York's corrupt union sector in this era. Lasky had started his career with Teamsters Local 138, a long-standing Brooklyn-based organization of workers in the grocery industry. In 1948, he pleaded guilty to Taft-Hartley charges that involved demanding money from employers. After receiving a suspended sentence, Lasky left Local 138 and operated on his own. He continued to act as a union representative for a group of shops with about three hundred members, but now he did so as the head of an independent union. In 1950, when Dio had helped Zakman receive a charter for Local 102 from the UAW-AFL, Lasky brought his members into the new organization and became vice president of the local. About a year later, he and his brother obtained a charter from the UAW-AFL to operate a new union, Local 136, in Long Island's Nassau County, with another branch of that same union, Local 136A, organizing in Brooklyn.

Thus by the time that Dioguardi had entered the field, Lasky was clearly an independent player. When Dioguardi sought to assert control over Local 136A by appointing a trustee, Lasky simply withdrew from the UAW-AFL. Once again he operated his organization as an independent union, affiliating with other groups when it suited his purposes. By 1954, he had a charter from the Retail Clerks Union. When the McClellan Committee investigators stopped by his office in Long Island City to interview him in 1957, they found signs there listing it as the headquarters for four different locals that Lasky now ran: Local 136 Retail Clerks International Association; District 100, Barbers and Beauty Culturalists; Local 631 Textile Workers of America; and Local 142 Conference of Independent Unions, AFL-CIO. A couple of years later, after the Retail Clerks revoked his charter, he moved again, this time to a group called the National Independent Union Council, where Lasky now titled himself the Eastern Regional Director. When this group ousted him, he responded nonchalantly, "Who needs them? They're just a bunch a hayseeds. We already got a new organization on our own." As late as 1965, news reports would appear on his continued activity, running the same types of unions under a seemingly endless series of organizational titles.[11]

There were other self-styled union leaders operating with very similar profiles. Hyman Powell got his start in the labor movement working in the Building Service Employees International Union in the 1930s. His last name back then was Palatnick. When prosecutors went after the head of that union, George Scalise, Palatnick was one of the lesser officials caught up in the resulting cases, and charged with extorting money from building service contractors. He avoided prosecution, apparently by cooperating with the District Attorney's Office, and later changed his name to Powell. In 1947 he resurfaced as an officer in the International Jewelry Workers Union. One of the smallest affiliated national unions in the AFL, the IJWU had about 28,000 members, most of them black or Puerto Rican low-waged laborers working in a range of the city's industries. In 1959, the Association of Catholic Trade Unionists labeled it "the worst dealer in sweetheart contracts in the entire Metropolitan New York area."[12] Another small AFL affiliate with a problematic reputation was the Doll and Toy Workers Union; it too had a membership overwhelmingly made up of black and Puerto Rican workers laboring in various industries in the New York metropolitan region. The union had eighteen thousand members total; among the leaders of its seventeen local unions were individuals such as Milton Gordon and Harry Davidoff, whose checkered careers matched those of Powell and Lasky. Other labor leaders in the city saw the Doll and Toy Workers as "substantially controlled by underworld rackets."[13] There were more organizations, and more union officials, just like these—a lot more. In 1962, a Department of Labor official produced a listing of such "Racketeer Organizations" located in the New York City region that included just under a hundred entries.[14]

This type of union leader found it fairly easy to gain a union charter, or to operate as an independent union and then affiliate with an existing international union. In 1953, after two officials in Chemical Workers Union Local 496 were indicted, the group found itself under increased scrutiny from the organization's national leadership. Fearing that a trusteeship might be imposed on their local, these officials started looking around for charters from other national unions. They had no problem finding them. After a short search, the group ended up with two charters, one from the Sheet Metal Workers Union and one from the Doll and Toy Workers Union. A wiretap on the local union's phones recorded the leaders consulting with their attorney about which union charter they should pick. According to the police summary, the attorney "paused for a moment and finally told him to take both, telling him [one of the local union leaders] to put some shops on one and some on the other." However, Dioguardi must have been more persuasive—eventually they brought their shops over to Teamsters Local 284.[15]

The ability of these kinds of union operators to move their membership so easily stemmed from the basic characteristic of their organizations. Paper local union leaders had not mobilized groups of workers in underserved industries; instead, they made their arrangements directly with small business owners. The relationship was akin to a kind of service agreement, like an insurance policy, which is how these officials sometimes pitched it. The businessman was the client and the pitch made to him could be quite straightforward. One employer described the offer he received this way: a couple of organizers from the Jewelry Workers Union "called on him and outlined a scheme whereby Mr. Benjamin could avoid any labor difficulties by signing a contract with Local 222." They told him that he could essentially draw up the contract however he liked, "naming his own terms." In fact, "he was told that he didn't even have to tell his employees that they had joined a union, just pay their dues and keep the dues books himself." As long as Local 222 got these dues payments, the union officials assured him that they "would guarantee no labor trouble from any other union." Another employer remembered being told, literally, the union officials "were selling insurance. . . . They told him eventually he would have to sign up with somebody, so he might as well sign up with them." Given the terms being offered, the arrangement made a good deal of sense.[16]

Sometimes employers went looking for this kind of agreement as a preemptive move. According to one investigator's report, a condiment packager in Brooklyn with a twenty-person shop remembered that "in the early part of 1953 . . . that there was an undercurrent of dissatisfaction he could feel among his personnel. He analyzed the situation and came to the conclusion it could only mean trouble for the company because it involved unions." He talked his situation over with a friend of his, whose name he could not recall; these friends somehow always had names that were hard to recall. His friend recommended Joe Levine, one of the paper local union leaders, who at that time was affiliated with the Retail Clerks International Union. When Levine moved over to Teamsters Local 875, he brought the condiment packager over to the new organization with him.[17] A manufacturer in Brooklyn told investigators he began to get nervous after organizers from the International Association of Machinists showed up at his shop. He too talked with a friend (name not recalled), who advised him "to sign up with a local that wouldn't try to strangle him and that he could do business with." This same friend put him in touch with the leaders of Local 136A, UAW-AFL, one of the paper locals.[18]

For their part, union officials operating in this sector weren't above manipulating employers' concerns. Wiretaps caught them conspiring to have picket lines from other unions show up at a prospective client's shop just before, or just after, they had made their pitch. In one case, an official from the Chemical Workers Union discussed with his colleague about reaching out to someone they knew in the Metal Polishers Union to help them out with an employer who was hesitant about signing a contract: "Have one of Weisler's men go in front of the joint and make believe he's organizing, then they'll get scared and call Bill right away."[19] When Teamsters Local 250 was looking for a better deal with one of its shops in 1951, an informant remembered the leadership using a similar tactic. He told investigators that one of the local's leaders "got a hold of some organizers from District 65 (Wholesale Warehouse Distributors, located at 8 Astor Place, NYC) to go over and bother Hudson Optical. It was believed the reason he [the Teamster official] did this was to 'scare' Hudson into upping the ante."[20]

These kinds of union officials were unscrupulous, and the hardsell approach might come across as very hard indeed. The McClellan Committee hearings featured testimony by an employer who recalled being warned that, unless he made a deal with a paper local, his business could be destroyed by an organizing campaign that imposed a union contract with costly terms. He also described a paper local leader asking suggestively ominous questions about the well-being of his children.[21] But almost none of the cases reported by the committee's investigators involved any kind of direct physical threat. This may have been because if a union leader played the heavy, it always carried the risk of backfiring. It might scare the customer, in this case the small employer, away. The wiretap on Chemical Workers Local 496 refers to an employer who was refusing to meet one of the group's organizers who had come on too strong. "She thinks he sounds like a gangster," another union official was told.[22] In the case of the frightened employer profiled by the McClellan Committee hearings, the businessman simply closed down his shop for seven weeks and signed a contract with another paper local, one that had approached the business on another occasion and made a much friendlier impression.[23] In the end, the menacing paper local leader lost out on that contract.

Indeed, if an employer did want to resist, he or she had plenty of options. Small shops with minimal equipment could easily shut down, relocate, and open under a different name. This was why, in fact, this sector was so unappealing for legitimate, mainstream unions to try to organize. Employers could also, and did, sign up with a different union if they felt threatened; they could choose another paper local–type organization, one that featured a less abrasive pitch but included similar lenient terms, or they could turn to a legitimate union. In a period of union resurgence, there were many unions operating in New York City, and the McClellan Committee investigators came across numerous accounts of paper local organizers competing with each other for employers.

The environment was so competitive, and resisting union pressure was so easy, that some employers simply created their own paper locals. A group of auto body repair shops did exactly this in 1955 when an organizer for UAW-AFL Local 362 began showing up. They hired an attorney, rented a postbox, and created their own fake local, calling it Independent Auto Workers Union 101-A. The local had its own business cards and ornately printed contracts that looked in style and terms a lot like the ones issued by UAW Local 362. Some two hundred shops ended up "signing contracts" with Independent Auto Workers Union 101-A, and for a minimal price they warded off all future overtures from Local 362 or any other paper locals. When paper local organizers came around, the auto shop owner just showed them the union contract with Local 101-A. "If the organizer persisted," an investigator explained, "the proprietor would state that he washed his hands of the matter and would leave it up to the state labor board to resolve any jurisdictional difference that might exist." The tactic was "100 percent successful so far." [24]

The hearings in August 1957 would portray these types of arrangements as shocking examples of how racketeers were invading the business world, expanding out from their usual underworld haunts to corrupt a growing range of economic sectors. *U.S. News & World Report* summed it up this way, with a subheading that disparaged the unions themselves as "racket unions": "Currently, the Senate Committee is hearing testimony that known racketeers have taken charge of various local unions in New York, and that these unions are used 'as instruments for the commission of extortion from employers.'" [25] The term "extortion," like the "racket union" label, placed the onus on criminality within the labor movement while tagging the employers in general as hapless victims. Most of the prosecutions that grew out of law enforcement's investigations of this activity also involved extortion charges. This prosecutorial strategy reinforced the apparent validity of the media's categorization of two clashing groups: criminal racketeers and victim employers. Businessmen testified that they made payments out of fear—fear that their business would be destroyed if they didn't make an arrangement with one of the paper local leaders, or with an organized crime figure like Dioguardi who would broker this kind of deal.

It was a problematic conception of fear, something that prosecutors would acknowledge privately to themselves, but depicting these arrangements as extortion made it possible to prosecute someone for the obviously shady deals made between employers and union officials.[26] These were transactional crimes, and prosecutors needed the testimony of a participant to win a conviction. Describing these payments as bribery might have better captured the role that the employer's self-interest played in the transaction, but that option was unlikely to generate much in the way of cooperation. Employers, or their attorneys, were well aware of the fact that admitting to paying a bribe brought negative legal consequences. As one investigator, after asking a balky employer if he was masking payments for a lenient contract, recounts being told, "He said he couldn't answer that question because he was just as guilty as they [the union officials were]." [27] When the committee later pressed this same employer's attorney about having his client co-operate, they were told he would likely take the Fifth if called to testify. The attorney explained that the employer was "concerned with Federal and/or New York State prosecutions for having paid bribes."[28] Employers simply would not cooperate in any proceedings that portrayed these transactions as bribes and without their cooperation no legal prosecution was possible. Similarly, public hearings that gained impact from their trial-like characteristics, including dramatic testimony, required cooperative businessmen. As a result, the public was presented with a skewed image of the nature of the corruption and of the conditions of its expansion.

Perhaps the greatest shortcoming of the perspective reinforced by the hearings was that it presented the corruption as an aberration in the New York business world, the result of a purported underworld invasion. The reality was that cash payments to persons in a position of trust, made with the goal of gaining an untoward advantage, were anything but an aberration in the New York business world of the 1950s. That was how the business world, at least this sector, worked.

The committee's investigators were well aware of this angle as they diligently combed employers' account books looking for evidence of cash payments made to paper local union leaders. What they found was evidence of cash payments made by employers to many people. Typically, payoffs showed up on a business's books as checks made out to cash and written to one of the company's officers. In the case of a tool manufacturer in Brooklyn with a paper local union contract, investigators found a steady record of such checks being issued and listed as "cost of expediting." The only problem was that the amounts were way too large, some years totaling up to $119,000. "It is probable that payoffs to labor officials came out of these expediting costs," the investigative memo concluded, "but because of the size of them it is most likely that considerable sums went to 'five percenters' [i.e., persons of influence who steered a government contract to a business in return for a portion of the profits] and/or government officials and inspectors." The company produced tools for the Air Force, and, the investigator noted nonchalantly, "there are three resident inspectors" located at the factory.[29]

The same company had other checks made out to cash and listed under the heading "Sales Expediting."[30] In this same period, FBI agents probing labor racketeering in the Garment District encountered a similar pattern. Garment manufacturers had a range of explanations for the cash payments listed on their company books; one of the most common was that they needed to make payments to chain store buyers. Technically this too was bribery, but in legal terms it fell under the heading of commercial bribery, a widely practiced activity. Indeed, commercial bribery was such an accepted practice that many states had no law on their books against it, and those that did have such laws had almost never enforced them.[31]

None of these practices made it onto the record during the course of the McClellan Committee hearings. The result was a skewed image of the world in which the paper locals existed—one that depicted employers operating in a principled environment that was altered with the entrance of a seedy union organization, which itself had been invaded by Dioguardi and the collection of crooks and communists he had brought into the labor movement. This scenario fit the Cold War trope of infiltration though it had little foundation in reality.

But if the hearings provided scant information about the business practices of the employers, the Senate proceedings delved deep into the business practices of the paper locals and the financial improprieties of the union officials. In this way the McClellan Committee hearings promoted a negative public image for organized labor, doing so by documenting in great detail how unscrupulous union leaders had misused the labor movement and were milking it solely for their personal gain. Senator McClellan's statement introducing the hearings on the paper locals explained that they would explore how unions' "initiation fees and dues of members constituted a steady source of income for these hoodlums and their henchmen who were put on union payrolls."[32]

And the paper local union leaders did appear to have entered the labor movement solely out of a desire for economic gain. Seen from the perspective of the investigators' reports, however, one is struck by the degree to which their locals resembled small companies whose revenues were based on pushing a particular product. Organizers were in fact often hired on a simple commission basis that consisted of a portion of each new member's initiation fee. It was, to be sure, dingy exploitation; and stripped of portentous rhetoric, the day-to-day operations had the feel of a shady business operation, with union officials in the role of unscrupulous salesmen scrambling to make a buck. Even the notorious gangsters at times slipped into this kind of scenario. In 1955 a wiretap caught a paper local union official describing a recent scene where Anthony Corallo, a ranking member of the Lucchese crime family, was giving a kind of pep talk to the union's officials. "Get out and work, or else," Corallo told them, warning that unless business improved they could expect to be replaced. And, like any boss in a similar situation, he also used positive incentives. "I want everybody to get a raise and I want this organization to be the biggest . . . I want to see what happens in the next four or five weeks and I want to see you guys with members."[33] Other wiretapped conversations include paper local officials using coded language to discuss payoff amounts, but the terminology suggests the small-scale character of the transactions, and perhaps the officials' limited ability at subterfuge. Payoffs were referred to as "potatoes," as in, "Chester then said he had a deal for Chippie that would get him two potatoes ($200) for the month."[34]

As the McClellan Committee investigators made their rounds, interviewing paper local union officials and employees, poring through their filing cabinets, and moving from rented union office to rented union office, the outlines of these kinds of organizations became clear. They were small in scale, with lean payrolls. Teamsters Local 258, with about a thousand members scattered across thirty-eight shops, was a typical example. It came into existence when its two officials, Harry Davidoff and Sidney Hodes, took their shops and left another paper local, Local 649, to strike out on their own. They landed in a small rented office in Queens Plaza, Long Island City, with a staff that consisted of themselves, one other man, and a secretary hired through a service known as Bookkeepers Unlimited. Besides the income from the members' dues, there were also contributions paid to the benefits plan, known as the Welfare Fund, which Davidoff and Hodes managed and used to cover Local 258's general payroll and expenses. In this way, Davidoff earned a salary of $225 a week from the Welfare

Fund and $75 a week from the union. For Hodes it was vice versa, with the bulk of his salary coming from the union. In today's terms each man was grossing about $130,000 a year.[35]

At least that was their regular taxable income. Figuring out the actual earnings would be more complicated. Some employers were making payoffs to maintain particular contract terms or to limit the proportion of their workforce covered by the union. Those sums would have made up part of a paper local union leader's actual income, though it would never show up on the payroll or on someone's taxes. Income also came from money siphoned from a local union's funds through fictitious expense vouchers, compensation for picket lines that never existed, relatives listed as executive officers, or drawing a salary while working full-time at other occupations like bartending. A 1955 wiretap transcript captured the flavor of these arrangements as a paper local secretary discussed various ways to disburse the union's income without putting those amounts into a standard payroll for the organization's three leaders. "Can't they supply you with someone you can charge with expenses and vary it?" the accountant asks. "Make it car expenses." They discuss other tactics and the need to limit the amounts in each category to avoid suspicion. The accountant ends with straightforward advice: "Find somebody you can use on the payroll as an organizer. That's what's being done with other places."[36]

These kinds of funds would have gone to supplement a paper local union official's income, but one assumes the money also went to that official's sponsor, the organized crime figure who had helped arrange for the charter, the person one turned to in cases of a conflict, the guy you paid so his thugs wouldn't beat you up. Dioguardi was one such sponsor, but he was far from alone; just as there were lots of unions operating like the paper locals, there were also many potential organized crime sponsors. In the case of the paper locals, the Lucchese crime figure Corallo was a sponsor; so too was a Jewish gangster in the Garment District, Solly Cotliar.[37] The payments to Dioguardi, Corallo, Cotliar, and whichever other organized crime figures were involved amounted to a form of licensing arrangement. Crooked union officials, like other kinds of criminal entrepreneurs, such as bookmakers and drug dealers, paid organized crime figures because they could not turn to law enforcement for protection, and so these payments were a type of extortion. But one could also see this licensing relationship as having elements that were not extortionate. Organized crime figures offered a forum to resolve disputes between such illegal entrepreneurs and provided useful networking services that one could turn to if, for instance, you were looking for a place to buy yourself a union charter.

The ultimate source of the money working its way through this system could be found in the myriad little manufacturing shops whose owners had made the arrangements with various paper local union leaders. This money came out of the wages of the largely black and Puerto Rican workforce who labored in those shops and who had union dues and initiation fees deducted from their wages in return for a collective bargaining contract that offered them nothing. Often enough, the workers had no knowledge of the terms of those contracts. There were no union meetings, and if there was a shop steward he often was also the company's foreman. Asking questions, or making a complaint, did nothing but put a worker at risk of losing their job. While the employers enjoyed tangible benefits from a paper local union contract, the situation was just the opposite for the workers. For them, the paper locals represented one more form of exploitation, in what was already a hard life of minimum wage work in the small workshops and factories of industrial New York.

This was what racketeering meant in places like the Newcraft cellophane bag factory in Long Island City: the exploitation of a largely non-white workforce in a city with one of the strongest labor movements in the country, but one that had little impact for these workers and in this sector of the economy. Instead, the labor movement's strength had created an opportunity for paper local union leaders to peddle their services, offering anxious employers a reincarnation of the old company union. In a time and place where the union movement was weaker, this service would have had little appeal. In a time and place where the union movement was better, reputable unions would have organized these workplaces and left no opportunities for the paper locals.

At this moment, unions were not some distant abstraction, and so the victims—the workers in these shops—were often keenly aware of how little their local resembled a reputable union. This was especially true for the workers who found themselves appointed shop steward; often these were longtime employees, and those with the best English language skills. The investigators' reports occasionally documented their voices directly, providing a frontline perspective on labor racketeering. On Bancroft Place in Brooklyn, a shop steward named Peter Thomashefsky described all the ways he and his fellow workers lacked any real membership ties with the union that had been foisted upon them about four years earlier: "I don't get regular notices of meeting—I don't know when they're supposed to be held—and honestly I don't know what the officers' names are and honestly I don't know when we elect them." [38] Esmeralda Suarez had been working at the F&B Novelty Shop, located on Manhattan's West Side, for five years. When the plant's employees were enrolled into a paper local, she found herself appointed steward. She knew enough about how unions worked to know that new employees were supposed to sign cards designating their membership in the local and acknowledging that dues would be deducted from their wages. No such cards were ever signed. She also clearly understood the significance of the union's contract with her employer. "She has asked Sidney Hodes [one of the local union's leaders] for copies of the [union] contract, many, many times," the investigator's report explains. "But he has never given it to her. He keeps stalling her on it, and actually she does not know what the terms of the contract are." [39]

Reading the reports from the McClellan Committee's staff, one can sense the visceral reaction of investigators who encountered articulate members of this exploited workforce. In October 1956, one of these investigators took extensive notes on his conversation with a fifty-four-year-old African American man named Walter Campbell who worked at a pharmaceutical plant in Long Island City: "He stated that there has never been a vote for union officers; that no one has ever gone to the local headquarters on 23rd Street; that the union does nothing for the men; that no one knows what happens to union dues; that although he is shop steward, he has never been instructed to telephone the Local whenever any member has been hospitalized; and he never heard of anyone in his shop ever getting anything from the local.

He summed it up by stating, 'We pay our dues regularly and they give us nothing.'" The report ends with a line that reveals how the encounter had managed to bridge a gap in circumstances, background, and race that divided the committee's staff from these victims: "This very intelligent Negro would make a good witness."[40]

In fact, Walter Campbell never appeared as a witness in the August 1957 McClellan Committee hearings on the paper locals. The hearings, and especially the coverage they received, did present the plight of these workers, but the focus of the proceedings and the bulk of the coverage revolved around issues quite different than the mundane reality of the paper local's corruption. They kept the spotlight firmly directed on Dioguardi and Hoffa, focusing public attention on the specter of organized crime and its ties to the menace of unscrupulous union power.

The hearings were a show, staged with the intent of attracting as much media attention as possible, and this shaped the content of the proceedings as well as the message that they conveyed. By August 1957, the McClellan Committee had held a series of hearings over the previous six months on union corruption in other parts of the country. It had developed a standard procedure for previewing its upcoming proceedings. Typically this involved statements from the committee's chairman and more informal briefings by the chief counsel. A newspaper headline from late July aptly summarized McClellan's preview of the upcoming Paper Local Hearings and the emphasis on Dioguardi's ties to Hoffa: "Teamster-Dio Links Face Inquiry July 30." A story in the *Chicago Tribune* quoted McClellan explaining that "these hearings will show the methods by which known hoodlums and racketeers have muscled into the labor movement—and how some of the top leaders of labor have used these underworld forces in grabs for power."[41]

Coverage of the hearing's opening day framed the issues in terms of a stark threat to national security. Summing up the opening statement by Senator McClellan and the two-hour introductory presentation by Chief Counsel Robert Kennedy, the *New York Times* asserted, "James R. Hoffa of the Teamsters Union was accused today of aiming for a position where he could throttle the Eastern Seaboard and

New York Herald Tribune coverage of Robert Kennedy, chief counsel, at the McClellan Committee hearings. *Getty Images*

part of the Midwest." "Working hand in hand with his lieutenants," a group that included "John (Johnny Dio) Dioguardi, extortionist and racketeer," the article reported, Hoffa "is alleged to have made the Port of New York his first target." It also quoted McClellan: "The economic factors involved are tremendous. Such power placed in the hands of persons affiliated with racketeers is a danger to the welfare of the nation."[42]

The committee's chief counsel offered a more detailed explanation of just how such a nightmarish scenario might occur. He began by listing all the vital materials transported by Teamsters, using an array of impressive charts to demonstrate their ability to bring New York City's economy to a standstill, if they so chose.[43] Next he offered an explanation of why they might do such a thing; it could happen if their leadership was controlled, or beholden, to some hostile force. In Hoffa's case, that hostile force was evidently organized crime, but Kennedy's warning tended to blur the distinction between mobsters and communists, asserting a similar method of infiltration and control by these two Cold War domestic threats. Both conspiracies exploited vulnerabilities in America's system of labor relations. Unscrupulous union leaders like Hoffa, Kennedy explained, "have an obligation to gangsters and hoodlums because they would not have achieved their position of power unless they had made a deal a year or 2 years or 4 years earlier." The situation mirrored the domestic menace that communists presented to the labor movement. "Now the same risk applies certainly as far as Communists are concerned. If you make an arrangement with a Communist that you are going to get a position of power, if they do a favor for you, you in turn cannot turn your back on them in 2 years." In both cases, the deal had allowed a nefarious conspiracy to gain power over the union, and by extension over a vital part of the nation's economy.[44]

The results of such bargains, Kennedy warned, endangered the nation's security. "If the Teamsters are controlled or run by hoodlums, or gangsters, or run by people who have an obligation to hoodlums or gangsters, or communists, then the lifeblood of New York City, and really of the United States, can be cut off."[45] It was an assertion that was widely repeated in the media coverage of the hearings. This was a distinctive Cold War framework for the perception of labor racketeering that emphasized the menace of powerful union leaders, and that kept two domestic conspiracies closely linked. The *New York Herald Tribune* noted Senator McClellan's charge that Hoffa, "in his drive for power, derived strength from gangsters." The newspaper then went on to inform its readers of Senator McClellan's assertion that "the underworld was assisted by Communists and that both elements gained from the association."[46]

This focus on Hoffa directed attention to the issue of union power, a central concern for the conservative congressmen who made up a significant portion of the committee's membership. In early August, as the paper local hearings were beginning, Senator McClellan responded to reports that Hoffa was considering forming an alliance of unions involved in the transportation field. The result would be, McClellan warned, the creation of a dangerous "super-government." Other conservative members of the committee argued that Hoffa's proposal confirmed the central danger that the committee's proceedings had uncovered in its investigation of Teamsters corruption. "Control the nation's transportation and you control the country," Senator Goldwater observed. "There never has been any doubt in my mind that's what Hoffa wants."[47] In this way the hearings sought to direct public attention by linking union power and racketeering together as threats to Cold War America's national security.

The drama of the testimony, televised live, constituted another key aspect of the hearings' impact. By the time of the McClellan Committee, such televised coverage of hearings had become familiar enough that viewers could expect it to follow a set of conventions that played up its dramatic potential. A *New York Times* article on the broadcast of the paper locals hearings noted, "Of course, by now Congressional hearings are nothing new to television, but nonetheless they are still prime viewing fare." What made them such prime viewing fare was the way they appeared to offer viewers a chance to see a real-life contest, one that involved a search for truth, a struggle to force conspirators to reveal hidden information. "Watching members of the Senate probe for information and witnesses carefully weigh every reply is something that cannot be reproduced theatrically. When TV covers actuality, the medium continues to be at its best."[48]

Ironically, some of the best drama came at times when witnesses responded by repeatedly claiming their Fifth Amendment rights. This was true in the testimony of Dioguardi, which came during the second week and which was considered one of the dramatic high points of the hearings. Already notorious by this point, Dioguardi's appearance received significant buildup in advance. "This week Chairman McClellan would be ready to show the world the top dog himself," *Time* magazine gushed. "Scheduled to take the stand: Johnny Dio."[49] Reporters paid lavish attention to Dioguardi's clothing and invoked gangster-movie comparisons in their descriptions of his appearance. "He was a vision from an old George Raft movie," another *Time* article asserted, describing him dressed in a "plaid summer suit, white shirt, dark gray-flecked hair." "He gave himself a final reassuring pat of his breast handkerchief when one woman cooed, 'He's beautiful.'"[50] Dioguardi then proceeded to spend the next two hours reading the same answer, over and over again, from a preprinted script: "I respectfully decline to answer . . ." The televised broadcast included a numerical counter in the lower right-hand corner of the screen, which provided viewers with a running tally of how many times he had invoked the Fifth.[51] Before his testimony was complete he had taken it 140 times; *Newsweek* informed readers it was "a record for any one session of the Rackets Investigating Committee."[52] The effect was apparently electrifying. Dioguardi's appearance, the entertainment reporter for the *New York Times* asserted, "provided viewers with one of the season's most interesting programs."[53]

One suspects that part of the impact of such Fifth Amendment testimony was the way in which it allowed the committee to depict Dioguardi and his role in the most portentous terms possible, with no risk of contradiction by the witness. By the 1950s, rules regarding testimony before congressional committees limited a witness to two stark choices: answer every question, or take the Fifth on every question. Once a witness like Dioguardi had claimed the Fifth, the senators knew that he would have to do the same thing throughout the rest of his testimony and they could lay out their version of his role in the most hyperbolic of terms, using his refusal to contradict them as confirmation of their claims. If they chose, senators could use this kind of Fifth Amendment testimony to depict a witness as brazenly defiant, or as part of broader conspiracies. Or, senators could imply links between a witness and union leaders, characterizing those ties in whatever fashion they wanted. With Dioguardi's testimony, they took the opportunity to do all of these things. Dio was asked if he was one of Hoffa's "lieutenants." "Does he give orders to you?" "Have you ever been in the narcotics business?" Dio was apparently so brazenly defiant that, according to the *Chicago Tribune*, "while spectators gasped, [he] refused to tell whether he is an American citizen on the grounds that an answer might incriminate him."[54]

As documented by *Life* magazine, he had slugged a news photographer in the hallway outside the hearing room before the proceedings began, and that episode heightened the drama of his appearance while offering a compelling reminder of the violent underworld that he represented. One newspaper report explained, "Dio's attack on the

Hugh Hutton's political cartoon appeared on August 10, 1957, in the midst of the Mc-Clellan Committee's Paper Local Hearings. It references John Dioguardi's attack on a news photographer. The cartoon also illustrates the widespread belief that even though witnesses such as Dioguardi invoked the Fifth Amendment in response to every question the hearings were still providing important revelations about the menace of racketeering. *Syracuse University Library*

photographer was the first violence of the week's hearing, although labor terrorists, acid throwers, and extortionists have been parading to the witness stand."[55]

That "Runyonesque rogues' gallery," as one article described it, came to shape how the hearings were understood and what they communicated about the pattern of corruption embodied by the paper locals. During the first week, the hearings had presented testimony that offered a realistic understanding of the details of that corruption. These proceedings offered explanations of how employers benefited from the sweetheart contracts they signed with paper local leaders. The fate of workers trapped in such contracts also received attention. One of these workers, Bertha Nunez, an immigrant from Honduras, testified about the awful working conditions in her factory and described the frustrations of having to battle both her employer and her local union in an effort to improve those conditions. But this perspective was overshadowed by the more sensational issues presented by the hearings. On the day Nunez testified, for example, the newspaper headlines focused on Dioguardi's upcoming testimony and his ties to Hoffa: "Rackets Probers to Question Dio on Hoffa Alliance."[56] *Newsweek's* article for that week included a reference to Nunez's testimony, but it appeared at the back end of a piece entitled, "Labor Rackets: Johnny Dio's Role." The magazine gave more prominent placement to an inset photo of Kennedy pointing to one of his charts, which appeared with the caption "Unions That Can Choke a City."[57] The impact of the corruption on workers in the paper unions was not a focal point of the media coverage.

By the second week of the hearings, in the wake of Dioguardi's appearance, it was as if no one had ever presented evidence of employer culpability. Employers were once again depicted as the victims, plagued by a labor movement that had been infiltrated by ruthless mobsters. In a *Time* magazine article, the employers were compared to hapless victims of a shark attack: "Johnny Dio's man-eating sharks were everywhere, fanning out among makers of dog food, candy, zippers. . . . In most instances, the 'organizers' operated under phony union charters traceable to Dio, and ultimately to Teamster Big Shot Jimmy Hoffa."[58] *Newsweek's* article offered a similar frame. The lede asked, "What does an ordinary small employer go through when a mob like Dio's singles him out? The chilling picture of what really happens was given last week to the Senate Rackets Investigating Committee. It was far more revealing even than the appearance of Silky Dio himself."[59] The editors of the *New York Herald Tribune* adopted a similar slant, asking, "How many other employers have been victimized this way?"[60]

By the final part of the month, the hearings had turned away completely from the day-to-day operations of the paper locals. The committee focused instead on the contested election in the New York City Teamsters Joint Council and Hoffa's role in bringing Dioguardi's local unions into the Teamsters. Hoping to become the next president of the International Brotherhood of Teamsters, Hoffa avoided taking the Fifth Amendment in his testimony. AFL-CIO provisions barred union officials from invoking the amendment's protections in order to stymie a legitimate investigation; resorting to using the Fifth would have undercut Hoffa's claim that as a champion of his membership's interests he had nothing to hide. But in eschewing the Fifth Amendment, Hoffa put himself in a vulnerable position of having to respond to every committee question. The result was a dramatic contest of wits as Hoffa sought to carefully hedge his answers to avoid either perjury or contempt charges, while the committee played wiretapped conversations from 1955 that suggested strong links between Dioguardi and the Teamsters leader. *Business Week* labeled it "the liveliest show in Washington," with Hoffa in the role of "star performer."[61]

In this way the McClellan Committee hearings forefronted the issue of unscrupulous union leaders and their ties to organized crime figures. *U.S. News & World Report* summed up the impact with a caption to a photo of the hearing room: "Around this table in Washington— repeated charges of wrongdoing in unions. Senate investigations of specific labor officials have cast a shadow over union leaders everywhere." The article noted that the AFL-CIO leaders who were gathered in Chicago that month for the labor federation's executive council meeting were deeply worried: "Their anxiety is over the effect on people and on legislatures of disclosures by investigating committees of Congress."[62] According to the *New York Herald Tribune*, the labor federation's top leaders had concluded that the McClellan Committee's "methods are giving the public the impression that all organized labor is corrupt and that the committee is not going out of its way to dispel that impression."[63] Other observers agreed with that assessment of the hearings' impact. *Time* magazine's story on "Labor Day, 1957," asserted that throughout the preceding months "the United States watched with fascination as a Senate investigating committee poked into labor's darkest corners." The resulting revelations of union leadership's misdeeds, "piling relentlessly up throughout 1957 . . . threaten a historic change in the political climate in which organized labor lives and breathes."[64]

The expected result was the weakening of the labor movement as a whole, at a time when a stronger union movement could have offered better protections against corruption and exploitation. This point was made most clearly by John McNiff, a spokesman for the Association of Catholic Trade Unionists, a group that had sought to aid those workers exploited under paper local contracts. Summing up the solutions that would curb these practices, he asserted "the only effective cure" would have to come "through trade union action." Minority workers laboring in New York City's low-wage industries needed to be organized by legitimate unions, and that process would necessarily call for a measure of labor militancy. The solution to racketeering would come through bringing these exploited workers into a "bona fide union in New York City." For that kind of real reform to occur, however, "many strikes must ensue," McNiff explained.[65] It was a conclusion that reflected the findings that the McClellan Committee's own staff had collected, but its positive depiction of organized labor's role was not one that would be made apparent to anyone following the hearings that summer.

Conservatives, including some of the key senators on the McClellan Committee, ardently worked to shape the substance of the hearings in ways that would heighten their inimical effect on labor. Senator John McClellan and Senator Barry Goldwater invoked the menace of labor racketeering to call for new restrictions on the power of organized labor; indeed it was through this committee that Goldwater rose to national prominence as a powerful opponent of unions. In March 1958, at the behest of Republicans on the McClellan Committee, and against the wishes of the committee's general counsel, Robert F. Kennedy, hearings were held on a couple of bitter strikes waged by the progressive United Auto Workers led by Walter Reuther. The goal was to equate the violence involved in those conflicts with the corruption, abuses of power, and goon squad tactics that were earlier uncovered in other unions such as the Teamsters.[66] Conservatives hoped to depict Reuther—by association—as simply another type of racketeer.

In so doing, conservatives drew on an anti-racketeering discourse whose potency had first been demonstrated by the columnist Westbrook Pegler back in the 1930s. Conservatives opposed to unions invoked a broad definition of corruption and racketeering that included a range of legal but aggressive tactics used by unions. Later that year, Senator McClellan would tell the *U.S. News & World Report* that organizational picketing by unions and secondary boycotts were equivalent to racketeering.[67] In organizational picketing, the union mounted a picket line outside a shop that had not yet signed up with the union, and as a result, the picket line was staffed by people who were not employees of the targeted employer. The goal was to pressure the employer by giving other workers, and the general public, a reason to boycott the shop. Similarly, in a secondary boycott, union members working for one company would refuse to make deliveries to or pick-ups from another company if that latter employer was the target of a union strike or organizing campaign. Both practices were powerful tactics used by unions faced with small shops that could be easily moved to a different location in order to stymie organizers. For the same reason, employers' groups objected to both practices and were eager to seize on the chance to label them as criminal activities. A statement issued by the U.S. Chamber of Commerce in September 1958 offered a concise example of how anti-racketeering rhetoric could be invoked to justify new legal restrictions on union power. Citing the revelations of the McClellan Committee, the Chamber asserted that "union racketeering and corruption abuses are symptoms or manifestations of excessive economic power wielded by unions and union leaders. This is the heart of the problem."[68]

Union members faced with the reality of organized crime–connected employers would strongly disagree with such a stance. In the spring of 1958, at about the same time as the McClellan Committee's hearings on Walter Reuther and the UAW, garment workers in northeast Pennsylvania invoked the same anti-racketeering discourse to justify militant trade union actions of the very type that provoked the objections of the Chamber of Commerce.

8

THE 1958 DRESS STRIKE AND THE ETHICAL PRACTICES COMMITTEE: RESISTANCE AND RESIGNATION

The Pennsylvania State Police report described the picket line incident with the laconic tone of the truly disinterested observer. On the morning of April 18, 1958, two troopers in plainclothes rolled up to the Harvic Sportswear plant in rural Sweet Valley, Pennsylvania. They stayed in their car to watch as the local sheriff tried to enforce a *writ of replevin* and help the employer get his finished garments shipped back to Budget Dress Company, which had contracted to have them made. The International Ladies' Garment Workers' Union (ILG) had declared a strike weeks earlier on March 5, 1958, and though most dress manufacturers had quickly settled, employers based in northeast Pennsylvania continued to hold out. A core group of those employers had organized crime connections, including both Harvic and Budget, which were controlled by Thomas "Three Finger Brown" Lucchese, the head of the Lucchese crime family in New York. The troopers watched as a dozen deputy sheriffs arrived at Lucchese's plant to escort a truck that backed up to the loading platform.

Five minutes later all hell broke loose. A busload of two hundred women pickets swooped down on the plant, and in the words of the police report: "The pickets began to sing and shout, calling the truck driver and his helper vile names." The ILG picket captain, Dorothy Ney, told the trucking company official who was there that "they could back their truck into the loading platform and take everything, even the son-of-a-bitch three finger Brown." But once the truck had parked, the pickets refused to let it leave. Some of the women tried to let the air out of the truck tires, others put boards with protruding nails under the tires, and apparently still others quietly put sugar into the gas tank. Meanwhile, "after much bickering and arguing" between Ney and the trucking company official, the truck was allowed to pull away from the plant, but without having loaded any of the dresses for which it had come.[1]

This same scenario, captured in more picturesque language by other observers, was repeated again and again in northeast Pennsylvania in late March and April 1958. Seven days earlier a reporter from the *New York Post* watched another blocked attempt to move dresses out of the plant in Sweet Valley. This time the women pickets were led by Min Matheson, the district manager of the ILG in the Wyoming Valley, who announced, "The only way Mr. Lucchese can get his dresses out is to take his machines out too and leave the valley lock, stock and barrel. We don't want his kind here." A day before that, women pickets in downtown Pittston demolished a truck that had pulled up to their struck factory. They ripped out the dashboard wires, smashed the cab windows, deflated the tires, and for good measure threw the ignition key into the Susquehanna River. At another plant, Tony Pardini, a mother with five children, stood behind a loaded truck and refused to move. "You got to kill me before you move that truck," she told the driver even as he gunned the engine in warning. Here too the effort to get goods across the picket lines was abandoned. The trucker called his boss and warned him, "We're sitting on a keg of dynamite."[2]

Observers were struck by the militancy of these women strikers who stood up to employers who were all the more menacing because of their mob reputations. A visiting ILG staff member from New York City told a reporter, "Believe me, I don't want to take anything away from the pickets in New York, but there it was sort of a family affair with laughing and all. Here it is different. It is a strike from way back." One article called it a "demonstration of picket-line militancy not seen since the early days of the United Mine Workers." In a region where mine shutdowns had drawn wives into the workforce to support their families, it was a determination born out of necessity. "Half this town is out of work," one news report explained, "and it is the women who are the breadwinners. That's part of why they fight like they do." These were strikers like Margaret Shinski, from a small town outside of Wilkes-Barre; she had gone to work as a waistmaker to provide for her husband and two children after his twenty-three years in the mines came to an end. Though they had very different connections to the ILG than their counterparts in New York City, these women were often just as appreciative of its importance. "I know that if it wasn't for the union, the boss would cut me [from my wages] and I wouldn't have a place to turn," asserted Carmello Chellino.[3]

In April 1958, Chellino, Shinski, and their fellow women garment workers stubbornly faced down notorious racketeers such as Lucchese, winning the strike in northeast Pennsylvania after most of the holdout employers abandoned their association and made individual settlements with the union.[4] But their picket line battles made up just one facet of the labor movement's response to the issue of labor

ILG pickets in Scranton, 1958. *Kheel Center, Cornell University*

racketeering in the late 1950s. If the 1958 Dress Strike demonstrated labor's spirit of resistance, other aspects of labor's response amounted to a kind of resignation. Labor's top leaders made a show of adopting anti-corruption measures in this period, but they did little to back those measures up with meaningful action. Selective purges took the place of consistent self-policing. Privately, union officials expressed a pragmatic perspective on corruption, discounting the possibility that it could ever be totally eliminated. They also voiced their skepticism of the McClellan Committee hearings and the political impulses that lay behind the ongoing wave of revelations.

Perhaps no one better embodied this tension than the organizer whose brother was murdered in broad daylight by labor racketeers. Min Matheson had come out to northeast Pennsylvania in the 1940s and worked tirelessly to organize the mob-dominated dress shops that had located there. In the early 1950s, she and the ILG had reached an accommodation with the mob. It was by its very nature a tenuous arrangement, undercut by organized crime figures who expanded their operations at the expense of legitimate manufacturers, and constantly challenged by those same manufacturers who complained that they faced more rigorously enforced union contracts. It was in this context that in November 1957, Matheson agreed to meet with an investigator from the McClellan Committee named Arthur Kaplan.

The timing of the interview with Kaplan was significant. When she spoke with him that November, the ILG was preparing to wage its first general strike in over two decades, and a central goal of that strike was to confront the mob-connected firms who were circumventing the union contract. It might seem, therefore, that Matheson would have welcomed contact with the Senate rackets committee. But she didn't. She told the investigator that she had reservations about the committee and its investigation; throughout the interview her position wavered back and forth between wanting to take a stand against racketeering and questioning the methods and goals of the Senate committee. Matheson told Kaplan that she had encountered another committee investigator a year and a half earlier and concluded afterward she would not cooperate with the committee. "She states that she felt at that time that the Committee was anti-labor and she then decided that although she had cooperated with Mr. Duffy [the other McClellan Committee investigator], she would not do so in the future," Kaplan noted. Still, Matheson continued, she was opposed to racketeering. The committee's recent revelations about corruption within the Teamsters "and her own knowledge of racketeering in this area, both by employer representatives and within the confines of her own union, the ILG," made her sympathetic to the anti-racketeering cause. "She does believe," the memo reported, "that it is necessary that the corrupt influences in trade unionism be exposed and perhaps wiped out, and she would be willing to cooperate in every way that she is able." But her reservations continued, as demonstrated by Kaplan's very next sentence: "In spite of this statement by her, however, a good part of the ensuing several hours was spent in arguing against her reiterated review that there was not much point in continuing to give information because it made her vulnerable, and such investigations were generally futile." Yet, despite those concerns, she proceeded to give Kaplan some useful background about the leading Mafia figures in the area and their various business interests.[5]

It was an arm's length embrace. The skepticism reflected, in part, a realistic assessment of the political bias of at least some members of the McClellan Committee. But Matheson also raised the issue of just what this kind of investigation might achieve. As she noted in the Kaplan interview, "such investigations were generally futile." And yet, for all of that, she found herself drawn into helping the committee because in fact she did want to curb the corrupt influences inside and outside the Garment Workers' Union.

The history of the 1958 Dress Strike reflects this mixture of resistance and resignation. So too does the history of the Ethical Practices Committee (EPC), which was the anti-corruption body created by U.S. labor leaders in 1956, at the same time as the acid attack on Riesel and the subsequent congressional hearings, which placed the issue of labor racketeering at the top of the public's agenda. Taken together, the strike and the committee represent the range of labor's response to this issue and the limits of that response.

In an article subtitled "AFL-CIO's 'Cleanup' Squad," the *U.S. News & World Report* in 1957 described the EPC as the "mainspring of organized labor's effort to rid itself of gangster influences and unde-sirable union officials." The article depicted the committee as part of a major anti-corruption initiative within the AFL-CIO, with the EPC assigned a watchdog role comparable to that of an inspector general's office. "Its function," the magazine explained, "is to be continuously on watch for violations of the strict code of conduct that the big labor federation has set for itself."[6]

In fact, the role of the EPC was more limited. In its brief period of activity, beginning in 1956 and ending in 1960, it provided a way for the AFL-CIO's leadership to respond to scandalous revelations that emerged from congressional hearings. George Meany, the president of the AFL-CIO, used the committee to overcome the long-standing claims of national trade union autonomy which the federation's affili-ates had traditionally used to forestall anti-corruption initiatives. The committee also allowed the AFL-CIO to demonstrate to the American public that the Federation took the issue of corruption seriously. Pub-lic relations trumped anti-corruption actions in this campaign. The records of the EPC's hearings, internal committee documents, and oral histories from some of the participants highlight the AFL-CIO's pragmatic perspective and limited goals. Federation leaders had a real-world perspective on the issue of corruption. The result was a limited purge, one that would oust selected individuals and target cer-tain unions, but by no means would involve the EPC aspiring to the continuous, widespread watchdog role that the *U.S. News & World Report* had pictured.

In the Cold War era in which this history unfolded, commenta-tors often paired the EPC with the CIO's earlier purge of communist-affiliated unions, which took place at the end of the 1940s. Lester Velie's 1957 article in the *Reader's Digest* described it as "Labor's Two Front War." "They will fight [racketeers] as the unions have already fought another enemy: the Communists," he wrote. Velie quoted an EPC of-ficial who asserted, "It's like fighting the Communists all over again." The article explained that the communists and the racketeers em-ployed similar tactics: infiltration and "invoking the 5th Amendment to avoid talking." Labor leaders in turn would draw on their successful experience in curbing the communist menace. Or as Velie phrased it,

"Labor's racket-busters have the lessons of the old anti-Communist fight to guide them." These lessons included accepting the short-term loss in membership that came with expelling tainted affiliated unions, and the willingness to "create rival unions to 'liberate'—i.e., raid—the members of the ousted unions."[7]

In a speech made in 1956, Walter Reuther, the former head of the CIO, invoked this same comparison, but added an important component to it: "I say that just as we in the CIO did a good job of cleaning out Communists out of leadership, we [now] need to do the same kind of thorough job to clean out the crooks and racketeers." But he then clarified the goal of these anti-corruption efforts, which he centered on the need to court public opinion. "As long as this small handful continues to blacken our name, so long we shall be vulnerable in the eyes of the American public, so long will the reactionary political forces . . . exploit this problem and use it against us."[8] The goal in both campaigns, Reuther explained, was to address the presence of elements within the labor movement that made it politically vulnerable.

Nelson Cruikshank, who served on the staff of the AFL and later the AFL-CIO, where he played an important behind-the-scenes role on the EPC, recalled that during the negotiations to merge the AFL and CIO this Cold War comparison was often invoked. According to Cruikshank, the CIO's leaders "felt: 'Look we've done our purging. We purged the Communist elements. Now it's up to you guys to do your purging and get rid of these right wing racketeers.'"[9]

From Cruikshank's perspective, AFL president Meany "probably welcomed that pressure." Cruikshank pointed out that just months after assuming interim leadership of the AFL following the death of its previous president, and not yet having been formally elected by the convention delegates, Meany had pushed through the expulsion of the International Longshoremen's Association (ILA). The AFL had acted after the ILA's leadership refused to take remedial action in response to the scandalous revelations emerging from the New York State Crime Commission's 1953 hearings on waterfront corruption.[10] Albert Woll, the general counsel for the AFL at that time, held a similar view of Meany's aims. Woll asserted that Meany had welcomed the chance to strengthen the Federation's power to intervene in cases of corruption.

"It wasn't the lily-white C.I.O. talking to the dirty-handed A.F. of L. to clean up," Woll explained. "We wanted to clean up ourselves. But we never had anything in the [AFL] constitution [to do that]." In 1953, in moving to expel the Longshoremen, Meany had boldly asserted an authority that wasn't really there. "There was nothing in the constitution which gave us direct authority to do it," Woll said. "He just interpreted the constitution as meaning that you had to be pretty clean or else get out." During the AFL-CIO merger talks, Meany had happily taken advantage of the opportunity to use the CIO's advocacy of this issue and insert constitutional language that dealt with corruption. "He was all for it," Woll recalled. "No one took George and dragged him by the heels to make him do something. No one ever does." [11]

George Meany was a commanding figure on the American landscape in the mid-1950s. A big man, weighing over two hundred pounds, his was a scowling visage framed by a prominent jaw and a balding head, with horn-rimmed glasses and an ever-present cigar. A profile of him in the *New York Times* described him as "a cross between a bull dog and a bull." Gruff and direct in his public comments, he was known for refusing to mince words, even in his periodic meetings with U.S. presidents. News articles often titled him "Crusty George Meany." "The adjective was so often tied to his name," *Time* magazine noted, "that Meany would growl (he never just spoke, of course, always growled): 'Don't they know my first name isn't Crusty?'" The son of an Irish Catholic plumber in the Bronx, Meany had followed his father into the trade as a teenager, leaving school at sixteen and starting out as an apprentice. By his late twenties he had become a union official in his local plumbers' union and then steadily moved up the ranks of labor officialdom, becoming secretary-treasurer (the number two position) of the AFL in 1939 and then president of the Federation in 1952. "Stolid in appearance, sometimes slow of speech, he was easy to underestimate," *Time* observed. He was in fact an adept union politician, forceful in advocating his positions, but also able to broker compromise, and trusted for holding to the positions he took in public. Fellow union officials respected his intelligence, as did the Federation's lawyers, who found him capable of quickly marking out the gist of complicated legal cases. [12]

Having built his career in the New York City trade union movement, starting out in the construction trades, Meany was not unac-
quainted with the issue of labor racketeering. A model of rectitude
himself, he had rubbed shoulders with, and even had friendships with,
labor leaders notorious for corruption, such as Joseph Fay of the Operating Engineers Union. Fay had been sentenced to prison for eight
years in 1945 for extorting money from a contractor. But to Meany,
Fay was an old family friend, an occasional golfing companion, and
"a pretty nice guy except when he was drunk." At Fay's request Meany
visited him when he was in prison, becoming one of many influential
contacts the Operating Engineers leader drew on in efforts to get his
prison sentence commuted.[13] By the 1950s, however, Meany's stance
narrowed. As a national leader of a labor movement under assault by
anti-union forces—forces who had grasped the potency of the union
corruption issue—Meany concluded he needed to take a strong stand
on the issue. Failure to do so would lead to the erosion of public support, which in the long run would be fatal to the movement. For this
reason, Meany supported inserting language in the AFL-CIO constitution that gave the leadership of the Federation authority to intervene
in the affairs of national union affiliates.

The results were a series of provisions in the new AFL-CIO's 1955
constitution empowering Federation leaders to investigate an affiliated
union when "there is reason to believe that any affiliate is dominated,
controlled or substantially influenced in the conduct of its affairs by
any corrupt influence." Here too the Cold War context was much in
evidence. The same provision empowered the AFL-CIO's leaders to
keep watch for evidence of Communist influence. The constitution
provided for an ethical practices committee to assist the executive
council in its efforts to "keep the Federation free from any taint of
corruption or Communism." When the executive council deemed it
necessary, it could direct an affiliated union to take specific actions
to curb a corrupt influence, or, failing that, it could suspend a recalcitrant union and ultimately expel it from the Federation.[14]

As general counsel for the AFL, Albert Woll had helped draft these
provisions, and he noted that they encountered no real opposition at
the time even though they contravened long-standing traditions of

union autonomy. Ironically, Dave Beck, the head of the Teamsters Union, had even voted for them. "The thing was," Woll explained, "we didn't know what was meant by 'corrupt influence.'"[15] It would turn out to be a term that was open to interpretation, allowing President Meany a great deal of latitude in choosing when and how to act.

A subsequent resolution, adopted in June 1956, authorized the EPC to draft a set of guidelines for union governance. The results were six Ethical Practices Codes that covered governance issues such as the need for affiliated local and national unions to safeguard the democratic rights of their members and to maintain a set of standard accounting practices to protect the members' financial interests. The codes also specified abuses that were to be avoided, such as the granting of local union charters to known gangsters, or labor leaders accepting kickbacks from companies doing business with the union. After approving these codes, the AFL-CIO's executive council sent them out to the affiliated national unions with instructions to ratify them. A union's failure to abide by these codes then became the basis for the EPC to make charges against an affiliate. In this way, the AFL-CIO imposed a system of regulations on its member unions, creating a set of rules governing their internal practices and providing justification for intervention.[16]

Though no one in the labor movement wanted to appear to be defending corrupt practices, the loss of autonomy rankled many union leaders. A.J. Hayes, the president of the International Association of Machinists, who became the head of the EPC, recalled that among those who complained in private about these provisions were the heads of the AFL-CIO's Building Trades Department and the Metal Trades Department.[17] But opposition also existed among the industrial unions. When the executive board of the United Steel Workers union was first asked to approve these Ethical Practices Codes, several district leaders balked. Arthur Goldberg, who as general counsel to the AFL-CIO had overseen the creation of the codes, sought to mollify such opponents. Appearing before the Steel Workers board, he argued that the codes did nothing more than set out long-standing union practices in writing. "These are not new codes," Goldberg asserted, "the [Ethical Practices] Committee has been attempting to restate some fundamental principles of trade union morality that have always governed the trade union movement and, God willing, always will govern the trade union movement." [18]

In fact, the AFL-CIO was doing more than that—it was trying to forestall a potential political disaster. This process of drafting guidelines and convincing the affiliates to accept them occurred in the context of congressional investigations into union corruption, investigations that gave this internal union anti-corruption initiative a powerful impetus. A series of high-profile probes into labor racketeering occurred in this era, beyond the McClellan Committee, with over a dozen different congressional investigations taking place from 1947 to 1960. These investigations included hearings by a Senate Subcommittee of the Committee on Labor and Public Welfare, known as the Douglas Committee, which occurred at the same time as the AFL-CIO merger and which revealed union pension fund and health insurance abuses in several unions. The trend culminated with the McClellan Committee hearings, which began in early 1957, soon after the AFL-CIO merger, and continued to 1959.

AFL-CIO leaders described the disastrous impact of these investigations. David McDonald, the president of the United Steel Workers, recalled how these probes undercut the gains that he and other leaders had anticipated from the AFL-CIO merger: "I was hopeful. I thought we could do greater things than we did. . . . Of course, you know, you had these big investigations, the McClellan Committee, people like that. The way they were reported in the newspapers, and on the TV and radio, why you'd have thought the unions were headed up by a bunch of communists or racket guys. That made it very difficult." [19] A.J. Hayes, of the International Association of Machinists, shared a similar view. He told an interviewer in 1979, "I think that in that period of time, because of the publicity given to the investigation of the McClellan Committee, that the anti-labor forces in the United States probably launched more attacks against organized labor, officials of organized labor, and specific unions than at any time that I recall." [20] According to the AFL-CIO's chief lobbyist at the time, Andrew Biemiller, Meany held similar views. "Meany thought McClellan was an anti-labor nut." But he was a nut who led a committee that could cause the labor movement serious damage. Biemiller recalled McClellan "had a hell of a lot of nasty material, so we had to walk carefully with him. You don't mess around with people who can kill you." In discussing this history with an interviewer decades later, Meany said, "Very, very frankly, we were concerned on the question of public opinion. . . . We know we cannot ignore public opinion."[21]

These congressional probes created a dilemma for the AFL-CIO's leadership. Revelations began emerging in January 1957 about the activities of Teamster Union leaders, such as Dave Beck and, by the summer of 1957, James R. Hoffa. The AFL-CIO general counsel Goldberg warned Federation officials, "We are in a grave problem in this country as a result primarily of what has occurred in the Teamsters union. We have provided the enemies of labor with tremendous ammunition which they are using at this time." From the point of view of the Federation's leadership, these anti-labor forces clearly hoped to seize the opportunity provided by this negative publicity to push through new legislation that would hamstring the labor movement. Goldberg, Meany, and others might well have concluded that the Mc-Clellan Committee's probe reflected political bias, but they could not on that basis simply dismiss the investigation. "We cannot say that there was not a legitimate basis for investigating the situation which has been disclosed with respect to the Teamsters Union," Goldberg observed. The probe was uncovering real problems that could not be easily ignored or excused. Nor could AFL-CIO leaders justify the revelations by pointing out that businessmen engaged in similar activities. "Because, after all," Goldberg argued, "the trade union movement is not a business enterprise, and things that businessmen take for granted are not applicable to the trade union movement, which is founded on different principles."[22]

The solution to this dilemma was a pragmatic combination of policies. Despite their jaundiced view of the McClellan Committee, AFL-CIO leaders moved to cooperate with the probe. Meany and Goldberg met privately with Senator McClellan and his chief counsel, Robert F. Kennedy, and worked out an arrangement: Kennedy would run potential investigations past Goldberg, who would get the opportunity to try to forestall probes that lacked merit.

Kennedy and his investigators had little experience with the labor movement, and Goldberg recalled that he often interceded in cases where the committee members' naiveté had led them to overreact. Goldberg cited an example where Kennedy intended to subpoena a labor leader whose only infraction had been to accept moving expenses from his union. In return for the committee allowing this input, Meany agreed to push AFL-CIO leaders to cooperate with investigators. Publicly he spoke in favor of the investigation. At the same time, the AFL-CIO's Ethical Practices Committee published its Codes of Ethical Practices and conducted internal probes into several of the unions and union leaders who had figured in the hearings of the Douglas Committee and the McClellan Committee, a group that tended to overlap.[23]

This response led to conflict with the Teamsters, who were the initial primary target of the McClellan Committee. When Teamster officials balked at cooperating with McClellan Committee investigations, the EPC produced the fifth Code of Ethical Conduct entitled "Regarding Cooperation with All Appropriate Public Agencies Investigating Racketeering." This particular code asserted that "if a trade union official decides to invoke the Fifth Amendment for his personal protection and to avoid scrutiny by proper legislative committees . . . into alleged corruption on his part, he has no right to continue to hold office in his union." The code generated serious debate when it came up for approval before the AFL-CIO's executive council. Woll noted how it stripped union officials of their basic constitutional rights. But in response Meany focused on the issue of public opinion. If they failed to take this stand, he asked, "what would be the public reaction to the AFL-CIO?" He warned the executive council that if the group "equivocates on this question, we will get legislation that will hurt every one of our members."[24] He took the same stand a few months later, after Dave Beck invoked his Fifth Amendment rights before the McClellan Committee. The executive council debated the legality of a proposal to remove Beck from his seat on the council because he had violated the EPC's Code of Ethical Conduct. In response, Meany asserted, "The big question is what we must do at this particular point from the standpoint of public relations." Even if Beck's removal turned out to lack a legal basis and was overturned later by the courts, Meany asserted it would be worthwhile because it would demonstrate the executive council's commitment to take a stand against corruption.[25]

Meany's strategy focused on combating the labor movement's slide in public opinion by taking a visible stand on the issue of corruption. Demonstrating the Federation's willingness to cooperate with the Mc-Clellan Committee was one way of pursuing that strategy. Another involved using the EPC to provide a public response by the Federation to revelations of particular misdeeds in particular unions. The result was not a widespread campaign against corruption, but a carefully targeted response to the hearings—one that pursued limited goals with very limited means.

One indication of the limited scale of the AFL-CIO's effort was its choice in staffing the EPC. In what amounts to the committee's charge letter, Meany wrote to its chairman, A.J. Hayes, in June 14, 1956, to inform him that he was assigning four AFL-CIO staffers to the EPC. These staffers would do the legwork of the committee to support its members, made up of five national union leaders who sat on the AFL-CIO's executive council. In making these assignments Meany drew on existing staff who worked for the AFL-CIO's Legal Department and its Social Security Department.[26] Cruikshank was one of those staffers and later recalled that essentially ethical practices became one more administrative assignment layered on top of his existing work to promote Social Security reforms. "It was a kind of extra-burden on us at the time."[27]

As laid out in Meany's letter, the EPC's initial assignment consisted of reviewing the final report of the Douglas Committee. In his June 14 charge letter to Chairman Hayes, Meany wrote, "The Douglas Report referred to three International Unions in particular and a number of local union situations, which would appear to require attention and action on the part of the International Unions concerned." In the months that followed, the four staff members worked through Douglas Committee records, crafting reports for the EPC. These reports summarized the findings of the Douglas Committee and established how the practices of the targeted unions constituted violations of various Ethical Practices Codes. In this way, the unions and labor leaders pursued by the AFL-CIO's anti-corruption campaign were determined by the focus of the Douglas Committee hearings. By the fall of 1956, this review led the EPC to hold hearings on three small national unions, each with less than one hundred thousand members: the Distillery Workers, the Laundry Workers, and the Allied Industrial Workers Union (formerly known as the United Auto Workers-AFL), as well as one federal local—a local union directly chartered by the AFL that belonged to no national union.

In 1957, as the McClellan Committee began holding its hearings, the same pattern emerged. The EPC reviewed the testimony and findings of the Senate investigation, then crafted reports that marked the codes violations demonstrated by these hearings. By the summer of 1957, the EPC had produced staff reports on violations in the Teamsters, the Bakery Workers, and the Textile Workers unions, all specifically targeted by the McClellan Committee.

The EPC limited itself to responding to the revelations coming out of the congressional hearings. It avoided expanding its purview, making no effort to search out corruption in other unions, or inviting whistle-blowers to provide leads. Complaints that came in from local union members were forwarded to the relevant national union leadership. Nelson Cruikshank recalled that even if the EPC became aware of conduct by a national union leader that violated an Ethical Practices Code, the committee did not feel bound to pursue the case. He cited as an example a case in which they had learned of a violation by the president of the Upholsterers' Union, who was accepting an extra salary for his union duties and receiving that compensation from the union's welfare fund. This was a practice explicitly banned by one of the Ethical Codes. "I certainly was not asked to investigate it, and the staff was not," Cruikshank said, "although we knew this was going on." [28] In effect, the EPC's operating policy meant that an "open violation of the ethical practices" simply "went unchallenged," Cruikshank explained. "We didn't need to stir up any business. We had more than we could do." [29] He could not recall any case that the EPC pursued that had not first figured in a set of congressional hearings. [30]

The results of this campaign were necessarily limited. Faced with the threat of expulsion from the AFL-CIO, which would have resulted in raiding from other unions, the Allied Industrial Workers and the Distillery Workers accepted a limited period of probation, which included oversight from a Federation official. In contrast, the leadership of the Laundry Workers rejected the penalty of holding a special convention in which its delegates would be read the Ethical Practices Report and then face re-election; as a result the AFL-CIO expelled the recalcitrant Laundry Workers.[31] All three unions were small bodies, ill-equipped to defy the executive council; and in the case of expulsion, they would amount to a relatively small loss to the AFL-CIO.

This was not true regarding the Teamsters. The largest affiliate in the AFL-CIO, the Teamsters played a strategic role in the labor movement, where other unions often needed the cooperation of delivery drivers to win their strikes. By the summer of 1957, as the EPC moved to hold hearings on the union, Teamsters leadership balked and refused to accept the committee's authority. Beck's position within the union plummeted in the wake of McClellan Committee hearings, which had demonstrated his financial ties to a management consultant and revealed a variety of disreputable financial practices. But as Beck's fortunes declined, Hoffa moved to the fore and positioned himself to be elected president of the Teamsters Union at its October 1957 convention.

Meany recalled a one-on-one meeting with Hoffa at the AFL-CIO headquarters at that time. The presumptive president-elect arrived at Meany's office with an entourage of Teamster officials; there he made it clear that, regardless of what the AFL-CIO's constitution said, the Federation would face real risks if it tried to impose its will on the Teamsters. "Oh, but he was confident," Meany remembered. "They threw around a lot of figures about how big and powerful they were, that they were twelve percent of the [AFL-CIO] membership, and that sort of stuff." To his apparent surprise, Hoffa discovered that Meany intended to continue with this selective anti-corruption campaign despite such risks. "I told Hoffa right to his face that if he did not care to abide by the Constitution, I was going to move that they be expelled, period. Well, he almost fell out of his chair, he was so surprised."[32]

In the months that followed, Meany proved to be as good as his word. There were attempts to negotiate a compromise, with various go-betweens seeking to craft a deal with the Teamsters Union that would keep it in the AFL-CIO but also push it to make reforms that would address the revelations of the McClellan Committee hearings. According to Cruikshank and Goldberg, the gist of the deal involved an arrangement where Hoffa would turn the union's insurance and pension business over to a financial management firm agreeable to Meany. In his conversations with these intermediaries, which included David McDonald of the United Steel Workers, Hoffa appeared eager to agree to such a deal. But he always backed out at the last minute. Goldberg and Cruikshank said it was understood that Hoffa was unable to take the deal because his Mafia connections would not let him. "That was the heart of it," Goldberg concluded. "They could not extricate themselves from that Mafia connection. It was a Mafia deal involving millions upon millions of dollars with their funds." And for his part, without such an arrangement, Meany would not accept Hoffa as the president of the Teamsters. McDonald remembered the executive council meeting where the question of Teamster expulsion came up for debate. McDonald was one of those who urged compromise, but he recalled Meany pounding his fist on the table, saying, "Hoffa's gotta go. Hoffa's gotta go." [33]

In his effort to win the support of the executive board, Meany focused once again on the issue of public opinion. To those who argued that, despite all of the damaging revelations coming out of the McClellan Committee hearings, Hoffa had yet to be convicted of a crime, Meany responded that waiting for a conviction would involve a serious political cost. It had become clear, he noted, that there were "elements with strong underworld connections that have access, and companionship even, with officials of the Teamsters Union." In the face of such evidence, "if there were no action taken by the trade union movement itself to try to eliminate those conditions, I am quite sure you all can realize the amount of criticism that we would be subjected to by the press and the public." [34]

Taking action against the Teamsters, however, offered a very public, very high-profile demonstration of the AFL-CIO's commitment to opposing corruption. Critics could easily dismiss the EPC when it confronted only the smaller unions. Cruikshank recalled, "Some of the talk was: 'Oh, you can expel the little unions like the Laundry Workers, or somebody like that, but wait till you tangle with the Teamsters!'" The act of expelling the AFL-CIO's largest affiliate, giving up one and a half million members and a union that paid in almost $800,000 year in per capita dues, showed, as Cruikshank put it, that the AFL-CIO "meant business."[35]

The decision to expel the Teamsters, therefore, should be seen as a serious and costly effort to affect public opinion of the labor movement; it should not be confused as part of a committed campaign to curb union corruption by the AFL-CIO. No such campaign occurred. It did not occur because of the perspective of the AFL-CIO's leadership.

Meany opposed union officials who used their position to profit themselves at the cost of their membership. For example, he expressed visceral contempt for Beck's actions. Meany also disliked the open ties between Hoffa's Teamsters and organized crime figures. The AFL-CIO president targeted Hoffa's most important Mafia contact, a Chicago union official named Paul Dorfman, who led a small local waste handlers' union that had been directly chartered by the AFL-CIO. According to the Federation's general counsel Goldberg, Meany considered "this fellow Dorfman" to be "an evil influence" and to have been in effect "the Mafia inside the A.F. of L." For this reason, the EPC held hearings on Dorfman's six-hundred-person local in 1956, which resulted in his permanent expulsion from the organization. For Goldberg, who oversaw those proceedings, it was a frightening experience. As his biographer notes, "So chilling was the look Dorfman gave Goldberg at their final meeting that he told his wife that same day about it, remarking, 'If anything ever happens to me, you call the FBI and tell them that's the man who did it.'"[36] But having expelled Dorfman, Meany apparently felt no compulsion to target other individual labor leaders with similar profiles, although he could easily have identified many by looking at union officials within the historically racket-ridden sectors of the economy, such as construction or the meat industry. The former plumbers' union leader was not an anti-corruption crusader.

In general, Meany maintained a pragmatic perspective on the issue of union corruption. He understood how a strictly legal definition of corruption might well be used against well-intentioned union officials who were operating within recognized norms of the labor movement. This awareness meant he had a realistic sense of the limits of reform, including an awareness that long-standing patterns of corruption and collusion were unlikely to be changed.

As a career union official leading an association of other union officials, Meany recognized that there were gray areas of conduct. Like their employer counterparts, unionists operated in a real-world context where getting things done often involved cutting moral corners. According to the scholar of corruption Michael Reisman, such practices fit into the category of "operational codes." These codes allow standards of behavior that differ from, or even contradict, the "mythic norms" of proper conduct. The operational codes also did not necessarily conform with the legal code.[37] Thus a legitimate garment manufacturer might follow accepted industry practice and regularly make surreptitious payments to a department store buyer, technically violating the commercial bribery statute, as well as the general public's understanding of accepted business practices. Similarly, union officials adhering to their own operational codes might at times take actions that were illegal, and which society at large defined as immoral. They might do so even as they worked tirelessly to promote the welfare of their union's membership.

Such operational codes complicated how union leaders viewed the issue of corruption. Meany and other AFL-CIO leaders understood that well-intentioned union officials sometimes made deals that could not bear public scrutiny, and sometimes hired individuals for activities that could bring legal complications, if such acts ever came to light. Such practices would leave a unionist vulnerable to corruption charges and legal prosecution, even though he had in no way violated the trust of his union members. Here the public's understanding of corruption would differ from the union's.

This ambiguity surfaced during the executive council's debate over the Teamsters expulsion. Joseph Beirne, the president of the Communication Workers of America, raised the issue of which union might next be the target of the McClellan Committee, noting that they were all vulnerable to scrutiny that pursued strictly legalistic violations.

Beirne recalled that in the CWA's 1955 strike against Southern Bell they had received a $25,000 loan from the United Steel Workers. He had used that money to help win that strike, but "if you demanded to know where it was spent I'd be up the creek without a paddle."[38]

Meany acknowledged this distinction, promising that he would keep the EPC away from matters that involved union officials who were adhering to this operational code. "Each union has to make its own decisions," he asserted, "but when we think in terms of this constitution we think in terms of trade union morality. And if a union is fighting for its life and it has got to spend its money in a way that will enable it to live—and we know what that means—well, that is not coming before the ethical practices committee—not by my say so— and I am quite sure the ethical practices committee wouldn't want to have anything to do with that sort of case."[39]

Essentially, Meany was laying out a scenario where, despite the newly ratified Ethical Practices Codes, the AFL-CIO would not in practice demand that a union official cooperate with a congressional probe. "If a trade union official has to sit before a committee of the United States Senate or any other place and has to say, 'Well, I don't know what happened to that money I used in that case; it was sent out there to try and help us win.' . . . I am sure we are not going to be greatly concerned because he is not able to spread out in detail on the record where the money went in an industrial dispute."[40]

The fuzzy nature of this distinction was again illustrated during the EPC's hearing on the Allied Industrial Workers Union (perhaps better known by its earlier title, the United Auto Workers-AFL). In the early 1950s, the AIW, headquartered in Milwaukee, Wisconsin, had issued a charter to a local union controlled by John Dioguardi. Later, Dioguardi became an official in the AIW, overseeing several local unions whose officials engaged in a range of dubious practices. In a hearing before the EPC in October 1956, the AIW's leaders were questioned about their decision to employ such a notorious gangster. Their response was that they understood he had previously done organizing work for the International Ladies' Garment Workers' Union, whose president, David Dubinsky, was now one of the members of the EPC. Questioned about this allegation, the AIW secretary-treasurer,

Anthony Doria, testified that he had spoken directly with Dubinsky about this in the early 1950s: Addressing Dubinsky directly, Doria testified: "You said that [Dioguardi] 'worked for us but never was on the inside.' You said he never was on the inside." [41] Dubinsky took the charge seriously enough to offer a detailed, and carefully worded, rebuttal on the last day of the hearing. He told his fellow EPC members that he had "checked with the office of the ILGWU, the General Office of the ILGWU, and they don't know the name [Dioguardi] and no such name was ever employed by the ILGWU." [42]

The allegation resurfaced during the McClellan Committee hearings, when the AIW's leadership was called to testify in August 1957 about their ties to Dioguardi. Again, Dubinsky issued a careful rebuttal that specified he had no personal knowledge of Dioguardi being employed by the Garment Workers' Union. He did not address the more likely scenario that Dioguardi had done work for one of the ILG locals or one of its industrial councils. [43]

However, during a private briefing with McClellan Committee investigators in March 1957, Dubinsky said that he suspected Dioguardi had worked for the ILG. He indicated that Dioguardi "may have been a pull-out man" for the union. According to a committee investigator's memo, Dubinsky "frankly described a 'pull out man' as nothing more than a 'strong arm man' used to unionize shops. He added that in unionizing shops, union representatives can sometimes expect some rough stuff, so for their protection 'pull out men' accompany them." Dubinsky told the investigators that there would be no union employment records for Dioguardi "since individuals of this type are paid by voucher." [44]

Although he publicly denied it, it is clear that a member of the AFL-CIO's Ethical Practices Committee, Dubinsky, led a union that had likely employed a notorious gangster; moreover, this was the same gangster that the Allied Industrial Workers had named as their regional director in New York City, an act for which the EPC condemned the AIW's leadership. Apparently, the distinction made by Dubinsky was that although his union might have hired Dioguardi, they never brought him inside the union—they never made him an officer. An AIW leader recalled Dubinsky telling him, "Sometimes we hire people for special assignments, but we don't keep them."[45] Or, as Dubinsky had put the matter to Doria, Dioguardi was "never on the inside." Although that distinction was probably quite clear within the operational code of a union leader like Dubinsky, it would be far less apparent to the public at large. To the public it would seem that both unions had unseemly ties to organized crime. This explains why the Garment Workers leader so adamantly and publicly denied what privately he admitted.

To the extent that other AFL-CIO leaders shared Dubinsky's perspective and his experiences, they would have been wary about launching any indiscriminate anti-corruption campaign. Instead, the EPC remained limited to responding to the McClellan Committee hearings, and after those hearings came to a close in 1959, the AFL-CIO allowed the EPC to become dormant.

Internal committee records show that its staff devoted their efforts in the 1960s to the mundane task of writing to national union leaders and requesting that they officially confirm their organizations' compliance with the Ethical Practices Codes. Ideally, this was to be accomplished by endorsing the codes at the national union's convention and then integrating them into their union's constitution, making sure their union's governance structure matched the codes. In practice, the union affiliates often simply responded by noting that their executive board had received the codes and approved them.[46] The pro forma nature of this correspondence was evidenced by the handwritten notation made by a staff member on the letter it received from the Carpenters Union. The president of the Carpenters had replied to the EPC query with the assertion that his executive council members "are of the opinion and belief that our General Constitution conforms to the Ethical Practices Code that has been adopted by the AFL-CIO." Below that in pencil an EPC staff member noted: "Act of Nov. 15 [Carpenters] Convention rejected the Ethical Practices Code." Besides that notation, no other action was taken.[47]

Other committee records from this era reveal a semi-covert AFL-CIO campaign to support a geographically dispersed set of Teamster dissident movements, offering groups assistance if they sought to take their locals out of the national union. If enough locals pulled out, the AFL-CIO would have been positioned to charter a rival national union, thereby achieving meaningful reform by providing Teamster members with an alternative to the leadership that the Federation had denounced as corrupt.[48] The AFL-CIO had tried this tactic against the International Longshoremen's Association in New York in the mid-1950s. The strategy failed after the AFL-CIO's organization, the International Brotherhood of Longshoremen, lost two key National Labor Relations Board elections. A majority of longshoremen working in the Port of New York had voted to stick with their notoriously racket-ridden national union. Meany pointed to that experience to explain his wariness in attempting that same strategy against the Teamsters. He kept the AFL-CIO's support for the dissidents minimal, arguing that doing more would only allow the Teamsters' leadership to claim the Federation was attempting to take over the union, and use that claim to rally the membership to its side. But it also seems likely that Meany had serious doubts that these secession movements could succeed. After a particularly bitter defeat in 1963 involving a vibrant dissident group in Teamsters Local 107 in Philadelphia, the AFL-CIO apparently stopped actively working to support such groups. In doing so, the Federation tacitly accepted the futility of its actions against the Teamsters' leadership. Hoffa had remained firmly in power after the Teamsters' expulsion. The union had remained the largest labor organization in the United States. When Hoffa went to prison in the late 1960s, he handpicked his successor, whose ties to organized crime were arguably even stronger than Hoffa's.[49]

Years later, an interviewer challenged Dubinsky on the apparently disappointing results of the EPC. A key member of the AFL-CIO's executive council and also one of the five board members who sat on the EPC, Dubinsky had played a central role in its history. Interviewed by the veteran labor journalist A.H. Raskin, Dubinsky was challenged with the question of what had the EPC "accomplished in terms of a cleaner labor movement." Raskin suggested that the AFL-CIO had abandoned the EPC because the Federation's leadership had concluded that "the whole thing was a mistake." The disappointing outcome of the Teamsters' expulsion had demonstrated the failure of the whole campaign. The AFL-CIO's leaders must have realized "they were not eliminating corruption in a real sense." When the Teamsters were expelled, the Federation lost 12 percent of its membership. "They were simply leaving the Federation, in their judgement, weaker rather than stronger," Raskin said.

Dubinsky strongly disagreed. "The purpose was not to make the labor movement stronger," he said. "The purpose was to make it more respectable. When action was taken by the Ethical Practices Committee, it had an effect on the public and it had an effect on the membership." Corruption itself, Dubinsky argued, was not something that ever could be eliminated, "as long as you have a capitalist system, with profits and money and graft and everything else." Given that perspective, the real goal of a highly public anti-corruption campaign was to demonstrate to the public the labor movement's willingness to respond to scandalous revelations. Dubinsky asserted that the EPC had provided significant "help to the dignity, to the prestige . . . of the labor movement" when the public "saw the labor movement doing

David Dubinsky and George Meany, president of the AFL-CIO. *Kheel Center, Cornell University*

something."[50] The implicit explanation for letting the EPC fade away was that it had served its purpose in responding to the McClellan Committee; it had never really been expected to accomplish any other goal.

For his part, looking back, Meany also offered no regrets. In taped interviews from the 1970s, he expressed views similar to Dubinsky: "We will never eliminate all corruption [in unions], any more than we will eliminate all crime in the community." He "was never sorry that we kicked them [the Teamsters] out." The need to address public opinion had been paramount. "I felt we couldn't afford to keep them in because, in the public view, if we kept them in we would be condoning what they had done and what everybody felt they had done." The result, he feared, "would be really stringent legislation." In explaining why the EPC had gone dormant, however, Meany was less straightforward. The Landrum-Griffin Act, passed in 1959, "practically put our Ethical Practices Committee out of business," he asserted. It expanded the category of criminal charges that union officials faced, including a new set of regulations on union governance. Meany argued that the law made affiliated unions unwilling to cooperate with an AFL-CIO probe out of fear that any testimony or records they provided to the EPC could then be handed over to federal prosecutors. Of course, the AFL-CIO's constitution gave the executive council the authority to force affiliated unions to cooperate. And, if the AFL-CIO was truly committed to rooting out corruption, then a working partnership with law enforcement would have made perfect sense; in that scenario, the EPC might have become more active after 1959, the exact opposite of what actually occurred. But indirectly, Meany suggested that the AFL-CIO avoided that kind of partnership because the operational code that governed union officials' sense of right and wrong often contradicted the terms of the law. "Before the law came," Meany explained, "we were applying what I would call a trade union morality to the situation."[51] That contradiction, as well as the fact that the congressional hearings on labor racketeering had ended, offer a compelling explanation for why the AFL-CIO let its anti-corruption campaign fade away.

———

While the brief history of the EPC demonstrated one aspect of the labor movement's response to the issue of racketeering, the 1958 Dress Strike revealed a different approach, one that highlighted the investment that rank-and-file workers had in the issue of corruption, and that demonstrated the ILG's pragmatic approach to anti-corruption. This approach involved an acknowledgment of the role that organized crime had come to play in the New York garment industry; the union aimed to curb the mob's role but did not pretend its influence could be simply eradicated. For this reason the ILG was careful about when and how it invoked the issue of racketeering during this strike. It was not a concern that they chose to publicize on the eve of the strike, or even during its first few weeks. A flier issued by the union on the day the strike was declared, March 5, 1958, illustrates this point. It makes a concise but stirring case for the job action, which involved over one hundred thousand dressmakers in seven northeastern states. The flier argues that the employers had forced the conflict on the union as a "test of strength." It lays out the main goals of the strike, including the issue of strengthening contract enforcement. "We are fighting for fool-proof enforcement provisions that will guarantee that the gains we achieve will not just be on paper but will be reflected in our pay envelopes and actual improved conditions."[52] Although contract evasion was a hallmark of the mob-associated companies, no reference was made to that issue in this statement, or in any of the others in the early days of the strike.

But by April 1958, the conflict narrowed to the group of holdouts who belonged to the Pennsylvania Garment Manufacturers Association (PGMA), and tensions rose as the leadership of this group walked out of several initial settlement agreements. On April 15, 1958, ILG president David Dubinsky invoked the discourse of anti-corruption. A newspaper article on a speech he gave during a visit to northeast Pennsylvania to meet with strikers and employers reported that Dubinsky said "some of the 'hoodlums and their stooges' operating in the area hoped to obtain preferential agreement with the union."[53] According to the news article, the employers were being held back from a settlement "because of threats from racketeers, Dubinsky said." A few days later, as resistance folded and most of the holdout employers abandoned the PGMA to sign individual union contracts, an ILG news release depicted the outcome as an anti-racketeering victory: "Mr. Dubinsky described the settlements as a substantial victory against sinister elements who challenged the union's program of stability and enforcement of agreements." [54] Over the next year as the conflict narrowed even further to just a few remaining employers, Dubinsky's rhetoric returned to this theme with even greater emphasis, referring to "underworld elements centered in New York and Pennsylvania" who used violence "to carry out their sinister purposes." [55]

But if the ILG's leadership waited to raise this issue in public until April 1958, it was not because union leaders were unaware, or unconcerned, about the presence of organized crime figures in the garment industry. The union's leadership had, of course, been dealing with these figures since the early 1950s. Min Matheson was able to give the McClellan Committee investigator very specific information on this subject. But also, in discussions preparing for the strike, the union leadership put the growing role of organized crime at the center of the effort. Notes on a pre-strike conference in January 1958 by the top leadership of the strike, a group that included Julius Hochman, Lazare Teper, and Emil Schlesinger, referred to "the forces that spur on the development of irresponsible contracting—the role of the jobbers, truckers, underworld." [56]

A report by Julius Hochman to the ILG's Dress Joint Board in September 1957 described how the main goal of the coming strike was to win a contract system that would curb the role of gangster-protected contractors and jobbers. Hochman, who was manager of the Dress Joint Board, argued that the ILG's ability to achieve this goal would fundamentally decide the union's future. "I believe," he told his fellow union officials, "that our forthcoming negotiations are of utmost importance to our union. . . . I believe that 1958 is the year of decision for us." He also asserted, "This may be the last opportunity in our lifetime—at least in my lifetime—to re-establish our union on a solid foundation." [57]

But Hochman's assessment of the growth of such gangster-protected shops to dangerous proportions also reveals why—at this point—the union's public rhetoric tended not to raise the issue of racketeering.

The current problem had its roots in years past, when ILG leaders had made special arrangements with organized crime figures, bringing their businesses into the union under terms that offered them a competitive advantage. These arrangements belied the public perception of the ILG's leadership, including its president, whose reputations for honesty and rectitude were often contrasted with other segments of the labor movement, such as the Teamsters Union. Because Dubinsky and his fellow Garment Workers' Union leaders clearly cherished that image, the union's records tend to make only the most cryptic of references to any agreements made with gangsters.[58] Hochman's report appears to be the one exception, offering a fairly forthright account of these deals, on paper. Hochman apparently felt the need to document the history of these arrangements because by 1957 they had become untenable. They had been negotiated originally with the understanding (at least on the union's part) that these would be temporary accommodations. But as Hochman ruefully acknowledged, "these temporary arrangements tend to perpetuate themselves." They had fostered a group of jobbers based in New York "who, because of the special arrangements I referred to earlier, are able to compete at an advantage with other Joint Board jobbers. In other words, we have a double competition going on within the framework of our union."[59]

Hochman concluded his report to the union's Joint Board by laying out the solution to this situation, which involved winning a new contract that eliminated these earlier accommodations. "We must be determined not to allow exceptions, special arrangements or anything else that tends to create competition based on labor costs [among union organized shops], a competition that inevitably undermines standards and makes them unenforceable." Contract enforcement provisions were to be beefed up in order to make it impossible for jobbers to evade those new uniform contract provisions by simply allowing their contractors to pay substandard wages. The new contract would make the jobber financially responsible for seeing to it that the contract was adhered to by his contractors.[60]

It makes sense that the union did little to publicize the mob's role in the garment manufacturing association, the PGMA, with which the ILG had been working for years. But as the union's adamant unwillingness to continue those special accommodations became clear in late March and April 1958, the strike turned bitter. Certain garment manufacturers attempted to resume production and break the strike. It was at this point that the picket line contests escalated to the tense, and always potentially violent, standoffs described earlier. The mob responded and retaliated according to its own code. When a contractor who belonged to the PGMA resigned his membership in the group and signed an individual agreement with the ILG, a bullet was fired into his house. It was apparently intended as a warning to other contractors who might seek to break away from the mob-dominated employers association. "The contractors are full of fear," Matheson reported to her superiors in early April.[61]

There were also attempts by the mob leadership to reach out to the union's leadership, to draw on ties that had been established since the 1940s. Matheson described being summoned to a meeting in New York City with Abe Chait and a group of other Garment District mobsters and organized crime figures from Pittston.[62] Dubinsky's own records cryptically refer to a mob attempt on March 22, 1958, to make contact with him: "Had a telephone call in the morning from Min Matheson that someone told her for me to see somebody. That same afternoon, conference in Manhattan Hotel [with] Glassberg [an official with the PGMA] Min Matheson, Jack Spitzer, [Harry] Toffell [a prominent jobber with links to Chait] and somebody." The next pages of this document consist of a Dun & Bradstreet Report that profiles Abe Chait's interest in two garment firms, suggesting who the "somebody" might have been.[63] McClellan Committee investigators later documented that Chait had returned from a stay in Florida during this same part of March.[64] Later, apparently as those efforts to reach out to the ILG leadership failed, a red paint bomb was thrown at Matheson's house. This happened a few days after the ILG publicly declared in early April that it would no longer negotiate with the PGMA.[65]

Most of the firms that had belonged to the PGMA group ended up signing individual contracts with the union. The remaining holdouts were a collection of firms with the most evident ties to particular mobsters, like Thomas Lucchese and Russell Bufalino. The strike against these mob-connected holdouts dragged on through the rest of 1958 and into 1959.[66] It involved violence on the picket line and attacks on the ILG's leadership. Matheson's reports described how the holdout firms employed a crew of strong-arm men, and news articles included references to women pickets being beaten. As Matheson summed up the situation in April 1959, "the strike and the fights have been very, very rough."[67] In February 1959, a couple of thugs waylaid Sol Greene, an official with the Dress Joint Board, as he returned home from work, beating him so badly he had to be hospitalized. A few months later, while Sasha Zimmerman was attending the ILG's convention in Miami, someone went after him with a blackjack. The attack occurred right outside the convention hotel.[68] The choice of targets seems significant. Both Zimmerman and Greene had been personally involved in the arrangements with gangsters, such as Chait, that had first brought the mob-connected firms into the ILG. Now, when the union refused to continue those arrangements, they were singled out for public retribution.

Faced with this kind of physical intimidation, Dubinsky turned for help to the Department of Justice. He wrote to the attorney general, William P. Rogers, referring to "a growing pattern of violence by the criminal elements in the dress industry." Dubinsky invoked the discourse of anti-racketeering that was being circulated so readily by the McClellan Committee and conservative legislators then pushing hard for new restrictions on organized labor. He pointed to the "recent activities of underworld elements centered in New York and Pennsylvania" who had reached across state lines in their attacks on the Garment Workers' Union leadership. "It is time for the federal government to act," Dubinsky asserted. "I trust I can look forward to immediate action by the Federal Bureau of Investigation in this matter."

He quickly learned he could look forward to no such thing. Despite the fact that the Eisenhower Administration had publicly adopted an aggressive posture toward labor racketeering, launching fifteen hundred investigations by 1955, this was not a case that appeared to interest the attorney general. In a letter whose frigid tone speaks volumes, Rogers explained to Dubinsky that simply because a union official became a victim of physical assault did not make it a federal case. Rogers offered a loaded comparison to clarify his point: "Attacks against employers and or bombings of their property during a labor dispute" were also not federal crimes.[69] Similarly, although the McClellan Committee had conducted a preliminary investigation of organized crime influence in the 1958 Dress Strike, the committee chose not to hold any public hearings on the matter and closed their investigation after the Landrum-Griffin Act was passed in 1959.[70]

The case of the ILG in the 1958 Dress Strike offers a chance to look at how anti-racketeering discourse could be employed in ways quite different from its use by anti-union groups such as the Chamber of Commerce. For the ILG leadership, anti-racketeering rhetoric was useful because, in fact, the union did strive to curb the very real influence of organized crime in their industry. But because that influence was real, and because the ILG had had to find ways to respond to it over many years with methods both tactical and problematic, the union leaders' invocation of anti-racketeering rhetoric was more selective. For much the same reason, their relationship with groups like the McClellan Committee would be constrained; they necessarily accepted the congressional anti-corruption crusade, but at arm's length. Practically speaking, the union's leadership and its members were doing more than just political posturing in the halls of Congress; they were endeavoring to win better wages and working conditions for the workers in the garment industry and, given the conditions and geography of the industry, it may have seemed inevitable for that effort to require making accommodations with Abe Chait. When the union's leaders concluded that those arrangements weakened the union, they changed course and mounted an anti-racketeering effort that targeted specific organized crime figures and sought to curb the influence of those criminals in the industry. It was strikingly different from the activities of the McClellan Committee or the Eisenhower Administration, which were at the very same time loudly proclaiming their own anti-racketeering agenda.

Viewed from a long-term perspective, this episode highlights the ongoing contest over the ways in which union power in the United States would be understood in the twentieth century. By the turn of the twentieth century, employers had already come to label union tactics such as the secondary boycott as forms of corruption.[71] Andrew

Wender Cohen has demonstrated how the term "racketeering" was created in the late 1920s by the Chicago Employers Association, which deployed the term as part of its efforts to "equate certain local unions and trade associations with criminal gangs."[72] The news media popularized this use of the term, especially after the syndicated newspaper columnist Westbrook Pegler exploited a series of union corruption scandals in the early 1940s to depict the entire labor movement as racketeer-ridden. At the same time he demonstrated the rhetorical potency of labeling particular union tactics as forms of racketeering.[73]

Union leaders contested this anti-union use of the term. They insisted on a distinction between the actions of gangsters and those of legitimate union leaders whose efforts on behalf of their union members might lead them to facilitate cartel-like industry trade agreements, or to conduct militant strike actions. In 1928, a Chicago Federation of Labor (CFL) official objected to a newspaper headline that labeled a recently murdered Teamster official as a "racketeer." Noting the murdered man's long career of service to his union members and the vitality of the local union he had created, the CFL official asserted, "Racketeers don't leave any money in the treasury of any organization with which they are connected."[74] Such assertions involved a tenuously balanced acknowledgment of the degree to which union officials, like the murdered Teamsters leader, had been involved with organized criminal groups, or with employers' associations tied to such groups. The union's position asked the public to accept a more careful use of terms such as "racketeering" and "corruption," and to sympathize with the kind of moral dilemmas some union leaders found themselves facing, especially when the greater balance of power lay in someone else's hands. These arguments lacked the rhetorical punch of the blanket denunciations that critics like Pegler could make.

The limited success of union efforts to promote a more discerning use of the term "corruption" was demonstrated by the fact that their opponents adopted this anti-corruption rhetoric again and again as they argued for new legislation to curb the power and reach of organized labor. When the U.S. Congress passed the Taft-Hartley Act in 1947, a law that imposed new restrictions on union organizing, its defenders asserted the measure would mean the "end of the day of the labor racketeer."[75] Over a decade later, similar language served efforts to pass new restrictions on unions in proposals that emerged in the midst of the revelations produced by the McClellan Committee hearings. Anti-union groups seized on the opportunity to exploit these revelations. In 1957, as Elizabeth Fones-Wolf has noted, officials at the National Association of Manufacturers "concluded that the time was right 'to crystallize' the 'public reaction against labor abuses into specific reform legislation.'"[76]

Reform in this case meant provisions in the Landrum-Griffin Act of 1959 that banned organizational picketing and tightened existing restrictions on secondary boycotts, both measures long sought by business groups.[77] This law emerged out of a series of legislative battles that had followed the initial revelations of the McClellan Committee in 1957. Those revelations had spurred calls to amend existing federal labor laws in order to curb the union abuses and corruption that the hearings had brought to the nation's attention. An initial moderate set of reforms, co-sponsored by Senator John F. Kennedy and moderate New York Republican Senator Irving Ives, failed to win passage in 1958, after employer groups opposed it. Those same employer groups strongly supported the Landrum-Griffin Act a year later, because it included provisions to limit crucial union organizing tactics. The legislation combined new restrictions on union organizing, with a set of provisions put forward by Senator McClellan, a conservative Southern Democrat, who proposed to limit labor racketeering by strengthening union democracy. The legislation required labor organizations to submit public reports on their internal finances and set out guidelines intended to ensure fair union elections. An informed and democratically empowered union membership, McClellan asserted, could clean up their own labor organizations, and keep them clean. The law also provided new tools for law enforcement to help with this effort. Landrum-Griffin tightened existing restrictions on payments employers might make to labor officials. It also barred union officials convicted of a crime from holding any union office for a certain number of years.

Organized labor, including the AFL-CIO, viewed it as an anti-union measure. They noted the disparity between new regulations on union governance and the lack of any similar rules on corporate governance in this bill. Union democracy provisions, they complained, would empower dissent within trade unions, potentially undercutting the organizational unity needed in the ongoing battles against hostile employers. But most of all they cited the new restrictions on organizational picketing and secondary boycotts, tactics that had allowed labor to leverage union strength in particular trades and regions, to bolster organizing in more problematic terrain. Unions such as the Teamsters had used these tactics to make dramatic organizing gains in the traditionally anti-union Southern states, which may have been one reason why conservative Southern Democrats, such as Senator McClellan, were so interested in this particular type of union reform. For all of these reasons, organized labor had no success in defeating the legislation.[78]

The passage of this law, despite labor's apparent political power in this period, demonstrated the union movement's vulnerability on the issue of corruption, and its inability to sway the public's mind with its version of anti-racketeering discourse. George Meany, president of the AFL-CIO, ruefully discussed this situation with a *New York Times* reporter in 1959, as passage of the Landrum-Griffin Act loomed. "The issue of corruption in some unions," said Meany, "has been used as an excuse for the view that 'labor as a whole must be punished.'" He went on to describe how the potent public reaction to that issue had undone the apparent victory labor had won in the 1958 congressional elections. "We are supposed to have elected a good many friends and been successful in defeating those who would have foisted a right-to-work law on us in several states." But now with labor's opponents poised to score a major legislative victory, Meany acknowledged that the issue of corruption had rendered the electoral victory hollow; it had created a political environment where even congressmen elected with labor support would vote to limit union power.[79] And that aspect of the issue was the most telling: the proliferation of anti-racketeering discourse fostered a political climate in which liberals, the union movement's erstwhile allies, would support new curbs on union power in the name of reform.

Ironically, the Landrum-Griffin Act, promoted as an anti-racketeering measure, curbed the efforts of women garment workers in northeastern Pennsylvania, who had just waged a fierce struggle to limit the role of actual organized crime figures in their industry. At the ILG's executive board meeting in August 1960, one of the union's top officials explained how "due to the Landrum-Griffin Law it has become next to impossible to organize non-union jobbers." Since the law banned organizational picketing, it required the union to have the majority of a company's workers signed up before staging a strike. In the small shops that mob-connected jobbers used in northeast Pennsylvania, this requirement raised an insurmountable barrier to the union. The jobbers had their work "scattered in many shops, sometimes in several states. . . . If we succeed in getting all the workers [organized] in one shop, the jobber can withdraw the work and send it elsewhere." The results dramatically undercut the union's success in the 1958 Dress Strike, by eroding the organizing gains the workers had won in that conflict. "The restriction of the [Landrum-Griffin] law, prohibiting organizational picketing, is, therefore, playing into the hands of the worst elements in our industry."[80] This union official's comments demonstrate how the issue of anti-racketeering played out in ways that were both complex and, in the end, harmful for organized labor in this era.

Organized labor had not found a successful response to this issue. At the national level, the Ethical Practices Committee had amounted to a short-term, limited purge. It had failed to counteract the negative publicity generated by the McClellan Committee, and it had done little to effectively stem corruption within the labor movement. The 1958 Dress Strike demonstrated the commitment of rank-and-file union members to stand up for honest unionism and to confront racketeering in the form of mob-connected employers. But the union's history of accommodation with industry mob figures undercut its ability to exploit this stand. Moreover, the basic situation in the Garment District remained unchanged. The mob-connected jobbers continued to operate, and union officials such as Sasha Zimmerman and Sol Greene remained vulnerable, still subject to physical violence with no effective response from the state.

AFTERWORD: THE ENEMY WITHIN

The AFL-CIO's executive council gathered at Chicago's historic Drake Hotel in August 1957. The regularly scheduled meeting occurred in the shadow of the spectacular McClellan Committee hearings on the New York paper locals, a televised news media sensation that had featured testimony by the notorious John Dioguardi (aka Johnny Dio) and the combative James Hoffa. Questioned about the hearings during a press conference, the gruff Federation president, George Meany, acknowledged that they had given labor a "black eye." "I don't think the things that have been exposed are things that people in the labor movement can be proud of," Meany ruefully admitted. Worried about the political impact, he announced that the Ethical Practices Committee would begin holding its own hearings on Hoffa and the Teamsters in September.[1]

As the executive council members took their seats at 9:30 on the first morning of the gathering, David Dubinsky handed them copies of an affidavit he had prepared in response to the McClellan Committee's recent hearings; a witness had alleged that Dioguardi had once worked for the International Ladies' Garment Workers' Union and that Dubinsky knew about it. In the affidavit, Dubinsky vigorously denied any such connection and proudly touted his past efforts to resist racketeering. "My record is clear," he asserted, "that far from having had even the remotest connection with Dio or his ilk, I am a sworn enemy of his and every other racketeer in the labor movement." Dubinsky told his fellow council members that he had provided the McClellan Committee with a copy of this affidavit and expressed his willingness to appear before the committee to answer any questions they might have about its contents.[2]

In the midst of these efforts to repair the labor movement's sullied reputation, an old opponent reappeared. Westbrook Pegler had risen to prominence as a critic of unions in 1939, when he uncovered a long forgotten criminal conviction for pandering (i.e., sex trafficking) by a top official in the Stagehands Union, and then shortly afterward he reported that the president of the Building Service Employees International Union had served time for a Mann Act violation, commonly known as white slavery. Both labor officials had ties to organized crime and, after Pegler focused attention on them, both were convicted on labor racketeering charges. Pegler had followed those stories with other exposés and a steady stream of newspaper columns that mockingly contrasted the idealistic language of labor with the misdeeds of particular unscrupulous labor leaders. He was widely read and politically influential. *Time* magazine reported in December 1941 that Pegler had finished third in its reader nominations for Man of the Year, behind Franklin Roosevelt and Joseph Stalin. By August of 1957, however, his influence as a conservative columnist had waned, as his tendency to intemperate screeds had earned him the nickname "the stuck whistle of journalism."[3] But he remained an effective investigator, able to draw on contacts in law enforcement and willing to run down details. From time to time he still scored investigative coups. This was one of those times.

Pegler stationed himself in the lobby of the Drake Hotel and waited for the members of the AFL-CIO executive board to file out at the end of their morning meeting. When they emerged, he publicly confronted Dubinsky with the criminal record of the union organizer William Lurye, who had been stabbed to death in broad daylight in the heart of the busy Garment District seven years earlier.

As Pegler described the scene, he walked up to Dubinsky, who was still surrounded by his fellow board members, including Walter Reuther and George Meany. "I said I had a document for him. As he put on the fumble for his glasses, I said, 'that is the criminal record of your friend Lurye.'" Dubinsky's reaction, according to Pegler, was to immediately distance himself from the murdered union organizer.

"He was not my friend," Dubinsky asserted. "He was not my picket. What do you mean he was mine?" Dubinsky had not employed Lurye, he told Pegler. "He worked for the local." It was the same premise of bureaucratic separation that had allowed Dubinsky to issue a categorical public denial that Dioguardi had ever worked for the Garment Workers' Union, while privately admitting to McClellan Committee investigators that a local union might well have employed him. As a national union president, Dubinsky could claim ignorance of what went on in the local unions. He took a similar tack in regard to Lurye's criminal record. "I give you my word of honor as a man," he told Pegler, "this is the first I ever heard of it." Pegler was skeptical. "Didn't you ever investigate him?" When Dubinsky implied that he had no responsibility to conduct such a probe, Pegler responded: "But you indorsed this fellow and gave him a 40-hack funeral and now you tell me you know nothing about him and moreover he didn't even work for you."[4] Pegler used Lurye to support his complaint that Dubinsky was both a hypocrite and complicit in the Garment District's corruption. "Dubinsky poses as a gallant enemy of the very type of hoodlums who have prospered by his accommodation and Lurye was one such."[5]

In a series of columns that followed that scene, Pegler demolished the union's depiction of Lurye as a martyred "idealist," or as Dubinsky had described him in his memorial eulogy, a "noble soldier who had given his life to the advancement of labor's cause."[6] Although he had grown up in the same household as his sister, Min Matheson, William Lurye's youth was marked not by participation in radical politics, but instead by a string of arrests for robbery and related crimes. He had served time in jail, including two years in an Illinois State Prison on a house burglary charge. His last arrests in Chicago had been in 1934, when the police brought him in as a suspect in a series of robberies and two months later detained him as "a well known hoodlum."[7] Some time after that, he relocated to New York City and went to work as a presser in the Garment District. In the spring of 1949 he took a leave of absence from that job to work on the Garment Workers' Union's organizing drive, accepting a cut in pay as a result.

This should have been a problem because he had significant expenses. Married, with a wife and four children living in Brooklyn, he also shared a Manhattan apartment with an official in his pressers' local named Jack Spitzer. Members of the organizing crew that he worked with told police that Lurye gambled and dated women. As one of his fellow pickets put it, Lurye "likes to spend money and go with women."[8] He complained to them about needing money. It may have been his Manhattan roommate who showed him how to profit from his work with the union. Spitzer was later caught on tape taking bribes from an employer. For his part, leading a crew of pickets in the union's big organizing campaign provided Lurye with opportunities to engage in similar activities. One of the detectives who had investigated Lurye's murder told Pegler that Lurye was taking payments from non-union employers, charging them ten cents a garment to let their goods slip through the union's picket lines.

The police concluded that this corrupt sideline had led to Lurye's murder. One of the firms that had been making payments to him was the dressmaker Rosebelle; at the time of the organizing campaign, the company had switched tactics and given the mobster Tony Macri a partnership in their firm, turning over 25 percent of their profits in return for protection from the union. Unwilling to be double-billed for this kind of protection, Rosebelle's owners stopped paying Lurye. In retaliation, Lurye broke into a warehouse where the firm was storing dresses and slashed them with a knife. Another member of his union picket crew told the police that Lurye had bragged about what he did, saying, "I'll show them old time methods." The dress slashing called for a response by Rosebelle's mob protector. It was soon after the dresses were destroyed that Macri had brought along an old friend from the neighborhood, Tony Giusto, and together they tracked Lurye down and ambushed him in the building lobby on Thirty-Fifth Street.[9]

Lurye, it turned out, was not a martyr. Nor was the blinded journalist Victor Riesel, whose acid attack had nothing at all to do with any selfless, anti-racketeering crusade. The standard character archetypes who populate the true crime accounts of labor racketeering in this era—the victim, the villain, the crusading hero—make for dramatic narratives, but they obscure more than they reveal about how racketeering actually functioned. Endemic corruption had little to do with personal moral failures and reflected instead the pragmatic decisions of historical actors who saw themselves as adhering to well-understood operational codes. In the garment industry, businessmen operating on narrow margins did what they saw their competitors doing. They cut corners where and when they could, copying other firms' designs or shrinking the mark. At times, seeking an edge meant dealing with well-established industry insiders who could help them get steady work, dodge the union, or at least get a better union deal. For their part, organized crime figures like Abe Chait functioned as mobsters and as businessmen, playing a kind of naturalized role in the industry landscape that belied the hyperbolic language of Mafia infiltration and invasion that was so common in this Cold War era. Dedicated union leaders such as Min Matheson found themselves reaching accommodations with organized crime figures like Chait. She and other union leaders, vulnerable to violence and faced with an entrenched organized crime presence, made the best choices possible in a bad situation. They built a union movement that was flawed but that nevertheless brought vital changes to workers' lives. The union meant enough to garment workers like Tony Pardini, a mother with five children, that she would use her body to block a truck from crossing a picket line in the 1958 Dress strike.

In this era, labor was at its all-time peak of strength, with about one-third of the workforce organized, mostly in unions that had nothing to do with organized crime and free of any reasonable assertions of racketeering. But there were places and industries like the Garment District scattered across the industrial landscape, business settings where corruption was endemic and where union leaders had reached various kinds of accommodations with organized crime. Those accommodations left labor leaders such as Dubinsky vulnerable to the charge of corruption, or to allegations of complicity, by the likes of Pegler. And for the labor movement as a whole, these pockets of racketeering provided potent material for anti-union forces seeking to justify efforts to limit union power.

This complex history has never found a place in the standard true crime accounts of labor racketeering, which have instead reiterated a Cold War–era morality tale. The narrative of a gangster invasion stocked with archetypal good and evil characters follows a pattern first laid out in the McClellan Committee hearings. Those hearings threw a spotlight on the Teamster president Hoffa and a rogues' gallery of mobsters, including the snarling Dioguardi, who became the embodiment of the racketeer. The hearings drew on the Cold War–era tropes of invasion and infiltration to present labor racketeering as a threat to national security. This depiction may have justified new legislation, but it also inaccurately portrayed the problem of actual racketeering. The mundane reality of labor racketeering, small-scale shady operators peddling sweetheart contracts for "a couple of potatoes," the complicity of the employers, the exploitation of low-wage minority and women factory workers—all were obscured by the need to stage the hearings as a dramatic show and to promote this Cold War framework. And if the workers and complicit employers were obscured in the hearings, they disappeared almost entirely in the resulting news coverage.

Robert F. Kennedy enshrined that Cold War narrative framework in his best-selling history of the McClellan Committee hearings, a book he titled *The Enemy Within*, thus invoking a classic Cold War trope. Half a century after its publication, it still is one of the most read accounts of labor racketeering and has set out the basic framework that subsequent accounts have followed. It tells the story of a heroic band of investigators, led by Kennedy, who pursued an unscrupulous labor leader, Hoffa, and along the way encountered a colorful cast of mobsters, including Johnny Dio.[10] The conflict between Kennedy and Hoffa, sometimes labeled a "blood feud," or other times a "vendetta," became the central theme in media depictions of this probe. Over the decades it has remained the standard way to frame this history.[11]

That framework has political implications. Those accounts—at the time and ever since—established Hoffa as an enduring symbol of the problem of labor racketeering and a potent icon of the labor movement's tarnished public image. In this narrative, labor racketeering became the story of the moral failure of powerful union leaders like Hoffa. This, in turn, justified political efforts to limit union power. The historian Alan McAdams summed the cumulative effect of the prolific media coverage of the McClellan Committee hearings this way: "To many Americans 'labor' came to mean Teamsters, Teamster to mean Hoffa, and Hoffa to mean arrogance and power." [12] This equation led, inevitably, to public support for new limits on unions to the significant benefit of labor's opponents.

Alarmed by the merger of the AFL and the CIO in 1955, and fearful of the changes that a unified labor movement might achieve, the National Association of Manufacturers (NAM) had complained that the public seemed "relatively little concerned" about the menace of union power. Exploiting the outrage that had followed the attack on Riesel, NAM had pushed for congressional hearings in 1956, in hopes that it would change the public's perspective, and it did. The result was a dramatically different political climate for organized labor. A lobbyist for the Chamber of Commerce affirmed the political results: "The McClellan hearings gave us the train to ride on; they were the bulldozer clearing the path." [13] The political shift was evident by 1959. Labor supported candidates had swept the 1958 congressional elections, but faced with the specter of racketeering, those same congressmen voted in favor of new restrictions on union power. A legislative history explained, "The sordid complexion of some of the McClellan Committee revelations disenchanted many of labor's best friends on this issue." [14] Liberals found it difficult to oppose new restrictions on union power when they were packaged as anti-racketeering reforms. In fact, liberals did little to resist the tide of changes sought by labor's opponents. "On this issue," the political scientist Samuel C. Patterson observed, organized labor "did not get the support it often got on other issues from those of liberal political persuasion across the country." Racketeering functioned as a crucial wedge issue, dividing organized labor from its key supporters on the left. [15]

The result was the Landrum-Griffin Act of 1959, which provided new government oversight of union governance, but which also stripped unions of two of their most potent organizing weapons: the secondary boycott and organizational picketing. Secondary boycotts, in which union members working for one employer conducted a job action such as refusing to make a delivery across a picket line to another employer, had historically allowed labor to harness its strength in one area to aid organizing efforts in another. It was the method used by the Teamsters to organize warehouse workers in anti-union bastions. Organizational picketing involved union members demonstrating in front of an employer whose members had not yet joined a union. It provided a quick way to put pressure on those employers whose mobility, or geographically dispersed workforce, made them difficult to organize in a traditional fashion. The tactic had been crucial to the growth of the garment industry unions.

The new law played a significant role in shaping the fortunes of the labor movement. Dramatic union decline came later, with deindustrialization and globalization, but like the Taft-Hartley Act of 1947, the immediate effect of the Landrum-Griffin Act was to limit the ability of unions to organize in new areas and to maintain their strength in industries, such as garment manufacturing, where employers could easily shift plant location away from the areas of union strength. The new law rendered hollow the victory workers had won in the 1958 Dress Strike. In the years to come, garment manufacturers would shift operations out of the areas of union strength, including northeast Pennsylvania. Min Matheson had seen this coming and noted a trend of dress factories in her area moving south.[16] Without organizational picketing, the ILG's executive board acknowledged they faced a nearly impossible task in trying to follow these employers and bring their workers into the union. One Garment Workers' Union official noted the irony of how the putative anti-racketeering law, the Landrum-Griffin Act, was "playing into the hands of the worst elements in our industry."[17]

But perhaps the most enduring impact of this history was to tarnish labor's image in the public's perception. This was the metaphorical acid attack that left the labor movement intact but permanently scarred, with a reputation for corruption that endures to this day. It discredited the labor movement's status as the defender of American workers and cast it instead in the role of an exploiter, with corrupt labor bosses preying on their own members. Bruce M. Shanks illustrated this effect with a cartoon titled "The Thinker," which won a Pulitzer Prize in 1958 for its commentary on the McClellan Committee hearings. It depicts a "Rank and File" union member gravely contemplating newspaper headlines including "Crooked Labor Leaders" and "Fifth Amendment Dodge." In an article about the awarding of the Pulitzer Prize, the

New York Times explained that the cartoon portrayed "the dilemma of union members confronted by racketeering union leaders."[18] A prominent pundit of the time, Gerald Johnson, explained "the popularity of this cartoon" lay in the way that it reflected the response many Americans had to the revelations of the McClellan Committee. "The uproar was such that in many minds the words 'labor leader' became hardly more opprobrious than 'pickpocket,' conveying, in fact, pretty much the same impression." Johnson acknowledged that these revelations involved the conduct of "only a small percentage of the country's labor leaders, but how they stank!" The result, he asserted, was a dramatic decline in the reputation of all union leaders, and "as far as public confidence is concerned organized labor was set back twenty years."[19]

This was, of course, the nightmare scenario that George Meany had feared and hoped to avoid by demonstrating the willingness of organized labor to reform itself through the Ethical Practices Committee. His efforts had not succeeded, and he viewed the passage of the Landrum-Griffin Act as both tangible evidence of this shift in public opinion and the political result of that shift.[20]

Cartoonist Bruce M. Shanks's Pulitzer Prize–winning commentary of the rank and file union member's plight in "The Thinker." *Buffalo News*

In the years since, the image of labor has remained scarred by the public's association of union leaders with corruption. In his recent study of why many workers oppose unions, Lawrence Richards emphasized the common conception of a labor movement mired in corruption and racketeering. "Americans assumed that many, if not most, unions were run by organized criminals, an obvious threat to the safety and welfare of the membership," Richards wrote.[21] A recent article in the *Huffington Post* noted that public opinion polls taken since the 1970s have "found majorities or near-majorities believed many union leaders had known ties to organized crime and racketeers, were not to be trusted to tell the truth, and abused union funds." These concerns about union corruption present an enduring barrier to the labor movement. A majority of Americans (54 percent in the most recent poll) express approval of unions, but they remain wary of how the labor movement's power could be abused by its leadership. Paul Herrnson, executive director of the Roper Center for Public Opinion Research, recently spelled out this connection. "The negative attributes associated with union leaders," he explained, "impede unions' ability to garner more public approval."[22] That politically fatal link between the union movement and labor racketeering was cemented in the Cold War era of the McClellan Committee hearings. As long as this false notion remains uncorrected, the possibility of labor's revival remains dim, and without that revival America's continued slide down toward worsening inequality and working-class alienation seems destined to continue.

ACKNOWLEDGMENTS

This book has been over ten years in the making and never would have been completed without the assistance we received along the way. Penn State University generously provided sabbatical leaves as well as support for research in the form of Research Council Grants. In addition, David Witwer benefited from a semester residency at Penn State's Institute of Arts and Humanities in fall 2011 and a summer stipend in 2015 from the National Endowment for the Humanities. The Tamiment Library Center for the United States and the Cold War, the Hagley Museum and Library, the John F. Kennedy Presidential Library, and the Dwight D. Eisenhower Presidential Library each provided research fellowships that facilitated access to their respective holdings, expanding the breadth of the research significantly.

It has been our pleasure to work with a series of generous and expert librarians and archivists who offered crucial guidance and support for this project. We would like to especially thank William Davis, now retired but formerly an archivist at the National Archives and Records Administration Center for Legislative Archives; Bill provided early support and encouragement as we worked through the voluminous and recently opened records of the McClellan Committee. Cheryl Beredo and Patrizia Sione provided similar assistance with the impressive record collection of the International Ladies' Garment Workers' Union, which is stored at Cornell University's Kheel Center.

A number of people read portions of this work in the form of conference papers or journal article submissions drawn from the larger manuscript, and we benefited greatly from their incisive and perceptive comments. Among those we wish to especially thank are Robert Bussel, Dennis Deslippe, Rachel Batch, John Enyeart, Leon Fink, Lisa Phillips, Elizabeth Fones-Wolf, Liesl Orenic, and Michael Pierce. Liesl Orenic and Robert Bussel have become valued friends, and have generously shared research materials as well as valuable insights about the Teamsters and the McClellan Committee. Eric Arnesen, Nelson Lichtenstein, and Joseph McCartin have provided commentary throughout the book's development, as well as other forms of pivotal support over the years—for instance, writing what must have seemed like an endless series of letters of recommendation. This book would not have been possible without their help and we are deeply grateful for their generous support.

We are indebted to Sandy Dijkstra, our agent, for seeing something significant in this story and for pushing us to prepare it for the right publisher. Elise Capron and the team at the Dijkstra Literary Agency have been instrumental in this preparation and we thank them for their enthusiastic support and commitment. Through their hard work the book found a wonderful publisher in The New Press. There, our editor, Marc Favreau, brought his perceptive reading to the first draft, and has taken us through the process with skill and insight—it has been a great experience to work with him and his entire team. We wish to especially recognize Brian Baughan's razor-sharp editorial work. We believe that the book is so much more effective because of the contributions of these talented professionals.

Our daughter, Mira, was a toddler when we began this project and she literally grew up in a house cluttered with boxes of FBI files and parents who discussed mob-connected dress contractors while making dinner. She accompanied us on research trips and watched while we made academic conference presentations. All the while she charmed and amazed us with her wit and her quirky and cutting commentary as we worked through the material. This book is dedicated to her for all the joy she has brought to us, her parents.

Portions of this book appeared in a different form as "The Dress Strike at Three Finger Brown's: The Complex Realities of

Antiracketeering from the Union Perspective in the 1950s," *International Labor and Working-Class History* 88 (Fall 2015), pp. 166–189; portions of Chapter 7 appeared in a different form as "The Acid Attack on Victor Riesel and Fears of Labor Racketeering in Cold War America," *Labor History* 55, no. 2 (Spring 2014), pp. 1–20.

NOTES

Introduction

1. Adam Reich and Peter Bearman, *Working for Respect: Community and Conflict at Walmart* (New York: Columbia University Press, 2018), pp. 190–93, 248–49; Lydia De Pillis, "Video: What Every New Wal-Mart Employee Hears about Why Unions Are Terrible," *Washington Post*, May 19, 2015. One of Walmart's training videos can be viewed at: "Wal-Mart's Anti-union Training Video LEAKED!!," www.youtube.com/watch?v=z_VL4gqrCHc&list=PLKch 08HyNp_a9irDmnC3vR9qr-R4joAwZ&index=2&t=0s; Target's video: "Target Stores Anti-union Propaganda," www.youtube.com/watch?v=2j3ZNUxqo9M.

2. Barbara Ehrenreich, *Nickel and Dimed: On (Not) Getting By in America* (New York: Metropolitan Books, 2001), p. 145.

3. Nelson Lichtenstein, *The Retail Revolution: How Wal-Mart Created a Brave New World of Business* (New York: Henry Holt, 2009), pp. 139–40.

4. "Don't Risk It. Don't Sign It," https://dontriskitdontsignit.com/dangers -at-the-iam. See also Eli Rosenberg, "Delta Told Workers to Spend on Video Games and Beer Instead of Union Dues," *Washington Post*, May 10, 2019.

5. Phoebe Wall Howard, "Anti-union Campaign Blasts UAW 'Corruption' in Full-Page Ad," *Detroit Free Press*, April 17, 2019; Center for Union Facts, www.unionfacts.com.

6. Michael Hiltzik, "In Anti-union Campaign, Delta Becomes Latest Firm Offering Dumb Financial Advice," *Los Angeles Times*, May 13, 2019; Steven Greenhouse, *The Big Squeeze: Tough Times for the American Worker* (New York: Alfred A. Knopf, 2008), p. 242.

7. Jack Rosenfeld, *What Unions No Longer Do* (Cambridge, MA: Harvard University Press, 2014), p. 90; "Work Stoppages: Annual Work Stoppages Involving 1,000 or More Workers, 1947–2018," U.S. Department of Labor, Bureau of Labor Statistics, www.bls.gov/web/wkstp/annual-listing.htm.

8. Michael Corkery and Ben Protess, "How the Twinkie Made the Super-rich Even Richer," *New York Times*, December 10, 2016, https://www.nytimes .com/2016/12/10/business/dealbook/how-the-twinkie-made-the-super-rich -even-richer.html.

9. Economic Policy Institute, "Unions and Shared Prosperity," https://www .epi.org/news/union-membership-declines-inequality-rises. See also Rosenfeld, *What Unions No Longer Do*, p. 82.

10. Greenhouse, *Big Squeeze*, p. 244.
11. Greenhouse, *Big Squeeze*, p. 243.

1: A Murder in the Garment District: Power and Pressure

1. "Coolie" was an anti-Asian slur often used in that era to denote poorly paid work.

2. Jerome Weidman, "Garment Center," *Holiday* 5 (April 1949), pp. 80–89; "It's Fall in the Garment Center," *New York Times Magazine*, June 15, 1952, pp. 52–53; Andrew S. Dolkart, "The Fabric of New York City's Garment District: Architecture and Development in an Urban Cultural Landscape," *Buildings & Landscapes: Journal of Vernacular Architecture Forum* 18, no. 1 (2011), pp. 14–42; the 80 percent figure is from Eugene Lyons, "A Remarkable Union—and Union Leader," *Reader's Digest*, April 1946, p. 121.

3. "Funeral for Willie," *Time*, 53, May 23, 1949, p. 24; A.H. Raskin, "Job Stoppage Set in Murder Protest," *New York Times*, May 11, 1949, p. 1; Bruce Bliven to Charles Zimmerman, June 8, 1949, and no author, typed responses to query, *The Nation*, September 21, 1949; both in Folder 5, Box 24, ILGWU Collection 5780/014, Kheel Center for Labor-Management Documentation & Archives, Cornell University, Ithaca, NY (hereafter Kheel Center).

4. Kalman Siegel, "Gross Ally Tells of Payoffs to Midtown Police," *New York Times*, August 1, 1952, p. 1; "3 'Witnesses' Held in Lurye Murder," *New York Times*, June 11, 1957, p. 1; "Macri Trial Opens in Lurye Slaying," *New York Times*, October 12, 1951, p. 1; Bruce Bliven, "Murder on Thirty-Fifth Street," *New Republic*, June 20, 1949, p. 11.

5. "Police Hunt 2 Men in Lurye Killing in 48 States," *New York Times*, June 22, 1949, p.1; "Garment Area Vet Says Lurye Beat Him Up," *New York Journal American*, June 14, 1949, p. 1; "$25,000 Reward Up for Lurye Killers," *New York Times*, May 12, 1949, p. 24; "South Is Searched in Lurye Murder," *New York Times*, June 23, 1949, p. 34.

6. No author, no date, document entitled, "Possible, and perhaps probable, motive for the stabbing of William Lurye . . . on May 9, 1949, as a result of which he died." In Folder 7, Box 25, ILGWU Collection 5780/005, Kheel Center.

7. "$25,000 Reward," General Executive Board, Advance Tear Sheet, May 12, 1949, Folder 2B, Box 297, Collection 5780/002 ILGWU Papers, Kheel Center.

8. A.H. Raskin, "Thousands at Funeral of Lurye Hear ILGWU Pledge War on Thugs," *New York Times*, May 13, 1949, p. 1.

9. "Funeral for Willie," *Time*, May 23, 1949, p. 24.

10. Description of Dubinsky and quote from his speech in A.H. Raskin, "Thousands at Funeral of Lurye Hear ILGWU Pledge War on Thugs," *New York Times*, May 13, 1949, p. 1; advertisement quote, ad tear sheet, May 12, 1949, Folder 2B, Box 297, ILGWU Collection 5780/002, Kheel Center; on internal ILG plans for protest and funeral, see: "Synopsis of Proceedings in Mr. Dubinsky's Office," May 11, 1949, 1 p.m., Folder 5, Box 24, ILGWU Collection 5780/014, Kheel Center; "$25,000 Reward Up for Lurye Killers," *New York Times*, May 12, 1949, p. 21; A.H. Raskin, "Job Stoppage Set in Murder Protest," *New York Times*, May 11, 1949, p. 1.

11. Murray Kempton, "Anniversary," May 8, 1950, *New York Post*, clipping in Folder 8, Box 24, ILGWU Collection 5780/014, Kheel Center.

12. Harry Enten, "How Much Do Democrats Depend on the Union Vote?," *FiveThirtyEight*, July 1, 2014; "Bigger Big Labor," *Newsweek*, December 5, 1955, p. 25; Robert Fitch, "Organized Labor's New Leviathan," *Christian Century*, August 31, 1955, p. 99.

13. "Labor Day, 1957," *Time*, September 2, 1957, p. 11.

14. Max Danish, *The World of David Dubinsky* (New York: World Publishing Company, 1957), pp. 74–80; Robert D. Parmet, *The Master of Seventh Avenue: David Dubinsky and the American Labor Movement* (New York: New York University Press, 2005), pp. 82–86, 90–93; Daniel Katz, *All Together Different: Yiddish Socialists, Garment Workers, and the Labor Roots of Multiculturalism* (New York: New York University Press, 2011), pp. 123–26.

15. Katz, *All Together Different*, p. 124.

16. Parmet, *Master of Seventh Avenue*, pp. 92–93; Danish, *World of David Dubinsky*, pp. 78–80.

17. Joshua B. Freeman, *Working-Class New York: Life and Labor since World War II* (New York: The New Press, 2000), p. 41; Gerald Mayer, "Union Membership Trends in the United States," Congressional Research Service, Order Code No: RL 32553, August 31, 2004, p. 12.

18. Roy B. Helfgott, "Women's and Children's Apparel," in *Made in New York: Case Studies in Metropolitan Manufacturing*, Max Hall, ed. (Cambridge, MA: Harvard University Press, 1959), pp. 50–52, 55–57, 100–107, 114–16; Don Hogan and Peter Braestrup, "Dress Plague: Big Five Racketeers," *New York Herald Tribune*, June 22, 1958, p. 1; Paul Jacobs, *The State of the Unions* (New York: Atheneum, 1966), p. 118.

19. Jesse Thomas Carpenter, *Competition and Collective Bargaining in the Needle Trades, 1910–1967* (Ithaca, NY: Cornell University Press, New York State School of Industrial and Labor Relations, 1992), pp. 804–6; Educational Department, International Ladies' Garment Workers Union, *How the New York Joint Dress Board Works, 1940–1941 Term*, pp. 6–7, Folder: International Ladies Garment Workers Union, Box 23, Series 4, Vertical File, Xavier Institute on Industrial Relations, Fordham University Special Collections Library, New York; "Labor Costs in the Garment Industry," no author, no date, Folder: Father Philip A. Carey, S.J., Labor Movement, ILGWU, 1946–1981, Box 4, Series I, Xavier Institute of Industrial Relations.

20. *How the New York Dress Joint Board Works*, p. 8; Carpenter, *Competition and Collective Bargaining*, pp. 804–6.

21. Don Hogan and Peter Braestrup, "Chait One of the Biggest of 'Big 5' Racketeers," *New York Herald Tribune*, June 23, 1958, p. 1; Report by Anthony J. Maloney Jr., Title: Garment Trucking Investigation, April 17, 1956, FBI Serial No. 92-1795-29, pp. 137–40 (hereafter Maloney Garment Trucking Report).

22. Jenna Weissman Joselit, *Our Gang: Jewish Crime and the New York Jewish Community, 1900–1940* (Bloomington: Indiana University Press, 1983), pp. 108–17; The quote is from p. 117.

23. Julius Hochman, "Basic Facts Behind Demonstrations at 35 Street, on February 21, 1939," Folder 4, Box 35, ILGWU Collection 5780/047, Kheel Center.

24. No author, "Rosenbaum's Report on Out of Town: Conditions in Out of Town Areas Working for the New York Dress Market," August 1945, Folder 4, Box 28, ILGWU Collection 5780/047, Kheel Center; the quote is from

Carpenter, *Competition and Collective Bargaining*, p. 817; A.H. Raskin, "Production Slump Cuts Dress Jobs," *New York Times*, February 19, 1948, p. 15.

25. "Green Pastures Are Found Lush," *New York Times*, March 28, 1954, p. F1; "Max Blauner, 79, of Suzy Perette," *New York Times*, June 8, 1962, p. 31; Alfred E. Clark, "Sidney Blauner, Who Founded Dress House, a Leader in the Field," *New York Times*, December 23, 1979, p. 22; "$2,000,000 Garment Racket Bared as Dewey Wins Two Indictments," *New York Times*, March 2, 1937, p. 1; "Victim of Racket Seized for Perjury," *New York Times*, March 31, 1937, p. 1.

26. Sidney Blauner to Julius Hochman, February 7, 1949, Folder 8, Box 14, ILGWU Collection 5780/047, Kheel Center.

27. Sidney Blauner to Julius Hochman, February 4, 1949.

28. Notes on Meeting, Julius Hochman, Lazare Teper, April 6, 1948, Folder 4, Box 28, ILGWU Collection 5780/047, Kheel Center.

29. "What Happened on Monday, September 20, 1948," by H. Singer, Folder 4, Box 28, ILGWU Collection 5780/047, Kheel Center; "Organization Drive, Chronology of Events, September 20 to October 20, 1948, Folder 9, Box 27, ILGWU Collection 5780/047; A.H. Raskin, "Thugs Invade Union Office, Beat 3, ILGWU Pickets Set Upon in Street," *New York Times*, September 21, 1948, p. 1.

30. The quote "Open Shoppers and Their Gangster Henchmen" is from "War Declared" Publicity Sheet and "Open Shoppers and Their Gangster Henchmen," fliers dated September 29, 1948, in Folder 4, Box 35, ILGWU Collection 5780/047. See also: "Suggested Notes for Speech, Tuesday, September 28, 1948," Folder 4, Box 28, ILGWU Collection 5780/047; A.H. Raskin, "Union Plans Fight on Terrorist Gang," *New York Times*, September 23, 1948, p. 1; A.H. Raskin, "Grand Jury to Start Inquiry into Garment Racketeering," *New York Times*, September 24, 1948, p. 1; A.H. Raskin, "50,000 Quit Today in Garment Area: Will Walk Out at 3 P.M. as Token of Fight on Racketeers Getting Foothold," *New York Times*, September 29, 1948, p. 42; A.H. Raskin, "Thousands in Rally Defy Racketeering in Garment Trades," September 30, 1948, p. 1; Confidential Report on Meeting of Local Managers, September 24, 1948, Folder 4, Box 28, ILGWU Collection 5780/047, Kheel Center. The final quote is from Emil Schlesinger to Commissioner Wallender, September 23, 1948, Folder 4, Box 28, ILGWU Collection 5780/047, Kheel Center.

31. "Seamen Are Seized in Garment Area," *New York Times*, October 8, 1948, p. 1; "3 of ILGWU Board Held in Shop Raids," *New York Times*, October 16, 1948, p. 1.

32. "This will teach" quote from memo entitled "From the Files of Room 207, Ext 48, November 1, 1948, Folder 4, Box 28, ILGWU Collection 5780/047, Kheel Center; see also "Dress Organization after November 9, 1948," Folder 9, Box 27, ILGWU Collection 5780/047, Kheel Center; "Bare Attacks on ILGWU War," *New York Post*, November 10, 1948, p. 16.

33. "ILGWU Organizer Stabbed Second Time in 10 Days," *New York Post*, November 9, 1948, p. 1; "I.L.G.W.U. Aide in Hiding After 2nd Knifing," *New York Post*, November 11, 1948, p. 5.

34. Interviews by A.H. Raskin, Binder: DD Zimmerman 41, Box 2, Abe Raskin Collection 6036/012, Kheel Center.

35. Report on Organization Drive, September–October 1948, Folder 9, Box 27, ILGWU Collection 5780/047, Kheel Center.

36. Parmet, *Master of Seventh Avenue*, pp. 4–80; Danish, *World of David Dubinsky*, pp. 13–70.

37. "Labor: Little David, the Giant," *Time*, August 29, 1949, pp. 12–15; A.H. Raskin, "Dubinsky: A Study in Labor Leadership," *New York Times Magazine*, December 12, 1948, p. SM10; Sam Lubell, "Dictator in Sheep's Clothing," *Saturday Evening Post*, November 19, 1949, pp. 19–24, 66–72; "David Dubinsky, 90, Dies, Led Garment Union," *New York Times*, September 18, 1982, p. 1.

38. Lubell, "Dictator in Sheep's Clothing," p. 66.

39. Paul Jacobs, *State of the Unions*, p. 113.

40. "Little David, the Giant," pp. 12–15; Raskin, "Dubinsky: A Study in Labor Leadership," p. SM10; Lubell, "Dictator in Sheep's Clothing," pp. 19–21, 66–72; David Dubinsky, "How I Handled the Reds in My Union," *Saturday Evening Post*, May 9, 1953, p. 31, 145–46. For Dubinsky's role in post–World War II campaigns against communist influence in labor unions abroad, see: Parmet, *Master of Seventh Avenue*, pp. 203–204, 224–36; Anthony Carew, "The American Labor Movement in Fizzland: The Free Trade Union Committee and the CIA," *Labor History* 39, no. 1 (1998), pp. 28–41.

41. Danish, *World of David Dubinsky*, pp. 142–43, 180–82; Parmet, *Master of Seventh Avenue*, pp. 214–15, 249–57.

42. Parmet, *Master of Seventh Avenue*, pp. 221–24; Danish, *World of David Dubinsky*, pp. 178–79; David McCullough, *Truman* (New York: Simon & Schuster, 1992), pp. 679, 701–2.

43. Meyer Berger, "President in 9-Mile Tour Gets Spectacular Greeting," *New York Times*, October 29, 1948, p. 1; Warren Moscow, "Truman in Strongest Plea for Israel Backs Boundaries in First U.N. Plan," *New York Times*, October 29, 1948, p. 1.

44. Interviews by A.H. Raskin, Binder: DD Zimmerman 41, Box 2, Abe Raskin Collection 6036/012, Kheel Center; pistol in sleeve in Lubell, "Dictator in Sheep's Clothing," p. 70; gun permit in Parmet, *Master of Seventh Avenue*, pp. 42 and 350n68.

45. "Dress Unions War on $2,000,000 Racket," *New York Times*, July 15, 1930, p. 20; "New Names Widen Dress Racket Inquiry," *New York Times*, July 17, 1930, p. 14; Interviews by A.H. Raskin, Binder: DD Zimmerman 41, Box 2, Abe Raskin Collection 6036/012, Kheel Center.

46. The quote is from "Dress Unions War on $2,000,000 Racket," p. 20.

47. Parmet, *Master of Seventh Avenue*, p. 278.

48. Interviews by A.H. Raskin, Binder: DD Zimmerman 41, Box 2, Abe Raskin Collection 6036/012, Kheel Center.

49. Interviews by A.H. Raskin, Binder: DD Zimmerman 41, Box 2, Abe Raskin Collection 6036/012, Kheel Center.

2: Shots in the Dark: Violence and Apathy

1. The most detailed accounts of the shooting are "U.S. Labor Has a Week of Violence," *Life*, May 3, 1948, p. 27; "Who Shot Walter," *Time*, May 3, 1948, p. 21; Frank Cormier and William J. Eaton, *Reuther* (Englewood Cliffs, NJ: Prentice-Hall, 1970), pp. 254–57; Victor G. Reuther, *The Brothers Reuther and the Story of the UAW* (Boston: Houghton Mifflin, 1976), pp. 276–78.

2. Robert H. Zieger, *American Workers, American Unions*, 2nd ed. (Baltimore: Johns Hopkins University Press), p. 104.

3. Accounts of Reuther's career and his ambitions for the union move-ment include Kevin Boyle, *The UAW and the Heyday of American Liberalism, 1945–1968* (Ithaca, NY: Cornell University Press, 1995); Nelson Lichtenstein, *The Most Dangerous Man in Detroit: Walter Reuther and the Fate of American Labor* (New York: Basic Books, 1995). Details on the contracts, including the 95 percent supplemental unemployment benefits, are drawn from John Barnard, *Walter Reuther and the Rise of the Auto Workers* (Boston: Little, Brown, 1983), pp. 135–55.

4. Lichtenstein, *Most Dangerous Man in Detroit*, p. 230.

5. Cormier and Eaton, *Reuther*, pp. 12–46; Lichtenstein, *Most Dangerous Man in Detroit*, pp. 13–46.

6. The quote is from Lichtenstein, *Most Dangerous Man in Detroit*, p. 184; on Reuther's efforts to purge Communists in the UAW and CIO, see pp. 268–69, 308–10.

7. Jack Alexander, "What Does Walter Reuther Want?," *Saturday Evening Post*, August 14, 1948, pp. 15–16; Jack Alexander, "What Does Walter Reuther Want?" [part 2], *Saturday Evening Post*, August 21, pp. 5 and 88; "Who Shot the Reuthers?," *Newsweek*, June 6, 1949, p. 19; see also Lichtenstein, *Most Dangerous Man in Detroit*, pp. 184–86.

8. "Formidable crusader" in Jack Alexander, "What Does Walter Reuther Want?," p. 15; Raymond Moley, "What Does Reuther Want?," *Newsweek*, March 28, 1955, p. 101; "Walter Reuther Marches On," *Fortune*, 44 (July 1951), p. 41; Truman and Murray anecdote in Zieger, *American Workers, American Unions*, p. 107.

9. "The White Ceiling," *Time*, May 24, 1948, p. 28; Cormier and Eaton, *Reuther*, pp. 258–59.

10. Cormier and Eaton, *Reuther*, p. 258.

11. "Shot in the Dark," *Time*, June 6, 1949, p. 26.

12. "The Man on the Phone," *Time*, January 2, 1950, p. 16.

13. "Who's After the Reuthers?," *Business Week*, January 7, 1950, pp. 22–23.

14. "Who Shot the Reuthers?," pp. 19–20. The quote is from p. 20.

15. "The Man on the Phone," p. 16.

16. "Who Shot the Reuthers?," p. 20.

17. "Who Shot Walter?," p. 21.

18. "The Shot in the Night," *Newsweek*, May 3, 1948, p. 22.

19. Gerry Weeks, "Reuther in the Saddle," *New Republic*, July 18, 1949, p. 11.

20. H. Blankenhorn, "Summary of Facts on Reuther Shootings," presented to the Senate Committee on Crime, Senator Kefauver, Chairman, January 1950, Folder 31, Box 3, Blankenhorn Papers, Walter Reuther Library, Wayne State University, Detroit, Michigan.

21. Blankenhorn, "Summary of Facts on Reuther Shootings," pp. 23–24; Cormier and Eaton, *Reuther*, p. 267; Bob Morris, *Built in Detroit: A Story of the UAW, a Company, and a Gangster* (Bloomington, IN: iUniverse, 2013), p. 233.

22. John F. Herling, "Personal and Private," pp. 12–19, 24, Folder: Reuther File, Box 32, President's Office Files, John F. Kennedy Collection, John F. Kennedy Presidential Library; Cormier and Eaton, *Reuther*, pp. 163–267. In 1951, when a reform police commissioner took office, one of his first steps was to begin efforts to remove DeLamielleure from the force. Morris, *Built in Detroit*, pp. 291–92; Lichtenstein, *Most Dangerous Man in Detroit*, p. 273.

23. Stephen H. Norwood, *Strikebreaking and Intimidation: Mercenaries and Masculinity in Twentieth-Century America* (Chapel Hill, NC: University of North Carolina Press, 2002), pp. 177–78.

24. Lichtenstein, *Most Dangerous Man in Detroit*, pp. 101–3; "You may shoot some of us" in V.G. Reuther, *Brothers Reuther and the Story of the UAW*, pp. 206–9, quote from p. 206; Cormier and Eaton, *Reuther*, pp. 128–29.

25. Lichtenstein, *Most Dangerous Man in Detroit*, pp. 102–3; V.G. Reuther, *Brothers Reuther and the Story of the UAW*, pp. 208–9, quote from p. 209; Cormier and Eaton, *Reuther*, pp. 128–29.

26. Cormier and Eaton, *Reuther*, pp. 128–29.

27. "Former Detroit Mayor Indicted Along with 150 Others," *Chicago Tribune*, August 8, 1940, p. 2; "Detroit's Ex-Mayor and 22 Convicted in Rackets Trial," *Chicago Tribune*, December 16, 1941, p. 13; the quote is from "Indict Ex-Mayor and 134 Others in Gambling Quiz," *Chicago Tribune*, April 25, 1940, p. 19.

28. Herling, "Personal and Private," p. 23.

29. Lichtenstein, *Most Dangerous Man in Detroit*, pp. 166–67, 274.

30. V.G. Reuther, *Brothers Reuther and the Story of the UAW*, p. 281.

31. "Shot in the Dark," p. 26; "Senate Hears Plea to FBI on Reuther," *New York Times*, May 26, 1949, p. 16.

32. Memorandum from Alexander Campbell, Assistant Attorney General, to the Director of the FBI, May 26, 1949, in Folder 26, Box 8, Victor Reuther Papers, Walter Reuther Library, Wayne State University, Detroit, Michigan.

33. "Crime: War on the Reuthers," *Newsweek*, January 2, 1950, pp. 19–20.

34. Heber Blankenhorn to Senator Kefauver, August 1, 1950, Folder: 33, Kefauver Committee, Misc. Material; "Ralph Winstead Visit to the FBI, August 17, 1950, Folder: 32, Ralph Winstead FBI Interview, August 1950. Both documents in Box 3, Blankenhorn Papers.

35. "Blankenhorn Memo, Confidential for Files, Conference with FBI Deputy Director on Their Investigation," January 18, 1950, Folder: 29, Box 3, Blankenhorn Papers; Lichtenstein, *Most Dangerous Man in Detroit*, p. 506n10.

36. Joseph Rauh, Memorandum on McGrath Interview, June 28, 1950. Folder: 33, Kefauver Committee, Misc. Material, Box 3, Blankenhorn Papers.

37. "Blankenhorn Memo, Confidential for Files."

38. "Motive Hunted in Shooting of Teamster Aide," *Chicago Tribune*, June 2, 1950, p. A11.

39. "Union Leader's Death Causes Dual Mystery," *Chicago Tribune*, June 14, 1950, p. 7.

40. "Union Leader's Death Causes Dual Mystery," p. 7.

41. "Assassin Fires at Union Head," *Chicago Tribune*, September 20, 1950, p. 1; "Teamster Aide Shot in Gang Style Ambush," *Chicago Tribune*, January 10, 1951, p. 1; "Bomb Home of Teamster Union Agent," *Chicago Tribune*, January 3, 1951, p. 1.

42. "Flat Bombed; New Teamster Violence Seen," *Chicago Tribune*, April 10, 1951, p. 1; "Bomb Blasts Teamsters Union Agent and Filling Station," *Chicago Tribune*, May 17, 1951, p. 1; "Milk Union Chief Bombed," *Chicago Tribune*, May 16, 1951, p. 1; "$10,000 Bomb Reward Put Up By Teamsters," *Chicago Tribune*, August 21, 1952, p. 8.

43. "$10,000 Bomb Reward Put Up by Teamsters," p. 8.

44. Clayton Kirkpatrick, "Familiar Mob Pattern Veils Labor Bombing," *Chicago Tribune*, August 19, 1952, p. 1.

45. "Blast Bruises 3 Women with Teamsters Aide," *Chicago Tribune*, October 3, 1951, p. 1; "Hunt Witness to Kidnapping of Slain Baldino," *Chicago Tribune*, November 15, 1952, p. 17; "Trace Violence to Teamster Member Drive," *Chicago Tribune*, November 17, 1952, p. B9.

46. "Probe Motives for Torture of Slaying Victim," *Chicago Tribune*, June 13, 1951, p. A2; George Hartmann, "U.S. Crime Quiz May Extend to Teamsters Union," *Chicago Tribune*, August 24, 1951, p. 10.

47. "Impoliteness Week," editorial, *Chicago Tribune*, July 14, 1952, p. 22; "going to get busy" in "Shooting of AFL Teamsters' Aide Still Mystery," *Chicago Tribune*, January 11, 1951, p. A9.

48. "Shooting of AFL Teamsters' Aide," p. A9.

49. "Police, Boyle Sift Clues for Bomb Plotters," *Chicago Tribune*, August 20, 1952, p. 4.

50. Kirkpatrick, "Familiar Mob Pattern Veils Labor Bombing," p. 1.

51. "Union Chiefs Hit by Violence Spurn Lie Tests," *Chicago Tribune*, August 28, 1952, p. A2; "Police, Boyle Sift Clues," p. 4.

52. "Labor Official Tells Threats by Gangsters," January 9, 1951, p. 17.

53. "Shooting of AFL Teamsters' Aide," p. A9.

54. "Mob Menace in Chicago: Union Rule by Terror," *Chicago Tribune*, August 29, 1954, p. 1; "Good Citizen and His Reward," *Life*, October 29, 1951, p. 33.

55. "Mob Menace in Chicago," p. 3.

56. "Police Charge Union Holds Out Bombing Facts," *Chicago Tribune*, August 22, 1952, p. 17.

57. David Witwer, *Shadow of the Racketeer: Scandal in Organized Labor* (Chicago: University of Illinois Press, 2009), p. 42.

58. Witwer, *Shadow of the Racketeer*, pp. 51–55.

59. "Live by Violence, Die by Violence," editorial, *Chicago Tribune*, August 30, 1951, p. 16.

60. Albert N. Votaw, "Gangs and Goons," *New Republic*, September 24, 1951, pp. 12–13; the quote is from p. 13.

61. Cormier and Eaton, *Reuther*, p. 261.

62. Robert Bussel, *Fighting for Total Person Unionism: Harold Gibbons, Ernest Calloway, and Working-Class Citizenship* (Chicago: University of Illinois Press, 2015), pp. 1–7, 15–20, 55–63; "stately looking" is from p. 67, and the quote on broader union goals, p. 5. For more on Gibbons's role in St. Louis civil rights, see: Clarence Lang, *Grassroots at the Gateway: Class Politics and Black Freedom Struggle in St. Louis, 1936–1975* (Ann Arbor: University of Michigan Press, 2009).

63. David Witwer, *Corruption and Reform in the Teamsters Union* (Chicago: University of Illinois Press, 2003), pp. 172–75; Bussel, *Fighting for Total Person Unionism*, pp. 72–73; "Union Official Found Shot to Death in Auto," *Chicago Tribune*, March 14, 1952, p. B12; "Nab Ex-convict in Slaying of Union Official," *Chicago Tribune*, August 29, 1952, p. 17.

3: The Workings of Racketeering: Blood and Profit

1. Interrogation of Joseph Ross, May 27, 1949, Folder: Joseph Ross, May 27, 1949. Materials are in the New York County District Attorney's Case File,

Indictment No. 1405, People vs. Benedicto Macri, New York City Municipal Archives, New York.

2. The quote is from Interrogation of Joseph Ross, May 27, 1949, Folder Joseph Ross; the same folder contains canceled checks from Ross's firm, Jay Dean Frocks Inc., to Eddie Cohen, the trucker, and a memo, dated May 15, 1951, describing his arrangement. Background on Greenberg is from Interrogation of Leo Greenberg, June 1, 1949, Folder: D.A. Statements. Materials are in the New York County District Attorney's Case File, Indictment No. 1405, People vs. Benedicto Macri, New York City Municipal Archives, New York. See also: "Macri Associate on Stand," *New York Times*, October 16, 1951, p. 64; "Macri Trial Opens in Lurye Slaying," p. 22.

3. W. Michael Reisman, *Folded Lies: Bribery, Crusades, and Reforms* (New York: The Free Press, 1979), pp. 15–36, 41–54.

4. Hogan and Braestrup, "Dress Plague," p. 1.

5. "Ghost of Lepke," *Fortune*, September 1952, p. 67.

6. Leonard S. Bernstein, *"How's Business?" "Don't Ask": Tales from the Garment Center* (New York: Saturday Review Press, 1974), p. 4.

7. "Dress Man Jailed as Balky Witness," *New York Times*, April 9, 1957, p. 27; Report by Logan J. Lane, Title of Case: John Ignazio Dioguardi, victim Young Tempo, Inc., November 15, 1956, Serial No. 92-2084-4; Report by [name blanked out], October 18, 1956, Serial No. 92-2084-3; SAC, New York, to Director, FBI, Subject: John Ignazio Dioguardi, Victim: Young Tempo, Inc., February 12, 1957, Serial 92-2084-8. All three of the Dioguardi documents were found in Case File: 92-2084, Young Tempo, Inc., Federal Bureau of Investigation, obtained by Freedom of Information Act Request.

8. Peter Braestrup, "Life Among N.Y.'s City's Garment Workers," *New York Herald Tribune*, October 1, 1958, p. 15.

9. Edgar F. Borgatta, "The Social System of a Garment Plant in New York City" (PhD dissertation, New York University, 1948), pp. 11–25; the quote is from p. 16.

10. William Cherkes, interview by Robert Wolensky, July 20, 1994; transcript and recording provided to author by Wolensky.

11. Cherkes, interview.

12. Bernstein, *"How's Business?,"* p. 13.

13. Bernstein, *"How's Business?,"* pp. 40–48, 64–69, the quote is from p. 47.

14. Don Hogan and Peter Braestrup, "Dress Trade Is 'The Jungle' Ethically," *New York Herald Tribune*, June 25, 1958, p. 15.

15. Carpenter, *Competition and Collective Bargaining*, pp. 804–6.

16. [Name blanked out] of Marsha Young, Inc., interview by [name blanked out], June 29, 1959, part of Report by: [name blanked out], Title of Case: Ladies Garment—Trucking, July 31, 1959, Serial No. 60-5297-24, in Case File: HQ-60-5297, Garment Trucking Anti-Trust Case, Federal Bureau of Investigation, obtained via Freedom of Information Act request by author (hereafter FBI Garment Trucking Anti-Trust Case File).

17. In practice the union's system of registering the jobber to only a set number of contractors provided no real protection. If he wanted to, the jobber could choose to send only the bare minimum of work required by the union to one of his contractors, enough work just to keep a few of the contractor's sewing machines occupied, not enough to maintain the business. The contractor who had insisted on his full 30 percent would soon find himself facing

bankruptcy. Abraham Lustberg, interview by [name blanked out], December 2, 1959, in Report by [name blanked out], January 22, 1960, Title of Case: Ladies Garment—Trucking Industry, Serial No. 60-5297-78; [name blanked out] of Jeffrey Sportswear, interview by John J. Starner, July 13, 1959, part of Report by: [name blanked out], Title of Case: Ladies Garment—Trucking, July 31, 1959, Serial No. 60-5297-24; [name blanked out] of Universal Coat Company, interview, July 10, 1959, part of Report by: [name blanked out], Title of Case: Ladies Garment—Trucking, July 31, 1959, Serial No. 60-5297-24.

18. Paul Kamerick to Robert F. Kennedy, Subject: Garment Industry—Harry Toffel, May 16, 1958, No. 18-193-174, Case File 18-193, Records of the Select Committee on Improper Activities in the Labor or Management Field, Record Group 46, Center for Legislative Archives, National Archives and Records Administration, Washington, D.C. (hereafter McClellan Committee Records).

19. Quoted in Paul Kamerick to Robert F. Kennedy, May 9, 1958, Subject: Garment Industry: Interview with Irving Jackman, May 9, 1958, Serial No. 18-193-119, Case File 18-193, in McClellan Committee Records.

20. Paul Jacobs, *State of the Unions*, p. 124.

21. "Romans" quote is from Report by John F. Ganley, Title of Case: Ladies Garment—Trucking, July 1, 1959, Serial No. 60-5297-11; "gifts to policeman" is from SAC, Philadelphia to Director, FBI, July 2, 1959, Serial No. 60-5297-26. Both reports in FBI Garment Trucking Anti-Trust Case File.

22. John F. Burns, "Slaying of ILG Organizer Is Laid to Open Shoppers," *Providence Journal*, May 22, 1949; Bill Cherkes, interview; Benjamin Wexler, interview, in Report by E. Huyett Magee and John Conly, July 1, 1959, Serial 60-5297-11, FBI Garment Trucking Anti-Trust Case File; [name blanked out] of Whirlaway Frocks, interview by John B. Meade, September 22, 1959, in Report by [name blanked out], September 30, 1959, Serial No. 60-5297-42, in FBI Garment Trucking Anti-Trust Case File.

23. No author, "Report: Sam Berger, Manager of Cloak, Dress Drivers and Helpers Local 102, I.L.G.W.U.," November 5, 1948, Folder: Yale Trucking Company, Box 4197, District Attorney's Investigative Case File on John Dioguardi, June 1956, New York Municipal Archives. The quote is from p. 26 of this report. Descriptions of the seasonal pressures on contractors and jobbers can be found in Paul Kamerick to Robert F. Kennedy, Subject: Garment Industry, January 22, 1959, Serial No. 18-193-448, McClellan Committee Records.

24. Paul Kamerick to Robert F. Kennedy, Re: Garment Industry: Orientation Memorandum, May 21, 1958, Serial No. 18-193-181, McClellan Committee Records; Walter Goodman, "Muscling in on Labor," *New Republic*, April 30, 1956, p. 10; Lester Velie, "Gangsters in the Dress Business," *Reader's Digest*, July 1955, p. 62; Report by William J. Roemer, Title of Case: Harry Strasser, July 10, 1959, FBI Serial No. 92-1473, NARA Serial No. 124-10347-10072, FBI Subject Files: James Plumeri, Warren Commission Files, National Archives; Local 102 Report, 1941, Folder 3a, Box 14, ILGWU Collection 5780/047 (Joint Dress Board Manager's Correspondence), Kheel Center; Franz S. Leichter, *The Return of the Sweatshop: Part II of an Investigation*, New York State Senate, Albany, NY, February 1981, pp. 5–21. The business card quote is from [name blanked out] by [name blanked out], interview, January 6, 1960, in Report by [name blanked out], Title of Case: Ladies Garment—Trucking

Industry, January 22, 1960, Serial: 60-5297-78, FBI Garment Trucking Anti-Trust Case File.

25. No author, no title, FBI Report No. 92-7130-317, September 20, 1973, FBI Garment Industry New York City Case File.

26. Robert Gilroy to Paul Kamerick, Re: Garment Industry: Scranton Frocks and Joseph Riccobono, no date, Serial No. 18-193-548, McClellan Committee Records.

27. In 1958, Riccobono was identified as the consigliere of the Gambino crime family. John H. Davis, *Mafia Dynasty: The Rise and Fall of the Gambino Crime Family* (New York: HarperCollins, 1993), p. 82.

28. Investigation of Joseph Riccobono, enclosed with Thomas R. Sullivan to Myles J. Lane, August 19, 1958, in File No. 147, Joseph Riccobono, Master Case Files: Apalachin, New York State Commission of Investigation Records, New York State Archives, Albany, New York.

29. Frank Ward to File, Re: Garment Industry: Missy Judy Fashions—Leo Kleinman, Serial No. 18-193-455, McClellan Committee Records.

30. No author, Report on Imperial Juniors, Re: Ladies Garment—Trucking Industry, September 15, 1959, Serial No. 60-5297-35, FBI Garment Trucking Anti-Trust Case File.

31. Frank Ward to File, Re: Garment Industry: Missy Judy Fashions—Leo Kleinman, Serial No. 18-193-455, McClellan Committee Records.

32. FBI reports, for example, cite a Morris Shapiro as the "collector" for Ben Kutlow, who in turn oversaw street matters for the more influential Benjamin Levine; Louis Lieberman and Harry Strasser allegedly played similar lower-level roles. In Lieberman's case, he went to jail rather than provide information about the gangster on whose behalf he was collecting payments from Garment District businessmen. Maloney Garment Trucking Report, April 7, 1956.

33. Report by [name blanked out], Title of Case: John Ignazio Dioguardi, Young Tempo, Victim, October 18, 1956, Serial No. 92-284-3, FBI Young Tempo Case File.

34. "Garment Man Loses Plea on Jail Term," *New York Times*, May 13, 1959, p. 19.

35. FBI Report by [name blanked out], Title of Case: John Ignazio Dioguardi, October 30, 1956, FBI Serial No. 72-964-1, FBI Riesel File, acquired via Freedom of Information Request by author ; the quote is from p. 19 and the details of payments are from pp. 20–21.

36. Maloney Garment Trucking Report, April 17, 1956, p. 169.

37. Thomas E. Dewey, *Twenty Against the Underworld* (New York: Doubleday, 1974), pp. 305–9; Report by Arthur P. Duffy, Re: Abraham Telvi, was (Deceased) Et Al., Victor Riesel—Victim, April 24, 1957, Serial No. 72-964-770, pp. 6–8, FBI Riesel File. A full account of Plumeri and Dioguardi's activities can be found in W. B. Herlands to Mr. Grumet, October 15, 1937, Re: Garment Trucking Racket, in Series 1, Box 90, Thomas E. Dewey Papers, University of Rochester, Rochester, New York.

38. Re: Garment Trucking Racket, pp. 4–8. See also Richard Norton-Smith, *Thomas E. Dewey and His Times* (New York: Simon & Schuster, 1982), pp. 222–23.

39. FBI Report by Arthur P. Duffy, Serial No. 72-964-770, p. 8; Dewey, *Twenty Against the Underworld*, pp. 307–9. Quotes are from p. 309.

40. Local 102 Report, 1941, Folder 3a, Box 14, ILGWU Collection 5780/047 (Joint Dress Board Manager's Correspondence), Kheel Center.

41. Parmet, *Master of Seventh Avenue*, pp. 66–67; Roy B. Helfgott, "Women and Children's Apparel," in Max Hall, ed., *Made in New York: Case Studies in Metropolitan Manufacturing* (Cambridge, MA: Harvard University Press, 1959), pp. 54–57.

42. New York City Department of Traffic, *A Study of Trucking Problems in the Garment District* (New York: Edwards and Kelcey, Inc., 1961), pp. 5, 11–13, 24–25; Helfgott, "Women and Children's Apparel," pp. 104–6; no author, no title, FBI Report No. 92-1730-38, December 1, 1972; Don Hogan and Peter Braestrup, "Truckers Bleed Garment Industry," *New York Herald Tribune*, June 29, 1958, p. 1; Leigh David Benin, *The New Labor Radicalism and New York City's Garment Industry: Progressive Labor Insurgents in the 1960s* (New York: Garland Publishing, 2000), pp. 119–20, 126; Ideal Trucking, FBI Report by John J. Ryan, Title: Garment Trucking Investigation, September 24, 1957, p. 62; FBI Report No. 92-1795-133, FBI Garment Trucking Anti-Trust Case File. Braestrup and Hogan estimate that 25 percent of the truck traffic was made up of over-the-road haulers, which apparently were larger operations. But even the biggest of the garment trucking companies were comparatively small. Interstate Dress Carriers, one of the biggest, employed 150 people and serviced about 500 accounts. For a description of Interstate, see Ryan, Title: Garment Trucking Investigation, pp. 66–67.

43. Local 102 Report, 1941, Folder 3a, Box 14, ILGWU Collection 5780/047 (Joint Dress Board Manager's Correspondence), Kheel Center.

44. Early history of Chait is found in Malcolm R. Wilkey to Robert F. Kennedy, May 14, 1959, Serial No. 18-193-504; Robert F. Kennedy to William Rogers, April 28, 1959, Serial No. 18-193-447; Paul Kamerick to Robert F. Kennedy, Subject: Abraham Chait, June 28, 1958, Serial No. 18-193-512, all in McClellan Committee Records; Hogan and Braestrup, "Chait One of the Biggest of 'Big 5' Racketeers," p. 1; "Gurrah Jake Dies in Prison Hospital," *New York Times*, June 10, 1947, p. 56; "Two Linked Here to Killer's Escape," *New York Times*, November 6, 1933, p. 16; "Slain Man Linked to Verne Miller," *New York Times*, November 23, 1933, p. 42.

45. Maloney Garment Trucking Report, April 17, 1956, pp. 144–46; the quote is from p. 144.

46. See: no author, no title, FBI Report No. 92-7130-11, October 11, 1972; no author no title, FBI Report No. 92-7130-80, December 20, 1972; and no author no title, FBI Report No. 92-7130-79, December 21, 1972. This perspective is borne out by Helfgott, "Women's and Children's Apparel," pp. 104–6.

47. Maloney Garment Trucking Report, April 17, 1956, pp. 145–46.

48. Maloney Garment Trucking Report, April 17, 1956, p. 146.

49. No author, "Report: Sam Berger, Manager of Cloak, Dress Drivers and Helpers Local 102, I.L.G.W.U.," November 5, 1948, Folder: Yale Trucking Company, Box 4197, District Attorney's Investigative Case File on John Dioguardi, June 1956, New York Municipal Archives. The "Seigel and Lenikoff" quote is from p. 15.

50. Paul Kamerick to Robert F. Kennedy, Subject: Garment Industry Hearings, April 30, 1959, Serial No. 18-193-500, McClellan Committee Records.

51. Arthur Kaplan to Robert F. Kennedy, December 4, 1957, Serial No. 18-193-64; Paul Kamerick to Robert F. Kennedy, Subject: Garment

Industry-Fairfrox, June 3, 1958, Serial No. 18-193-129; no author, Memo Titled: John Ignazio Dioguardi, no date, in Folder 4, Box 204, Irving Ives Papers. Peter Maas, *The Valachi Papers* (New York: Putnam, 1968; New York: Perennial, 2003), p. 150. The quote is from the Perennial edition.

52. Maloney Garment Trucking Report, April 7, 1956, p. 102; Maloney Garment Trucking Report, April 17, 1956, pp. 149–51.

53. Re: Glassberg's business partnership with Sara Chait, see Don Hogan and Peter Braestrup, "I.L.G.W.U. Strike Hard on Rackets," *New York Herald Tribune*, June 27, 1958, p. 6. Re: Fishgold, see Maloney Garment Trucking Report, April 17, 1956, p. 146; John J. Pezzent, Pennsylvania State Police [untitled memo from head of the Criminal Intelligence Unit, at Troop "B," Wyoming, Pennsylvania], no date, Serial No. 18-193-573, Case File 18-218, McClellan Committee Records. During his tenure with the Pennsylvania Garment Manufacturers Association, Fishgold used the name Bert Fielding.

54. FBI Report by John J. Ryan, Title: Garment Trucking Investigation, September 24, 1957, FBI Serial No. 92-1795-133.

55. Hogan and Braestrup, "Chait One of the Biggest of 'Big 5' Racketeers," p. 1; Paul Kamerick to Robert F. Kennedy, Subject: Abraham Chait, June 28, 1958, Serial No. 18-193-512, McClellan Committee Records; "Ex-Convict's Gifts Put Son in Racing," *New York Times*, December 10, 1953, p. 37; "Combat Boots Defeats Ted M. After Thrilling Jamaica Stretch Duel," *New York Times*, April 18, 1952, p. 33.

56. Hogan and Braestrup, "Chait One of the Biggest of 'Big 5' Racketeers," p. 1; "Racket Links End in Race Track Ban," *New York Times*, January 15, 1954, p. 13.

57. No author, Report: Sam Berger, Manager of Cloak, Dress Drivers and Helpers Local 102, I.L.G.W.U., November 5, 1948, Folder: Yale Trucking Company, Box 41947, Case File Number 3091, John Dioguardi, New York County District Attorney's Records, New York City Municipal Archives, New York.

58. SAC, New York, to Acting Director, FBI, Subject: Garment Industry, New York, May 15, 1973, FBI Serial No. 92-7130-187, pp. 6–7.

59. No author, no date, document entitled, "Possible, and perhaps probable, motive for the stabbing of William Lurye . . . on May 9, 1949, as a result of which he died." In Folder 7, Box 25, ILGWU Collection 5780/005, Kheel Center.

60. Maloney Garment Trucking Report, April 17, 1956, pp. 147–48; the quote is from p. 144.

61. On Abe Chait's role, see: Hogan and Braestrup, "Chait One of the Biggest of 'Big 5' Racketeers," p. 1; FBI Report by Russell E. Hogg, Title of Case: Sam Berger, July 10, 1959, FBI Serial No. 92-1469, NARA Serial No. 124-10347-10073, pp. 5–6, in FBI Subject File: James Plumeri, Warren Commission Files, National Archives. An FBI report from 1956 referred to Lucchese as "the head of the Italian mob in the garment industry . . . He was believed to be a partner of Abe Chait, garment trucking czar." Maloney Garment Trucking Report, April 17, 1956, p. 221.

62. Paul Kamerick to Robert F. Kennedy, Subject: Abraham Chait, June 28, 1958, Serial No. 18-193-512; Paul Kamerick to Robert F. Kennedy, Subject: Abraham Chait—Garment Industry, May 2, 1958, Serial 18-193-99, McClellan Committee Records.

63. Report by Frank W. Cornett, Title: Joseph Anthony Stracci, File

No. 92-2836, in James Plumeri Subject File, National Archives and Records Administration.

64. Report by Ralph Martorelli, Title of Case: John Ignazio Dioguardi, November 21, 1956, Serial No. 72-964-622, p. 16.

65. Report by Richard A. Anderson, Title of Case: James Plumeri, July 8, 1958, FBI Case File No. 92-2854-25, National Archives and Records Administration. Thomas Lucchese was listed as the vice president of Brauneil Limited, a garment manufacturer with a showroom at 262 West Thirty-Eighth Street. Charles Grutzner, "Lucchese Presents a Study in Contrasts," *New York Times*, October 11, 1952, p. 26.

66. Untitled, no author, records from New York City Crime Commission, December 17, 1951, Serial 18-218-416, p. E42, McClellan Committee Records.

67. Arthur G. Kaplan to Robert F. Kennedy, Subject: Racketeering-Garment Industry-Mafia, December 11, 1957, Serial No. 18-193-164.

68. Maloney Garment Trucking Report, April 17, 1956, pp. 185–87.

69. The quotes are from [name blanked out], Assistant Attorney General to H.G. Foster, January 11, 1960, Case File No. 60-5297-77, FBI Garment Trucking Anti-Trust Case File; other memorandums that describe aspects of this episode include: [name blanked out] to H.G. Foster, January 5, 1960, Case File No. 60-5297-75; SAC New York to Director, FBI, July 2, 1960, Case File No. 60-5297-105; Report of George Johnson, Title: Ladies Garment—Trucking Industry, September 30, 1959, Case File No. 60-5297-39; all in FBI Garment Trucking Anti-Trust Case File. Foster's January 5th letter names two of the men who accompanied Chait as Joseph Rosato and Natale Evola.

4: An Organizer's Fight for Justice: Rage and Dignity

1. "Garment Area War Vet Says Lurye Beat Him Up," *New York Journal American*, June 4, 1949, p. 1; A.H. Raskin, "Job Stoppage Set in Murder Protest," *New York Times*, May 11, 1949, p. 1; "$25,000 Reward Up For Lurye Killers," *New York Times*, May 12, 1949, p. 24; Re: the pressers, Bernice Lurye to David Dubinsky, no date [1949], Folder 2a, Box 297, ILGWU Collection 5780/002, Kheel Center; Min Lurye Matheson, "The Murder of My Brother," pamphlet in Folder 2b, Box 297, ILGWU Collection 5780/002, Kheel Center.

2. Min Matheson, interview #1 by Alice M. Hoffman, September 7, 1983, Historical Collections and Labor Archives, Penn State University, University Park, Pennsylvania (hereafter Matheson Oral History #1 by Hoffman).

3. Min Matheson to Sasha [Charles Zimmerman], [probably April] 1950, Folder 5, Box 24, ILGWU Collection 5780/014, Kheel Center.

4. Min Matheson to District Attorney, March 20, 1950, Folder 2B, Box 297, ILGWU Collection 5780/002, Kheel Center.

5. "Family of Lurye Visits Prosecutor," *New York Times*, May 7, 1950, p. 62.

6. Min Matheson to Julius Hochman, December 16, 1951, Folder 6, Box 24, ILGWU Collection 5780/014, Kheel Center; Min Matheson to Sasha [Charles Zimmerman], [probably April] 1950, Folder 5, Box 24, ILGWU Collection 5780/014, Kheel Center.

7. Min Matheson, interview #3 by Alice M. Hoffman, October 27, 1983, Historical Collections and Labor Archives, Penn State University, University Park, Pennsylvania (hereafter Matheson Oral History #3 by Hoffman).

8. Statement of Albert Cipriani, Folder: Cipriani, Albert, New York County

District Attorney's Case File, Indictment No. 1405, People vs. Benedicto Macri, New York City Municipal Archives, New York.

9. Anonymous to Tony, Organizing Department, August 6, 1949, Folder 5, Box 24, ILGWU Collection 5780/014, Kheel Center.

10. Kenneth C. Wolensky, Nicole H. Wolensky, and Robert P. Wolensky, *Fighting for the Union Label: The Women's Garment Industry and the ILGWU in Pennsylvania* (University Park: Penn State University Press, 2002), p. 189.

11. Min Matheson, interview #1, September 7, 1983, Historical Collections and Labor Archives, Penn State University, University Park, Pennsylvania (hereafter Matheson Oral History #1 by Hoffman), p. 5.

12. Matheson Oral History #1 by Hoffman, pp. 1–16.

13. Matheson Oral History #1 by Hoffman, p. 4.

14. Min Matheson to Sasha [Charles Zimmerman], no date [1952], Folder 5, Box 24, ILGWU Collection 5780/014, Kheel Center.

15. Kenneth Teitelbaum, *Schooling for "Good Rebels": Socialist Education for Children in the United States, 1900–1920* (Philadelphia: Temple University Press, 1993), p. 11.

16. Matheson Oral History #1 by Hoffman, p. 3.

17. Matheson Oral History #1 by Hoffman; quotes are from pp. 3, 4, 13.

18. Matheson Oral History #1 by Hoffman, p. 13. In her interview, she says she was out of the Party by the age of twenty.

19. Matheson Oral History #1 by Hoffman, p. 25; Matheson Oral History #2, pp. 1–5, 11.

20. Matheson Oral History #2, p. 12.

21. Peter Braestrup, "Life Among the Garment Workers," *New York Herald Tribune*, September 30, 1955, p. 16. Edgar F. Borgatta, "The Social System of a Garment Plant in New York City" (master's thesis, New York University, 1948), pp. 5–10, 35–48; Carpenter, *Competition and Collective Bargaining*, pp. 90–104.

22. Borgatta, "Social System of a Garment Plant," pp. 36–39; Peter Braestrup, "Life Among Today's Garment Workers," *New York Herald Tribune*, September 29, 1958, p. 1.

23. Minnie Caputo, interview by Robert Wolensky, July 22, 1993, provided to author by Wolensky (hereafter cited as Caputo Oral History).

24. Braestrup, "Life Among the Garment Workers," p. 16.

25. Borgatta, "Social System of a Garment Plant," pp. 35–48, 64–78; Peter Braestrup, "Life Among City's Garment Workers," October 2, 1958, p. 13.

26. Peter Braestrup, "Life Among Today's Garment Workers," *New York Herald Tribune*, September 29, 1958, p. 1; Peter Braestrup, "Life Among the Garment Workers: Puerto Ricans Rebel Against Boss—and Union," *New York Herald Tribune*, October 8, 1958, p. 15; Peter Braestrup, "Life Among the Garment Workers: Color Still Bar to Skills, Union Office," *New York Herald Tribune*, October 6, 1958, p. 19.

27. Peter Braestrup, "Life Among the Garment Workers: I.L.G.W.U. Sets Pace for Labor," *New York Herald Tribune*, October 7, 1958, p. 23; quote is from Parmet, *Master of Seventh Avenue*, p. 258.

28. Borgatta, "Social System of a Garment Plant," p. 56.

29. Borgatta, 57–58.

30. Katz, *All Together Different*, pp. 66–67; 114–20; Joseph B. Treaster, "Charles Zimmerman Dies at 86," *New York Times*, June 5, 1983, p. 32.

31. Katz, *All Together Different*, pp. 126–52; the quote is from p. 129.

32. Matheson Oral History #3 by Hoffman, p. 3.

33. Katz, *All Together Different*, pp. 126–52, the quote is from p. 129.

34. Matheson Oral History #3 by Hoffman, p. 7.

35. Sasha Zimmerman to Min Lurye, August 29, 1941, Folder 4, Box 20, ILGWU Collection 5780/014, Kheel Center.

36. Min Matheson to Alice [no last name given], March 3, 1943, Folder 4, Box 20, ILGWU Collection 5780/014, Kheel Center.

37. Min Matheson to Alice [no last name given].

38. Min Matheson to Sasha Zimmerman, February 12, 1944, Folder 4, Box 24, ILGWU Collection 5780/014, Kheel Center.

39. Matheson Oral History #3, pp. 10–14.

40. Min Matheson to Sasha Zimmerman, November 2, 1944, Folder 4, Box 24, ILGWU Collection 5780/014, Kheel Center.

41. Min Matheson to Charles S. Zimmerman, September 25, 1946, Folder 4, Box 20, ILGWU Collection 5780/014, Kheel Center.

42. Borgatta, "Social System of a Garment Plant," p. 67; Cherkes, interview; Wolensky et al., *Fighting for the Union Label*, pp. 37–38.

43. Thomas Dublin and Walter Licht, *The Face of Decline: The Pennsylvania Anthracite Region in the Twentieth Century* (Ithaca, NY: Cornell University Press, 2005); Wolensky et al., *Fighting for the Union Label*, pp. 25–37.

44. Caputo Oral History, p. 12.

45. Cherkes Oral History, p. 10.

46. [no name given] to Mr. President Dubinsky, February 18, 1956, Folder 12B, Box 319, ILGWU Collection 5780/002, Kheel Center.

47. Matheson Oral History #3 by Hoffman, p. 21.

48. Caputo Oral History, p. 8.

49. Matheson Oral History #3 by Hoffman, p. 21 and p. 22.

50. Matheson Oral History #3 by Hoffman, p. 14.

51. Matheson Oral History #3 by Hoffman, p. 22.

52. Matheson Oral History #3 by Hoffman, p. 14.

53. Min Matheson, interview by Robert Wolensky, December 5, 1988, provided to author by Wolensky, p. 2 (hereafter Matheson Interview by Wolensky).

54. Matheson Oral History #3 by Hoffman, p. 16.

55. Thomas Hunt and Michael A. Tona, "Men of Montedoro," *Informer* (April 2011); Robert Wolensky and William A. Hastie, *Anthracite Labor Wars: Tenancy, Italians, and Organized Crime in the Northern Coalfield of Northeastern Pennsylvania, 1897–1959* (Easton, PA: Canal History and Technology Press, 2013); the figure of thirty homicides is from p. 95.

56. "Bomb Kills Union Official," *Chester Times*, October 27, 1951, p. 1; "Bomb Kills Miner Leader," *New York Times*, October 27, 1951, p. 23.

57. Matheson Interview by Wolensky, p. 9.

58. Matt Birkbeck, *The Quiet Don: The Untold Story of Mafia Kingpin Russell Bufalino* (New York: Berkeley Books, 2013), pp. 54–55, 109; Bufalino's threat is from Arnold H. Lubasch, "Reputed Mafia Boss Guilty of Extortion," *New York Times*, August 11, 1977, p. 21; Frank Sheeran's recollections are from Charles Brandt, *"I Heard You Paint Houses": Frank "The Irishman" Sheeran and the Inside Story of the Mafia, the Teamsters, and the Last Ride of Jimmy Hoffa* (Hanover, NH: Steerforth Press, 2004), mannerisms, p. 66; Sinatra, p. 125.

59. Paul Kamerick to Robert F. Kennedy, Subject: Garment Industry: Interview with Russell Bufalino, May 7, 1958, Serial No. 18-193-115; Paul Kamerick to Robert F. Kennedy, Subject: Russell Alfred Bufalino, June 30, 1958, Serial No. 18-193-193; both in McClellan Committee Records.

60. Intelligence Report 3-B-4288, Subject: Russell A. Bufalino, March 28, 1956, Serial No. 1-7-65; quote is from Detective Victor Nelson to Commanding Officer, Subject: Russell Bufalino, February 29, 1956, Serial No. 1-7-12; both in New York State Master File.

61. Intelligence Report 3-B-4288; quote is from Detective Victor Nelson to Commanding Officer; Commission of Investigation Individual Intelligence Profile—Organized Crime: Bufalino, Russell, no date, Serial No. 1-7-88; all in New York State Master File; Paul Kamerick to Robert F. Kennedy, Subject: Russell Alfred Bufalino, June 30, 1958, Serial No. 18-193-193, McClellan Committee Records.

62. The FBI charged that Sciandra had written a threatening note that Macedon had received shortly before his murder. "Extortion Charges Ignored by Jurors," *Gettysburg Times*, October 7, 1952, p. 7; Maloney Garment Trucking Report, April 7, 1956; no author, FBI Report, Serial No. 124-10347-10059, Subject: James Plumeri, September 27, 1960; A.F. Dahlstrom to John W. Ryan Jr., July 27, 1959, Dominick Alaimo File, Serial No. 1-1-33; George L. List to Joseph D. Milenky, July 12, 1959, Serial No. 1-1-27; George L. List to Joseph D. Milenky, June 15, 1959, Serial No. 1-1-25A; all in New York State Master File.

63. Matheson Interview by Wolensky, p. 3; Caputo Oral History, p. 5.

64. Wolensky et al., *Fighting for the Union Label*, p. 72.

65. Wolensky et al., p. 73.

66. Dorothy Ney, interview by Robert Wolensky, July 3, 1990 (made available to the author by Wolensky), p. 7 (hereafter cited as Ney Oral History).

67. Caputo Oral History, p. 21.

68. Ney Oral History, p. 3.

69. Ney Oral History, p. 9.

70. Caputo Oral History, p. 4.

71. Ney Oral History, p. 3.

72. Matheson Oral History #2 by Hoffman, pp. 17–19.

73. Min Lurye Matheson to Sid Handler, January 19, 1952, Folder 4, Box 20, ILGWU Collection 5780/014, Kheel Center.

74. Fliers in Folder 4, Box 20, ILGWU Collection 5780/014, Kheel Center.

75. Caputo Oral History, p. 30.

76. Matheson Oral History #3 by Hoffman, p. 3.

77. Wolensky et al., *Fighting for the Union Label*, pp. 119–60.

78. Wolensky et al., p. 133.

79. Matheson Oral History #3 by Hoffman, p. 22.

80. Matheson Interview by Wolensky, p. 12

81. Matheson Interview by Wolensky, p. 12.

5: A Pattern of Accommodation: Allies and Enemies

1. "Grim Manhunt Casts Net for Lurye," newspaper clipping, Folder 7, Box 24, ILGWU Collection 5780/014, Kheel Center; "$50,000 Fund Set Up For Lurye Family," *New York Times*, May 14, 1949, p. 2.

2. "South Is Searched in Lurye's Murder," p. 34.

3. "3 Witnesses Held in Lurye Murder," *New York Times*, June 11, 1949, p. 3; "Major Break Seen in Lurye Murder," *New York Times*, June 17, 1949, p. 1.

4. "Police Hunt 2 Men as Lurye Killers in 48 State Alarm," *New York Times*, June 22, 1949, p. 1; "Lurye 'Killer' Held, *New York Post*, June 19, 1950, p. 1; Lawrence Lafer and Charles McHarry, "U.S. Jack Built Hoodlum House," *New York Daily News*, November 20, 1950, p. 1; Commanding Officer, 3rd Detective District, to Assistant District Attorney George Monaghan, Subject: Background on Benedicto Macri, August 12, 1949, in People v. Ben Macri, Indictment No. 1405, New York District Attorney (NYDA) Case Files, New York City Municipal Archives.

5. John Nothris, Memorandum Relative to Investigation in Easton and Surrounding Territory Concerning John Giusto, October 11, 1950; no author, Memorandum Relative to Investigation Conducted in Pennsylvania from November 15 to November 22, 1950, Case No. 631, 14th Squad, November 27, 1950, NYPD Criminal Record of John Guisto; both in People v. Ben Macri, Indictment No. 1405, NYDA Case Files, New York City Municipal Archives; "Lurye Suspects Defy Year-Long Manhunt," *New York Journal American*, June 4, 1950, p. 1.

6. Background on Benedicto Macri, August 12, 1949, NYDA Case Files.

7. "Lurye 'Killer' Held," p. 3; "Seek B.M. and J.G. as Killers of Lurye," *New York Journal American*, June 20, 1949, p. 1; "Lurye Suspects Defy Year Long Manhunt," p. L13; "Police Hunt 2 Men as Lurye Killers in 48 State Alarm," p. 1; "South Is Searched in Lurye Murder," p. 34.

8. "South Is Searched in Lurye Murder," p. 34.

9. Ira Henry Freedman, "The Harry Gross Story," *New York Times*, September 23, 1951, p. 156; Emanuel Perlmutter, "Gross Lists O'Brien, Moran, and Bals as Bribe Takers," *New York Times*, May 8, 1952, p. 1; Norton Mockridge and Robert H. Prall, *The Big Fix* (New York: Henry Holt, 1954), pp. 290–93.

10. Observers such as Sydney Lens have drawn on the history of the American Federation of Labor (AFL) and the Congress of Industrial Organizations (CIO) to assert that there were "two main currents" in American unions: "business unionism" and "social unionism," with the early CIO belonging to the latter group. Lens argued that the CIO resembled the kinds of labor organizations that had emerged in Europe. Left-wing social unionists, in Europe and in the U.S., had historical ties to radical political movements that "imposed mores, ethics, values and ideas, sharply at loggerheads with those of the business community." In America, on the other hand, business unionists, who led the AFL, "succumbed to business ethics and business mores," and as a result, "temptation [was] put in the way of some of their money-minded leaders." Because business unionists saw organized labor as nothing more than a business, Lens asserted, they were more susceptible to corruption than their social unionist counterparts. The result, Lens claimed, was "one of the unique features of the American labor movement"—the problem of racketeering. Lens termed it "the marriage of business unionism and crime, known as labor racketeering." Sidney Lens, *The Crisis of American Labor* (New York: A.S. Barnes & Company, 1959), p. 101.

11. Sidney Lens, *Unrepentant Radical: An American Activist's Account of Five Turbulent Decades* (Boston: Beacon Press, 1980), p. 16.

12. Lens, *Unrepentant Radical*, pp. 2–105; Joan Cook, "Sidney Lens Dies;

Activist of the Left," *New York Times*, June 20, 1986, p. D23; Ralph A. Pugh, "Sidney Lens: A Descriptive Inventory of His Papers," Chicago Historical Society, 2000.

13. Lens, *Crisis of American Labor*, pp. 101–2.

14. Lens, *Crisis of American Labor*, p. 23.

15. Lens, *Crisis of American Labor*, p. 198.

16. Lens, *Crisis of American Labor*, pp. 278–87.

17. [no author], Re: John Giusto, September 10, 1952, People v. Ben Macri, NYDA Files.

18. Neal Gabler, *Winchell: Gossip, Power and the Culture of Celebrity* (New York: Alfred A. Knopf, 1994), pp. 390–93; "Lurye Killer Held," *New York Post*, June 19, 1950, p. 1. Gabler's account of this episode doesn't mention the previous approach to Montgomery; I found reference to it in Winchell's papers, which were only opened after Gabler finished his well researched book. See handwritten note, no author, no date, with covering slip, "Dear Vic, . . . ," in Folder: Macri, Benedict, Box 4Zg43, Walter Winchell Papers, University of Texas, Austin, Texas.

19. Mark Ehrman and Erwin Savelson, "Gives Up in Lurye Slaying," *New York Daily Mirror*, June 20, 1950, p. 1.

20. "Garment Area War Vet Says Lurye Beat Him Up," *New York Journal American*, June 4, 1949, p. 1.

21. "Suspect Held in Extortion of Union Man," *New York Sun*, June 14, 1949, news clipping in Folder 7, Box 24, ILGWU Collection 5780/014, Kheel Center.

22. "Macri Trial Opens in Lurye Slaying," p. 22.

23. "Killing of Lurye Denied by Macri," *New York Times*, October 25, 1951, p. 26.

24. Brief of Appellant, in New York State, Court of Appeals, People of the State of New York Against George Futterman, 308 NY 734 (New York, 1954), via Google Books, https://books.google.com/books?id=SbuUyMesX7wC&pg=PA61&source=gbs_selected_pages&cad=2#v=onepage&q&f=false, accessed April 20, 2016.

25. "Macri Acquitted in Lurye Slaying," *New York Times*, October 30, 1951, p. 60; "Lurye Case Upset by Witness Error," *New York Times*, October 20, 1951, p. 8; "Macri Identified in Lurye Slaying," *New York Times*, October 18, 1951, p. 30.

26. Ira Henry Freeman, "Harry Gross's Story: Bets, Cops, and Corruption," *New York Times*, September 23, 1951, p. 156; see also: Norton Mockridge and Robert H. Prall, *The Big Fix* (New York: Henry Holt, 1954), pp. 1–38; Walter Arm, *Pay-off: The Inside Story of Big City Corruption* (New York: Appleton Century-Crofts, 1951). On Sherman and Blumenthal, see Emmanuel Perlmutter, "Gross Got Phones in War Scarcity, Witness Testifies," *New York Times*, July 31, 1952, p. 1.

27. Freeman, "Harry Gross's Story," p. 156; Mockridge and Prall, *The Big Fix*, pp. 33–38.

28. Ira Henry Freeman, "Brothers Anastasio—Toughest of the Tough," *New York Times*, December 14, 1952, p. E10; no author, FBI Report, February 25, 1954, Serial No. 62-98011, from General Investigative File: Top Hoodlum Coverage; quotes are from Davis, *Mafia Dynasty*, pp. 53–54, Mangano's disappearance, pp. 57–58.

29. Davis, *Mafia Dynasty*, pp. 52–54; FBI Report No. 62-98011-8, February 25, 1954, General Investigative File, AA, Top Hoodlum Coverage, pp. 7–9, FBI Files on Albert Anastasia; Selwyn Raab, *Five Families: The Rise, Decline, and Resurgence of America's Most Powerful Mafia Empires* (New York: St. Martin's Press, 2005), pp. 67–68.

30. Davis, *Mafia Dynasty*, pp. 57–59.

31. FBI Report No. 62-98011-8, February 25, 1954, General Investigative File, AA, Top Hoodlum Coverage, pp. 7–9, FBI Files on Albert Anastasia; Freeman, "Harry Gross's Story," p. 156; Mockridge and Prall, *The Big Fix*, pp. 289–93; 297–305.

32. "Prosecutor Feels Big Blow in His Battle Against Crime," *New York Times*, September 20, 1951, p. 1.

33. "Graft Trial Hears Eyewitness Name 2 as Lurye Slayers," *New York Times*, August 2, 1952, p. 1; "Ex-Convict Held in Witness Bribing," *New York Times*, February 28, 1952, p. 20; "Bookie Admits Perjury," *New York Times*, March 8, 1952, p. 30; "Tampering Trial Opens," *New York Times*, December 10, 1952, p. 44; "Bribe Demand Admitted," *New York Times*, December 13, 1952, p. 19; Brief of Appellant, People v. George Futterman.

34. Joseph Ingraham, "Moretti, Gambler, Slain by 4 Gunmen in New Jersey Café," *New York Times*, October 5, 1951, p. 1; FBI Report No. 62-98011-8, February 25, 1954, General Investigative File, AA, Top Hoodlum Coverage, pp. 7–9, FBI Files on Albert Anastasia.

35. "2 Attempts to Kill Anastasio Reported," *New York Times*, November 21, 1951, p. 26.

36. Examples of the standard depiction of David Dubinsky and the ILG can be found in: David Dubinsky and A.H. Raskin, *David Dubinsky: A Life with Labor* (New York: Simon & Schuster, 1977); Irving Bernstein, *Turbulent Years: A History of the American Worker, 1933–1941* (Boston: Houghton & Mifflin, 1970). A striking reinterpretation of Dubinsky's relationship to the corruption that occurred in his union can be found in Parmet, *Master of Seventh Avenue*. I have been strongly influenced by Parmet's reinterpretation of Dubinsky's posture regarding corruption. A far more skeptical interpretation of the ILG's leadership, but one that focuses on the period from the 1970s forward, is Herbert Hill, "The Mob and Labor-Management Corruption in the Garment Industry," *New Politics* 8, no. 7 (2000), p. 68.

37. Interviews by A.H. Raskin, Binder: DD Zimmerman 41, p. P.U. 9, Box 2, Collection 6036/012, Kheel Center.

38. Danish, *World of David Dubinsky*, pp. 190 and 191.

39. Dubinsky and Raskin, *David Dubinsky*, p. 9.

40. A recent account of organized crime's role in New York City, for instance, referred to Dubinsky as a "dynamic unionist with a record of fighting both Communists and gangsters." The author paired the ILG up with the Auto Workers Union as two exceptionally clean "national unions [that] avoided dealing with racketeers in union locals." C. Alexander Hortis, *The Mob and the City: The Hidden History of How the Mafia Captured New York* (Amherst, NY: Prometheus Books, 2014); the quotes are from pp. 116 and 108.

41. No author, no date, document entitled "Possible, and perhaps probable, motive for the stabbing of William Lurye . . . on May 9, 1949, as a result of which he died," in Folder 7, Box 25, ILGWU Collection 5780/005, Kheel Center.

42. "Possible, and perhaps probable, motive for the stabbing of William Lurye."

43. Julius Hochman, Report to Joint Board, September 4, 1957, Folder 3, Box 6, Joint Board of the Dress and Waistmakers' Union of Greater New York, Managers' Correspondence, 1909–1978, ILGWU Collection No. 5780/047, Kheel Center.

44. Julius Hochman, Report to Joint Board, September 4, 1957.

45. Julius Hochman, Report to Joint Board, September 4, 1957.

46. David Gingold, Daily Journal of David Gingold, March 14, 1950; quote is from April 3, 1950, Folder 17, Box 1, Series IIB, Northeast Department Records, ILGWU Collection 5780/050, Kheel Center.

47. Daily Journal of David Gingold, April 5, 1950.

48. See, for instance, Daily Journal of David Gingold, September 15, 1950.

49. Maloney Garment Trucking Report, April 17, 1956, p. 213.

50. Maloney Garment Trucking Report, April 17, 1956, p. 143.

51. Ralph Salerno, "The Assassination of President John F. Kennedy and Organized Crime: Report of Ralph Salerno, Consultant to the Select Committee on Assassinations," pp. 9–10, included in, U.S. House of Representatives, House Select Committee on Assassinations, *Investigation of the Assassination of President John F. Kennedy: Appendix to Hearings, Volume IX, Staff and Consultant's Reports on Organized Crime* (Washington, DC: U.S. Government Printing Office, 1979).

52. Maloney Garment Trucking Report, April 17, 1956, pp. 147–48; the quote is from p. 147.

53. Matheson Oral History #1 by Hoffman, p. 19.

54. Matheson Oral History #1 by Hoffman, p. 20.

55. "Picketers March in Garment Area," *New York Times*, July 30, 1952, p. 12; picket signs and fliers, dated July 19, 1952, in Folder 10, Box 18, ILGWU Collection 5780/014, Kheel Center.

56. "Violence Flares in Garment Strike," *New York Times*, August 2, 1952, p. 12.

57. No author, Memorandum: John Dioguardi, aka John Dio, January 16, 1952, Folder 14, Box 30, ILGWU Collection 5780/014, Kheel Center.

58. "Dubinsky Assails Independent Unit," *New York Times*, August 20, 1952, p. 18.

59. "19 Open Shops Sign with Cloak Union," *New York Times*, August 30, 1952, p. 21.

60. "Trust Suit Withdrawn," *New York Times*, September 17, 1952, p. 31.

61. Velie, "Gangsters in the Dress Business," p. 63.

62. "Dress Union Strikes Pennsylvania Shops," *New York Times*, August 11, 1953, p. 19.

63. Transcript Marked "Organizing Department, Wilkes-Barre, August 1953," in Folder 4, Box 20, ILGWU Collection 5780/014, Kheel Center.

64. Victor L. Nelson to the Commanding Officer, February 29, 1956, Subject: Russell Bufalino, Serial 1-7-12, New York State Commission Master File, New York State Archives.

65. Victor L. Nelson to the Commanding Officer, February 29, 1956.

66. "Dressmakers' Strike in Pennsylvania Ends," *New York Times*, August 13, 1953, p. 10.

67. Min Matheson to Charles S. Zimmerman, April 10, 1956, Folder 4, Box 20, ILGWU Collection 5780, Kheel Center.

68. Min Lurye Matheson to Charles S. Zimmerman, November 20, 1952, Folder 4, Box 20, ILGWU Collection 5780/014, Kheel Center.

69. Min Lurye Matheson to Charles S. Zimmerman, January 19, 1953, Folder 4, Box 20, ILGWU Collection 5780/014, Kheel Center.

70. Min Lurye Matheson to Angelo Sciandra, October 3, 1952, Folder 4, Box 20, ILGWU Collection 5780/014, Kheel Center.

71. Matheson Oral #1 by Hoffman, p. 20; see also Matheson Interview by Wolensky.

72. For a review of the ways in which labor historians have and have not addressed the problem of union corruption, see David Witwer, "The Chapter Left Untold: Labor Historians and the Problem of Union Corruption," *Labor: Studies in Working-Class History of the Americas* 8, no. 2 (2011), pp. 37–58. The article is part of a debate in that journal's issue over the sufficiency of such studies, which includes the following entries: Andrew Wender Cohen, "There Was a Crooked History," pp. 59–63; Rosemary Feurer, "How and Where to Look for Corruption," pp. 65–69; Joshua Freeman, "Corruption's Due (Scholarly) Reward," pp. 71–75; Jennifer Luff, "Historical Contributors Versus Sectoral Tendencies," pp. 77–82; and David Witwer, "Response," pp. 83–87.

73. Steven Fraser, *Labor Will Rule: Sidney Hillman and the Rise of American Labor* (New York: Macmillan, 1991), pp. 251–54.

74. Max Block and Ron Kenner, *Max the Butcher* (Secaucus, NJ: Lyle Stuart, 1982), p. 164.

6: The Uses of Fear: Ambition and Manipulation

1. Victor Riesel, "Veteran Gangster Goons," *Chester Times*, May 14, 1949, p. 6.

2. Louis Stark, "Labor News in the Secular Press," in Harold L. Ickes, ed., *Freedom of the Press Today: A Clinical Examination by 28 Specialists* (New York: Vanguard Press, 1941), pp. 240–41.

3. A.H. Raskin, "I Had No Voice and So Much to Say," *New York Times*, September 22, 1992, p. 9.

4. Westbrook Pegler, "Fair Enough," February 1, 1940, Box 120, [James] Westbrook Pegler Papers, Herbert Hoover Presidential Library, West Branch, Iowa.

5. David Witwer, "Westbrook Pegler and the Anti-union Movement," *Journal of American History* 92, no. 2 (2005), pp. 527–52.

6. "Labor Reporting: How Good Is It Now?," *Business Week*, October 20, 1951, p. 43.

7. Witwer, *Shadow of the Racketeer*, pp. 240–41; David Witwer, "The Racketeer Menace and Antiunionism in the Mid-Twentieth Century US," *International Labor and Working-Class History* 74, no. 1 (2008), pp. 124–47.

8. Nelson Frank to Gordon Greenfield, carbon copy, no date, enclosed with Richard Murray to Nelson Frank, August 3, 1953, Folder: DPOW, Box 7, Nelson Frank Papers, Robert F. Wagner Labor Archives, Tamiment Library, New York University.

9. Marilyn Nissenson, *The Lady Upstairs: Dorothy Schiff and the New York Post* (New York: St. Martin's Press, 2007), p. 119; "Between Issues," *New Leader*, April 16, 1956, p. 2; Fred J. Cook, "The Riesel Mystery: Case of the

Missing Motive," *The Nation*, September 29, 1956, p. 266; the quote is from Paul A. Tierney to Victor Riesel, September 16, 1947, Folder: Correspondence 1946–1950, Box 9a, Victor Riesel Papers, Robert F. Wagner Labor Archives, Tamiment Library, New York University (hereafter Riesel Papers).

10. Pegler, "Fair Enough"; "N.A.M. Leader Asks Business to End Fight with U.S. in Crisis," *New York Times*, December 7, 1950, p. 1.

11. Jay Lovestone to Victor Riesel, September 18, 1957, Folder: Correspondence 1956–1958, Box 7; Buck Harris to Victor Riesel, May 11, 1946, Folder: Correspondence 1946–1950, Box 9a; Clare Hoffman to Victor Riesel, February 2, 1954, Folder: Correspondence 1954, Box 9a; all in Riesel Papers; also Victor Riesel to Robert F. Kennedy, March 7, 1958, Folder: Personal Correspondence 1957–1959, Box 44, Pre-Administration Papers, Robert F. Kennedy Papers, John F. Kennedy Presidential Library.

12. "Labor Reporting," p. 43.

13. Victor Riesel, "How Some Union Chiefs Dip into Welfare Till," *New York Daily Mirror*, June 27, 1956, p. 3.

14. Victor Riesel to [Ted] Thackeray, October 8, 1941, Folder: Correspondence 1937–1945, Box 7, Riesel Papers.

15. Advertisement flier for "Inside Labor" column, no date, probably 1947, Folder 5, Box 16, Riesel Papers.

16. Victor Riesel, "Mobsters and Commies: They Go Together like Ham and Eggs," *Harrisburg Evening News*, April 16, 1956, p. 18.

17. Victor Riesel, "Crusading Labor Leaders Must Stop Mobs, Reds," *Milwaukee Sentinel*, December 27, 1952, p. 8.

18. "Labor Reporting," pp. 42–43.

19. Haynes Johnson, foreword to Malcolm Johnson, *On the Waterfront: The Prize-Winning Articles That Inspired the Classic Movie and Transformed the New York Harbor* (New York: Chamberlain Bros., 2005), pp. vii, xvii–xx; Nathan Ward, *Dark Harbor: The War for the New York Waterfront* (New York: Farrar, Straus and Giroux, 2010).

20. Mark Starr, the educational director of the ILGWU, observed the film's impact firsthand. Writing in 1955, he described the influence of the movie: "Its powerful impact strikes upon impressionable minds who only have heard about what is wrong with the labor unions." Because of his educational work, Starr had traveled widely while the film was in the theaters and met "hundreds of high school students." "I have been repeatedly told," he reported, "that the youngsters understand the longshoremen situation and the role of unions because they have seen this picture." Mark Starr, "Anti-'Waterfront,'" *New York Times*, April 10, 1955, p. X5.

21. Clark Mollenhoff, *Tentacles of Power: The Story of Jimmy Hoffa* (Cleveland: World Publishing, 1965), pp. 28–29.

22. Untitled wire service copy, November 10, 1955, Folder 2, Box 52, Wire Service Copy, 1953–1955, Clark R. Mollenhoff Papers, 1936–1975, Wisconsin State Historical Society, Madison, Wisconsin.

23. Clark Mollenhoff, "How Labor Bosses Get Rich," *Look*, March 9, 1954, pp. 38–45; the quote is on p. 45.

24. Edwin Guthman, *We Band of Brothers* (New York: Harper & Row, 1971), p. 3.

25. Louis J. Kramp to Clark Mollenhoff, December 7, 1955, Folder 9, Box 67, Teamsters General, Mollenhoff Papers.

26. Testimony by Victor Riesel, in U.S. vs. Dominic Bando, Case No. 151-65, U.S. District Court, Southern District of New York, November 13, 14, 15, 16, 19, 20, 21, 23, 26, 1956, pp. 2130–31, Record Group 21, Federal Records Center, Northeast Region, New York, New York.

27. Report by [name blacked out], Re: Unsub, Victor Riesel—Victim, May 8, 1956, Serial No. 72-964-82, pp. 6, 83, Victor Riesel Acid Attack File, Federal Bureau of Investigation, obtained via Freedom of Information Act Request (cited hereafter as FBI File); Victor Riesel, "The Night That Changed My Life," *Saturday Evening Post*, September 15, 1956, p. 97.

28. A.H. Raskin, "Thugs Hurl Acid on Labor Writer; Sight Imperiled," *New York Times*, April 6, 1956, p. 1.

29. "Riesel," *National Review*, May 23, 1956, news clipping in Folder: Clippings, Acid Attack, April–June 1956, Box 5, Riesel Papers.

30. "The Vicious Attack on Victor Riesel," editorial, *Los Angeles Tribune*, April 7, 1956, p. A4.

31. Raskin, "Thugs Hurl Acid on Labor Writer," p. 1.

32. Harold Hutchings, "Fight to Save Writer's Eyes in Acid Attack," *Chicago Tribune*, April 6, 1956, p. 1.

33. "Labor Racket Foe Hit by Acid," *Boston Evening American*, April 5, 1956, p. 1, clipping in Folder: Clippings, Acid Attack, April–June 1956, Box 5, Riesel Papers; "Assault Linked to Fight on Rackets," *Washington Post*, April 6, 1956, p. 1; "Acid Victim Worsening," *Los Angeles Times*, April 16, 1956, p. 1; Harold Hutchings, "Acid Victim Loses Sight in Both Eyes," *Chicago Tribune*, May 5, 1956, p. 1.

34. "Public Victim No. 1," editorial, *New York Herald Tribune*, October 4, 1957, p. 4.

35. "Acid on Broadway," *America*, April 21, 1956, p. 76.

36. "Cleaning House," *New Republic*, February 11, 1957, p. 5.

37. "Herald Tribune Photo Wins Top Press Award," *New York Herald Tribune*, October 9, 1956, clipping in FBI File 72-964-531, FBI File.

38. Mortimer Davis and Erwin Samuelson, "Riesel Vows He's Going to 'Get the Mob,'" *New York Daily Mirror*, May 18, 1956, p. 3.

39. "Victor Riesel, Labor Columnist," *Meet the Press*, June 3, 1956, CD of recording of broadcast provided by Jerry Haendiges Productions, Whittier, California, 2008.

40. "Hear Ike Plans Probe of Gang Entry into Unions," *Chicago Tribune*, June 6, 1956, p. 2.

41. M.J. Heale, *American Anticommunism: Combating the Enemy Within, 1830–1970* (Baltimore: Johns Hopkins University Press, 1990), pp. 135–40; Philip Jenkins, *The Cold War at Home: The Red Scare in Pennsylvania, 1945–1960* (Chapel Hill: University of North Carolina Press, 1999), pp. 98–99; Ronald L. Filippelli and Mark D. McColloch, *Cold War in the Working Class: The Rise and Decline of the United Electrical Workers* (Albany: State University of New York Press, 1995), pp. 100–103; Harvey A. Levenstein, *Communism, Anticommunism, and the CIO* (Westport, CT: Greenwood Press, 1981), pp. 216–17, 234–35; David M. Oshinsky, "Labor's Cold War: The CIO and the Communists," in Robert Griffith and Athan Theoharis, eds., *The Specter: Original Essays on the Cold War and the Origins of McCarthyism* (New York: New Viewpoints, 1974), pp. 125–27; Ellen Schrecker, "McCarthyism and the Labor

Movement: The Role of the State," in Steven Rosswurm, ed., *The CIO's Left-Led Unions* (New Brunswick, NJ: Rutgers University Press, 1992), pp. 139–42.

42. "Ives Urges Inquiry into Union Rackets," *New York Times*, July 6, 1956, p. 35.

43. "Racketeers in Labor," editorial, *Washington Post*, June 16, 1956, p. 12; "Labor Rackets Inquiry Urged," *Washington Post*, June 5, 1956, p. 30; Holmes Alexander, "A Labor House Cleaning?," *Los Angeles Times*, June 15, 1956, p. A5.

44. "Why the New Move to Investigate Racketeering in Labor Unions," *U.S. News & World Report*, June 15, 1956, p. 124.

45. John Fisher, "Demands Rise for Probe of Union Rackets," *Chicago Tribune*, June 5, 1956, p. 14.

46. "Labor's Black Eye," editorial, *Wall Street Journal*, August 14, 1956, p. 10.

47. "A Racket to Probe," editorial, *Reading Eagle*, June 8, 1956, p. 4.

48. Emanuel Perlmutter, "Dio Linked by U.S. to Telvi Murder in Riesel Case," *New York Times*, August 30, 1956, p. 1.

49. Max Frankel, "Johnny Dio and 4 Others Held as Masterminds in Riesel Attack," *New York Times*, August 29, 1956, p. 1; "No Ordinary Hoodlum," *New York Times*, August 30, 1956, p. 15; "Gangster Leeches on Labor," *Chicago Tribune*, September 1, 1956, p. 10; "Trouble for Mr. Dee," *Time*, August 5, 1957, p. 12; "Riesel Attacker Sought $50,000, Official Says," *Los Angeles Times*, August 30, 1956, p. 1.

50. Stanley Levey, "Rackets and Crime Linked in Riesel Case," *New York Times*, September 2, 1956, p. E10.

51. U.S. v. John Dioguardi, et al., Case No. C151-65, U.S. District Court, Southern District of New York, Trial Transcript, May 27, 1957, pp. 76–86; Bill Becker, "Key Dio Witness Refuses to Talk," *New York Times*, May 21, 1957, p. 1.

52. "Courtroom Show of Gang Power," *Life*, June 17, 1957, p. 49.

53. "Trouble for Mr. Dee," p. 12.

54. Robert F. Kennedy, interview by Kenneth Brodney, Newhouse Newspaper Features Syndicate, July 2, 1957, attached to, Kenneth Brodney to Robert F. Kennedy, July 4, 1957, Box 40, RFK Pre-Administration Working Files; "Labor—Kennedy Operation," [rough draft *Fortune* magazine article] enclosed with Daniel Seligman to Robert F. Kennedy, May 1, 1957, Box 51, RFK Pre-Administration Working Files; Mollenhoff, *Tentacles of Power*, pp. 124–29; Clark Mollenhoff, "New Labor Probe Will Reach City," *Minneapolis Morning Tribune*, December 5, 1956; Clark Mollenhoff, "Charging Teamster Scheme to Hide Evidence," *Des Moines Register*, January 18, 1957; Victor Riesel, "That Acid Attack Started Broad Scale Drive on Mobs," *Philadelphia Inquirer*, September 18, 1956; Willard Edwards, "Senate Groups Clash on Labor Rackets Probe," *Chicago Tribune*, January 8, 1957; all in Microfilm Newsclips, 1956–1959, Working Files, Robert F. Kennedy's Pre-Administration Papers, 1937–1960, John F. Kennedy Library, Boston (hereafter RFK Clipping File).

55. David Witwer, "'Pattern for Partnership': Putting Labor Racketeering on the Nation's Agenda in the Late 1950s," in Nelson Lichtenstein and Elizabeth Tandy Shermer, eds., *The American Right and U.S. Labor: Politics, Ideology and Imagination* (Philadelphia: University of Pennsylvania Press, 2012), pp. 207–28.

56. Edwards, "Senate Groups Clash on Labor Rackets Probe."

57. "pay dirt" in Joseph Loftus, "Rackets Inquiry a Political Plum," *New York Times*, January 11, 1957, p. 16; Joseph Loftus, "Senators Agreed on Racket Panel," January 26, 1957, p. 26; Edwards, "Senate Groups Clash on Labor Rackets Probe."

58. Robert F. Kennedy, interview by Kenneth Brodney; Robert F. Kennedy, *The Enemy Within: The McClellan Committee's Crusade Against Jimmy Hoffa and Corrupt Labor Unions* (New York: Harper & Row, 1960), pp. 160–61.

59. Elizabeth A. Fones-Wolf, *Selling Free Enterprise: The Business Assault on Labor and Liberalism, 1945–1960* (Urbana: University of Illinois Press, 1994), pp. 257–61; the quote is from p. 257.

60. "1956 Public Relations Program for NAM Campaign Against Labor Monopoly," February 1956, no author, p. 2, Accession No. 1411, Folder 2, Box 851.1, National Association of Manufacturers Papers, Hagley Museum and Library, Wilmington, Delaware. For more on NAM's leadership role in the postwar anti-union movement, see: Fones-Wolf, *Selling Free Enterprise*, esp. pp. 24–44, 50–57; and Kim Phillips-Fein, *Invisible Hands: The Making of the Conservative Movement from the New Deal to Reagan* (New York: Norton, 2009), pp. 87–114.

61. Sybyl S. Patterson to Coordinating Committee, memo, Subject: Suggested Draft of NAM's 1956 Campaign on Labor's Abuse of Its Monopoly Power, January 5, 1956, marked "Draft Confidential," Folder: NAM Industrial Relations Department, Union Monopoly Power, 1956, Box 139, Series 7, NAM Papers; the quotes are from pp. 1, 5, and 6.

62. "For Release in Morning Newspapers of Tuesday, April 17, 1956," from NAM Newsroom, Washington, Folder: NAM Industrial Relations Department, Union Monopoly Power, 1956, Box 139, Series 7, NAM Papers.

63. Victor Riesel, "My War with the Mob!": Chapter 6, "None So Blind as Those Who Blink at Rackets," *Daily Mirror*, June 26, 1956; clipping enclosed with Cola G. Parker to Members of Senate and House of Representatives, July 20, 1956, Folder: Labor, Box 195, Series 12, NAM Papers.

64. "quickie" in "House Inquiry Set on Labor Rackets," *New York Times*, January 21, 1954, p. 26. Witwer, "Racketeer Menace and Antiunionism in the Mid-Twentieth Century US," 133–34.

65. R. Alton Lee, *Eisenhower & Landrum-Griffin: A Study in Labor Management Politics* (Lexington: University Press of Kentucky, 1990), p. 48.

66. Kennedy, *The Enemy Within*, p. 18; Mollenhoff, *Tentacles of Power*, pp. 125–27.

67. Lee, *Eisenhower & Landrum-Griffin*, p. 50; "pull the wires" in Stephen Fox, *Blood and Power: Organized Crime in Twentieth-Century America* (New York: Morrow, 1989), p. 322.

68. Bob Devany, Memorandum to National Industrial Council, February 3, 1958, Folder: U.S. Government General 1958–59, Box 189, Series I, Accession No. 1411, NAM Papers.

69. Address by Philip M. Talbot before Wichita Chamber of Commerce, Wichita, Kansas, September 6, 1957, Philip M. Talbot, President, Binder Volume II, Box 30, Series I, Accession No. 1960, Chamber of Commerce Papers, Hagley Museum and Library, Wilmington, Delaware.

70. "Can Anything Be Done About Labor?" (chapter draft history of the 1958 campaign), n.d., Box 13, Robert Humphreys's Papers, Eisenhower Presidential Library, Abilene, Kansas.

71. James Reston, "G.O.P.-Labor Feud," *New York Times*, February 20, 1959, p. 17.

72. Elizabeth Tandy Shermer, "Origins of the Conservative Ascendancy: Barry Goldwater's Early Senate Career and the De-legitimization of Organized Labor," *Journal of American History* 95, no. 3 (2008), pp. 703–9.

73. Raskin, "Thugs Hurl Acid on Labor Writer"

74. Victor Riesel, "My War with the Mob!": Chapter 6, "None So Blind as Those Who Blink at Rackets," *Daily Mirror*, June 29, 1956, p. 3; editorial, news clipping in *Des Moines Register*, May 7, 1956, in Folder: Clippings, Acid Attack, April–June 1956, Box 5, Riesel Papers.

75. Report by Thomas L. Dunbar, Re: Abraham Telvi, Was (Deceased) Et Al., Victor Riesel—Victim, October 16, 1956, Serial No. 72-964-578, FBI File; regarding Riesel's view that journalists should not testify before a grand jury, see Fred J. Cook, "The Riesel Mystery: Case of the Missing Motive," *The Nation*, September 29, 1956, p. 267.

76. L.B. Nichols to Mr. Tolson, Office Memorandum, April 5, 1956, Serial No. 72-964-3, FBI File.

77. The notation is on a Washington City News Service Teletype, April 5 [1956], recorded by Bureau as received, April 9, 1956, Serial No. 72-964-8, FBI File.

78. FBI Report by [name blanked out], May 8, 1956, Serial No. 72-964-82, pp. 3–4, 10–11, FBI File.

79. U.S. v. Bando, et al., Trial Transcript, pp. 2126–36.

80. Bureau Teletype Report, from New York to Director, October 2, 1956, Serial No. 72-964-510; quote is from Memorandum from SAC, New York, to Director, FBI, Subject: USA Paul Williams, SDNY, September 28, 1956, Serial No. 72-964-513; both in FBI File.

81. Report by Nicholas Dunbar, Re: Abraham Telvi, Was (Deceased) Et Al., Victor Riesel—Victim, September 26, 1956, Serial No. 72-964-502, pp. 39–85, in FBI File. On the timing of when Dioguardi first requested an attack on Riesel, see the testimony of Joseph Peter Carlino, p. 248, and Miranti, p. 2041, both in U.S. v. Bando, et al., Trial Transcript.

82. Velie, "Gangsters in the Dress Business," pp. 59–64; for Riesel's piece, see Victor Riesel, "Inside Labor," April 2, 1956, in Report by Nicholas Dunbar, Re: Abraham Telvi, Was (Deceased) Et Al., Victor Riesel—Victim, September 26, 1956, Serial No. 72-964-502, p. 84, in FBI File.

83. Murray Kempton, "The Wrong Set (1)," *New York Post*, December 6, 1951; Kempton, "The Wrong Set (5)," *New York Post*, April 29, 1952; Kempton, "The Wrong Set (6)," *New York Post*, July 3, 1952; Kempton, "Paradise Lost," *New York Post*, February 19, 1953; Kempton, "The Brotherhood," *New York Post*, March 29, 1955; newspaper clippings in Serial 18-6-71, McClellan Committee Records.

84. Examples include: A.H. Raskin, "A.F.L. Pushes Drive to Oust Gangsters," *New York Times*, September 12, 1952, p. 43; Raskin, "Fight to Control Teamsters Eyed," *New York Times*, December 18, 1955, p. 43; Raskin, "Teamster Units Stirs New Storm," *New York Times*, February 4, 1956, p. 39.

85. Report by [name blacked out], Re: Unsub; Victor Riesel—Victim, May 8, 1956, Serial No. 72-964-82, pp. 19, 293, FBI File.

86. FBI Teletype to Director, April 27, 1956, Serial No. 72-964-73; SAC, New York, to Director, FBI, Re: Unsub: Victor Riesel—Victim Obstruction of

Justice, May 4, 1956, Serial No. 72-964-77, including photocopied enclosures; both in FBI File.

87. FBI Teletype, from SAC, WFO, to Director, and SAC, New York, September 28, 1956, Serial No. 72-964-499; also, Report by [name blacked out], Re: Abraham Telvi, Was (Deceased) Et Al., Victor Riesel—Victim, October 4, 1956, Serial No. 72-964-518, FBI File.

88. Report by Nicholas Dunbar, Re: Abraham Telvi, Was (Deceased) Et Al., Victor Riesel—Victim, September 26, 1956, Serial No. 72-964-502, p. 18, in FBI File. Riesel did, however, describe the offer of $1,000 or a television during a follow-up interview with the FBI in October 1956, as agents questioned him in detail about the information they had received from several individuals, including Cheyfitz. See Report by [name blacked out], Re: Abraham Telvi, Was (Deceased) Et Al., Victor Riesel Victim, October 9, 1956, Serial No. 72-964-534, pp. 5–6, in FBI File.

89. Report by Nicholas L. Dunbar, Re: Abraham Telvi, Was (Deceased) Et Al., Victor Riesel—Victim, October 16, 1956, Serial No. 72-964-578, pp. 2–5, 10; Betty Nevins's account is in Report by [name blacked out], Re: Unsub; Victor Riesel—Victim, May 8, 1956, Serial No. 72-964-82, p. 33; both in FBI File.

90. FBI Teletype, from New York to Director, October 1, 1956, Serial No. 72-964-509, FBI File.

91. "Good relations" in FBI Teletype, from the Director to NY, April 13, 1956, Serial No. 72-964-42; "source of information" in Report by [name blacked out], Re: Unsub, Victor Riesel—Victim, May 8, 1956, Serial No. 72-964-82, p. 33; both in FBI File.

92. FBI Teletype, from New York to Director, October 2, 1956, Serial No. 72-964-510, FBI File.

93. L.B. Nichols to Mr. Tolson, Subject: Abraham Telvi, Et Al.; Victor Riesel—Victim, October 3, 1956, Serial No. 72-964-528, FBI File.

94. Report by Nicholas Dunbar, Re: Abraham Telvi, Was (Deceased) Et Al., Victor Riesel—Victim, October 16, 1956, Serial No. 72-964-578, FBI File.

95. Sherman Willse to Robert F. Kennedy, Re: Victor Riesel—Permatex Company Inc., June 12, 1959, Serial 18-6-966, McClellan Committee Records. In November 1957, Riesel received a notification from the employer's representative about the IRS auditing his books and the fact of the $4,000 cash payment (made in October 1955) having to be explained to the agency. Donald D. Rowe to Victor Riesel, November 21, 1957; Folder 5, Box 9a, in Riesel Papers.

96. U.S. Senate, Select Committee on Improper Activities in the Labor or Management Field, *Hearings, Part 11: New York (Teamster Paper Locals)*, August 7, 8, 9, 12, and 13, 1957, 85th Cong., 1st Sess. (Washington, DC: U.S. Government Printing Office, 1957).

97. Kennedy, *The Enemy Within*, p. 200.

98. U.S. Senate, Select Committee on Improper Activities in the Labor or Management Field, *Hearings, Part 31: Maxwell Raddock and United Brotherhood of Carpenters and Joiners*, October 2 and 8, 1958, 85th Cong., 2nd Sess. (Washington, DC: U.S. Government Printing Office, 1958), "pair of scissors" in p. 12011; payment amounts detailed on p. 11997; "ghostwriter" p. 11916. Raddock's staff told investigators that Riesel had not done any research or writing for the book. Robert E. Dunne to File, December 20, 1957, Serial 18-217-76, McClellan Committee Records.

99. McClellan Committee, *Hearings: Part 31*, p. 11824.

100. Federal Trade Commission, *Decision in the Matter of the Trade Union Courier Corporation, et al.*, Docket No. 5966, Complaint, March 14, 1952, Decision, June 30, 1955, in *Federal Trade Commission Decisions* (Washington, DC: U.S. Government Printing Office, 1956), pp. 1275–318.

101. McClellan Committee, *Hearings: Part 31*, pp. 12016–156.

102. McClellan Committee, *Hearings: Part 31*, p. 11999.

7: The Congressional Hearings: Revelation and Rhetoric

1 "Strong Arm Dio Doing What Comes Naturally," *Life*, August 19, 1957, pp. 36–37.

2. Lester Velie, *Labor U.S.A.* (New York: Harper Brothers, 1959), p. 105.

3. Paul J. Tierney to File, June 30, 1960, Re: Local 875 Teamsters, Serial No. 18-179-235; Paul J. Tierney to File, January 5, 1961, includes anonymous, undated report, marked confidential, entitled: "Local 875 Teamsters and the International Ladies Garment Workers Union," Serial No. 18-179-339; Paul Tierney to Jerome S. Alderman, May 23, 1960, Re: Local 875, "Continued Control of This Local by Tony Ducks Corallo," Serial No. 18-179-130; Paul Tierney to Jerome Alderman, September 27, 1960, Subject: Toy Workers Union, Serial No. 18-179-299; Robert E. Dunne to Jerome Alderman, August 26, 1960, Re: International Union of Doll and Toy Workers of the United States and Canada; Harry O. Damino, Serial No. 18-179-283, McClellan Committee Records.

4. McClellan Committee, *Paper Local Hearings*, pp. 3636–72; Summary Memo on Local 102 and Local 649, UAW, no date, no author, Serial 18-6-668, McClellan Committee Records.

5. David Witwer, "The Acid Attack on Victor Riesel and Fears of Labor Racketeering in Cold War America," *Labor History*, 55, no. 2 (2014), pp. 228–47.

6. Summary Memo on Local 102 and Local 649, UAW, no date, no author, Serial 18-6-668, McClellan Committee Records.

7. Lisa Phillips, *A Renegade Union: Interracial Organizing and Labor Radicalism* (Urbana: University of Illinois Press, 2013).

8. Jerome Quinn and Morris Iushewitz to George Meany, [1957?], Folder 1a, Box 205, David Dubinsky Papers, President's Records, 1932–1966, International Ladies' Garment Workers' Union Papers, ILGWU Collection 5780/002, Kheel Center. A news report on August 4, 1957, quotes an AFL-CIO official offering a slightly different statistical snapshot of the problem: "Mr. Iushewitz estimated that of the 125,000 Spanish-speaking workers in the city, from 30,000–40,000 are victims of collusion between labor racketeers and employers." Francis Sugrue, "A.F.L.-C.I.O. Battles Labor Rackets Here," *New York Herald Tribune*, August 4, 1957, p. 1.

9. Freeman, *Working-Class New York*, pp. 6–20; Max Hall, ed., *Made in New York*.

10. Robert E. Dunne to Robert F. Kennedy, October 26, 1956, Re: Shops Switched from Local Union 227 to Local Union 284, Serial No. 18-6-28, McClellan Committee Records.

11. Paul J. Tierney and Robert E. Dunne to Robert F. Kennedy, January 15, 1957, Re: Interview with Lou Lasky, Serial No. 18-6-79, McClellan Committee

Records; A.H. Raskin, "8 Charters Lost by 'Paper Unions,'" *New York Times*, June 9, 1959, p. 27; Murray Seeger, "Right to Choose Union Is Upheld: NLRB Backs Employees of Brooklyn Warehouse," *New York Times*, May 31, 1965, p. 5.

12. Ralph Katz, "Meany Berates Jewelers' Union," *New York Times*, November 19, 1957, p. 23; "Grafters' Ejection Promised by Union," *New York Times*, May 22, 1952, p. 17; the quote is from Association of Catholic Trade Unionists, "The International Jewelry Union: A History of Betrayal," August 25, 1958, Folder 1, Box 4, SEIU/IJWU Collection, Accession No. 1542, Walter Reuther Library, Wayne State University, Detroit, Michigan.

13. Robert E. Dunne to Jerome Alderman, August 26, 1960, Re: International Union of Doll and Toy Workers of the United States and Canada, Harry O. Damino, Serial No. 18-179-283; Paul Tierney to Jerome Alderman, September 27, 1960, Subject: Doll and Toy Workers Union, Serial No. 18-179-299; both in McClellan Committee Records.

14. Paul J. Tierney to Files, May 10, 1962, Re: Labor Organizations—New York, Serial No. 18-21-959, McClellan Committee Records.

15. Carmine Bellino to Robert F. Kennedy, October 30, 1956, Subject: Local Union 227, Serial No. 18-6-69, McClellan Committee Records.

16. Edward M. Jones to Robert F. Kennedy, July 15, 1957, Re: Local 5 UAW, Confederated Unions of America, Serial No. 18-21-555, McClellan Committee Records.

17. John Aporta to Robert F. Kennedy, July 15, 1957, Re: Joseph P. Levine and His Carryover Locals, Serial No. 18-6-491, McClellan Committee Records.

18. Walter Sheridan to Jerome S. Alderman, July 11, 1960, Re: James Hoffa: Locals 239 and 875 Teamsters, Serial No. 18-179-160, McClellan Committee Records.

19. Carmine Bellino to Robert F. Kennedy, November 6, 1956, Subject: Labor Racketeering, Serial No. 18-6-69, McClellan Committee Records.

20. James P. Kelly and Edward M. Jones to Robert F. Kennedy, July 26, 1957, Subject: George Schneider and Local 362, IBT, Serial No. 18-6-467, McClellan Committee Records. District 65's leader, Arthur Osman, recalled being approached with a proposal to engage in a similar scheme, an offer that he turned down. He was, however, quite aware of a kind of symbiotic relationship in which his union's organizing activities provided opportunities for paper locals, who would make approaches to employers in areas where the Retail, Wholesale and Department Store Workers Union was becoming active. Phillips, *A Renegade Union*, pp. 63–64.

21. Allen Drury, "Dio Aide Accused of Terror Moves," *New York Times*, August 7, 1957, p. 1.

22. Carmine Bellino to Robert F. Kennedy, November 6, 1956, Subject: Labor Racketeering, Serial No. 18-6-69, McClellan Committee Records.

23. Sherman S. Willse, May 17, 1959, untitled memo, Serial No. 18-274-98, McClellan Committee Records.

24. Robert E. Dunne to Robert F. Kennedy, December 26, 1956, Re: LU362 of IBT, Serial No. 18-6-20, McClellan Committee Records.

25. "After Six Months of Hearings: What's Learned About Rackets," *U.S. News & World Report*, August 16, 1957, p. 100.

26. An example of this awareness can be found in a memo in the New

York district attorney's case file for its extortion indictment of Dioguardi in 1956, a charge involving a payment from an employer to Dioguardi's labor relations firm. No threats had been made to the employer, who had sought out one of Dioguardi's associates, and was then put in contact with Dioguardi himself. The memo notes that prosecution would have to argue that "the defendants took advantage of an existing fear in the minds of the corporation's officers to obtain money from them." "The Element of Fear," no date, no author, in Box 41947, People of the State of New York Against John Dioguardi, Indictment No. 3091, June 18, 1956, New York District Attorney Case Files, New York City Municipal Archives.

27. Walter Sheridan to Jerome S. Alderman, July 11, 1960, Re: James Hoffa—Locals 239 and 875 Teamsters, Serial No. 18-179-160, McClellan Committee Records.

28. Robert Emmet Dunne to Jerome Alderman, August 17, 1960, Subject: Bristol Dynamics Incorporated, Serial No. 18-159-247, McClellan Committee Records.

29. Robert Emmet Dunne to Jerome Alderman.

30. Walter Sheridan to Jerome Alderman, August 12, 1960, Re: Local 875 Teamsters Bristol Dynamics, Inc., Serial 18-179-237, McClellan Committee Records.

31. John J. Ryan, "Garment Trucking Investigation," September 24, 1957, FBI Serial No. 92-1795-133, FBI File, acquired via Freedom of Information Act Request by author. Regarding commercial bribery statutes, see John T. Noonan, *Bribes* (Berkeley: University of California Press, 1987) p. 578.

32. "Text of McClellan Statement on Rackets," *New York Times*, August 1, 1957, p. 15.

33. Walter R. May to Robert F. Kennedy, July 29, 1959, Re: Antonio Corallo, Serial No.: 18-179-111, McClellan Committee Records.

34. Carmine Bellino to Robert F. Kennedy, October 30, 1956, Subject: Local Union 227, Serial No. 18-6-69, McClellan Committee Records.

35. Robert E. Dunne to Robert F. Kennedy, November 21, 1956, Subject: Local 258, IBT, Serial No. 18-6-6; Robert E. Dunne to Robert F. Kennedy, November 21, 1956, Subject: Local 269, IBT and Local 649, UAW, Serial No. 18-6-5; and Robert E. Dunne to Robert F. Kennedy, November 20, 1956, Subject: Local 258 IBT and Interview with Keiko Ogura, Serial No. 18-6-4; all in McClellan Committee Records.

36. W.B. May to File, April 23, 1957, Re: New York Paper Local Case, Serial No. 18-6-235, McClellan Committee Records.

37. For example, see a reference to Cotliar's role in overseeing diversion of union funds from Teamsters Local 875, in W.B. May to File, April 22, 1957, Re: New York Paper Locals, Serial No. 18-6-240, McClellan Committee Records.

38. John Aporta to Robert F. Kennedy, July 15, 1957, Re: Joseph P. Levine and His "Carryover Locals" Serial No. 18-6-491, McClellan Committee Records.

39. R.E. Dunne to File, July 29, 1957, Re: F&B Novelty Company, Serial No. 18-6-455, McClellan Committee Records.

40. Robert E. Dunne to Robert Kennedy, October 23, 1956, Subject: Shops That Were Switched from Local 227 to Local 284, NYSCO Laboratories, Serial No. 18-6-32, McClellan Committee Records.

41. "Teamster-Dio Links Face Inquiry July 30," *New York Times*, July 22,

1957, p. 38; William Moore, "Probe to Sift Hoffa Role in N.Y. Rackets," *Chicago Tribune*, July 28, 1957, p. 1.

42. Joseph Loftus, "Hoffa Is Linked to Dio in Scheme to Control Port," *New York Times*, August 1, 1957, p. 1.

43. Loftus, "Hoffa Is Linked to Dio," p. 1.

44. McClellan Committee, *Paper Local Hearings*, p. 3600.

45. "Investigations: Making a Living," *Time*, August 12, 1957, p. 17.

46. "Hoffa and the Gangsters," editorial, *New York Herald Tribune*, August 1, 1957, p. 14.

47. "Assail Hoffa for Transport Union Program," *Chicago Tribune*, August 4, 1957, p. 4.

48. John Gould, "TV a Public Service," *New York Times*, August 1, 1957, p. 35.

49. "Investigations: Making a Living," *Time*, August 12, 1957, p. 17.

50. "Investigations: The Sharks," *Time*, August 19, 1957, p. 11.

51. J.P. Shanley, "TV Repetitive Script," *New York Times*, August 9, 1957, p. 24.

52. "Labor Rackets: Doing Dirty Work," *Newsweek*, August 19, 1957, p. 24.

53. Shanley, "TV Repetitive Script," p. 24.

54. William Moore, "Gangster Dio Defies Probe: Slugs Photog," *Chicago Tribune*, August 9, 1957, p. 1.

55. Moore, "Gangster Dio Defies Probe," p. 1.

56. "Rackets Probers to Question Dio on Hoffa Alliance," *Lebanon Daily News* [Lebonan, PA], August 3, 1957, p. 1; "McClellan Raps Hoffa Union Plan," *Brownsville Daily Herald*, August 4, 1957, p. 1.

57. "Labor Rackets: Johnny Dio's Role," *Newsweek*, August 12, 1957, pp. 33–34.

58. "Investigations: The Sharks," *Time*, August 19, 1957, p. 11.

59. "Labor Rackets: Doing Dirty Work," p. 24.

60. "Racketeers in Labor," editorial, *New York Herald Tribune*, August 8, 1957, p. 14.

61. "Curtain Rises on Hoffa Hearings," *Business Week*, August 24, 1957, p. 135.

62. "Trouble Ahead for Unions?," *U.S. News & World Report*, August 23, 1957, pp. 25–27.

63. Robert A. Bedolis, "Top Aids Urging Meany to Attack, Not Aid, Probe," *New York Herald Tribune*, August 12, 1957, p. 1.

64. "Labor Day, 1957," *Time*, September 2, 1957, p. 11.

65. McClellan Committee, *Paper Local Hearings*, p. 3764 and 3765. Another spokesman for this group, Norman C. DeWeaver, strongly defended organizational picketing, a practice often derided as a key tool for racketeers but one that was essential for organizing in this particular employment sector. DeWeaver noted that the ACTU's investigations revealed that racketeers were far more likely to simply approach an employer with a corrupt offer. "We have found that in most cases we have investigated it has been the employer who invited the racket union to sign a contract with him." "Employers Hit as Initiators of Pacts with Racketeers," *New York Herald Tribune*, August 12, 1957, p. 3.

66. Joseph Loftus, "Kohler Hearings Hit Three Ways: Committee, Union, Company Suffer," *New York Times*, March 16, 1958, p. E9; Joseph Loftus,

"Rackets Investigators Split over Reuther," *New York Times*, March 2, 1958, p. E4.

67. "Can the Labor Racketeer Be Stopped?," *U.S. News & World Report*, October 10, 1958, pp. 52–57.

68. Chamber of Commerce of the United States of America, Minutes of the Board, Directors Meetings and Executive Committee Meeting, April 29, 1958 to April 29, 1959, Board of Directors Meeting, September 26–27, 1958, p. 5, in Series I, Box 3, U.S. Chamber of Commerce Papers, Hagley Museum and Library, Wilmington, Delaware.

8: The 1958 Dress Strike and the Ethical Practices Committee: Resistance and Resignation

1. Sgt. Louis T. Shupnik and Trooper John A. Byerly to Commanding Officer, B-3, PSP, Wyoming, Pennsylvania, April 18, 1958, Folder: Strike Reports, Dresses, Eastern, Pennsylvania, March 5–May 25, 1958, Box 27, Record Group 30, Records of Pennsylvania State Police, Subgroup: Office of Commissioner Series: Strike Reports, Pennsylvania State Archives, Harrisburg, Pennsylvania.

2. Matheson quote and Pittston scene in Mitchel Levitas, "Dress Strikers Picket Pa. Shop," *New York Post*, April 11, 1958, news clipping in Folder 4E, Box 297; "dynamite" in Mitchel Levitas, "The ILG Pickets in a Tough Coal Town," *New York Post*, March 25, 1958, Folder 7, Box 297; both in David Dubinsky Papers, President's Records, 1932–1966, ILGWU Collection 5780/002, Kheel Center.

3. The quotes are from Mitchel Levitas, "'The Pajama Game' in Pennsylvania," *New York Post*, March 26, 1958; Shinski profiled in Mitchel Levitas, "A Striker's Pride . . . and Need," *New York Post*, March 28, 1958; both in: Folder 7, Box 297, ILGWU Collection 5780/002, Kheel Center.

4. David Melman, "The Cause and Effect of the ILGWU Dress Industry General Strike of 1958" (master's thesis, Baruch College, City University of New York, February 1994); Wolensky et al., *Fighting for the Union Label*, pp. 161–86.

5. Arthur G. Kaplan to Robert F. Kennedy, Subject: Pittston Area—Mafia-Garment Industry Rackets—Min Lurye Matheson, January 7, 1958, Serial No. 18-218-96, Case File 18-218, McClellan Committee Records.

6. "Will Unions Take Over Where Congress Leaves Off?," *U.S. News & World Report*, September 6, 1957, pp. 64–66, the quote is from p. 64.

7. Lester Velie, "Labor's Two Front War Against the Rackets," *Reader's Digest*, June 1957, pp. 37–42. The quotes are from pp. 38, 41, and 42, respectively.

8. Excerpts from Walter P. Reuther before the Textile Workers Convention, May 31, 1956, pp. 1–2, enclosed with Walter P. Reuther to George Meany, May 31, 1956, Folder 98/02, Box 98, Office of the President, George Meany Files, 1940–1980, RG1-038, George Meany Archives, University of Maryland (hereafter Meany Papers).

9. Oral History with Nelson Cruikshank, conducted by James Cavanaugh, August 21, 1979, George Meany Center for Labor History Oral History Project, transcript online at Digital Collections, University of Maryland Library, http://hdl.handle.net/1903.1/33983. The quote is from p. 14 of the transcript.

10. Cruikshank Oral History, p. 14.

11. Oral History with Albert Woll, conducted by Archie Robinson and

Alice Hoffman, March 19, 1979, George Meany Center for Labor History Oral History Project, transcript online at Digital Collections, University of Maryland Library, http://hdl.handle.net/1903.1/35186. The quote is from p. 11 of the transcript.

12. "bulldog" in A.H. Raskin, "The New Labor Leaders—A Dual Portrait," *New York Times*, December 21, 1952, p. 13; "crusty" in "Labor's Voice Is Stilled," *Time*, January 21, 1980, p. 37; "stolid" in "Giant Retires," *Time*, October 8, 1979, p. 26; other background and descriptive material from Joseph Goulden, *Meany* (New York: Atheneum, 1972), pp. 7–41; Archie Robinson, *George Meany and His Times* (New York: Simon & Schuster, 1981), pp. 17–49.

13. Goulden, *Meany*, pp. 189–90; Woll Oral History, pp. 11–12.

14. John Hutchinson, *The Imperfect Union: A History of Corruption in American Trade Unions* (New York: E.P. Dutton, 1970), includes the verbatim section of the AFL-CIO constitution, pp. 431–33.

15. Woll Oral History, p. 4.

16. Hutchinson, *Imperfect Union*, includes copies of the resolutions and the codes, pp. 421–54; for a description of how they were adopted and then sent out to the national union affiliates for ratification, see David L. Stebenne, *Arthur J. Goldberg: New Deal Liberal* (New York: Oxford University Press, 1996), pp. 161–62.

17. "Each of these people will deny that they oppose these things," Hayes told an interviewer, "and yet actually in any considerations or discussions of the matter, they did oppose them." Goulden, *Meany*, p. 235.

18. Stebenne, *Arthur J. Goldberg*, p. 162.

19. Oral History with David J. McDonald, conducted by Anthony Luchek, February 7, 1979, George Meany Center for Labor History Oral History Project, transcript online at Digital Collections, University of Maryland Library, https://digital.lib.umd.edu/image?pid=umd:690053. The quote is from p. 15 of the transcript.

20. Oral History Interview # II with A.J. Hayes, conducted by Gordon Cole, December 13, 1979, George Meany Center for Labor History Oral History Project, transcript online at Digital Collections, University of Maryland Library, https://digital.lib.umd.edu/image?pid=umd:689795. The quote is from p. 9 of the transcript.

21. Goulden, *Meany*, p. 235.

22. Stebenne, *Arthur J. Goldberg*, p. 163.

23. Stebenne, *Arthur J. Goldberg*, pp. 160–61.

24. Goulden, *Meany*, p. 236.

25. Goulden, *Meany*, p. 243.

26. George Meany to Albert J. Hayes, June 14, 1956; see also a memo on the staff assignments, George Meany to Nelson Cruikshank, Stanley Ruttenberg, John McCarty, and Boris Fishkin, June 14, 1956; both in: Folder 98/02, Box 98, Office of the President, George Meany Files, 1940–1980, RG1-038, Meany Papers.

27. Cruikshank Oral History, p. 16.

28. Cruikshank Oral History, p. 18.

29. Cruikshank Oral History, p. 19.

30. He suggested that the EPC had investigated the Laundry Workers Union without the probe being initiated by Congressional hearings, but in

fact the EPC's action had followed Congressional action. Cruikshank Oral
History, p. 22.

31. Hutchinson, *Imperfect Union*, pp. 306–33.

32. Goulden, *Meany*, p. 245.

33. Woll Oral History, p. 18; McDonald Oral History, pp. 12–13; Oral History with Arthur Goldberg, conducted by Alice M. Hoffman, October 8, 1979, George Meany Center for Labor History Oral History Project, transcript online at Digital Collections, University of Maryland Library, http://hdl.handle.net/1903.1/34118. The quote is from pp. 19–20 of the transcript; Cruikshank recalled that one these intermediaries, Paul Hall of the Seafarers Union, told him, "You know Jimmy would like to come clean, but he's under threat from the mob. He can't." Cruikshank Oral History, p. 24.

34. Goulden, *Meany*, p. 246.

35. Cruikshank Oral History, pp. 21–22.

36. Stebenne, *Arthur J. Goldberg*, p. 166.

37. Reisman, *Folded Lies*, pp. 15–36, 41–54.

38. Goulden, *Meany*, p. 246.

39. Goulden, *Meany*, p. 247.

40. Goulden, *Meany*, p. 247.

41. Hearing before the Ethical Practices Committee of the American Federation of Labor and the Congress of Industrial Organizations, Requested by the Allied Industrial Workers of America, October 3, 1956, Washington, D.C., Folder 111/16, Box 16, Office of the President, George Meany Files, RG1-038, Meany Papers. The quote is from p. 176.

42. Hearing before the Ethical Practices Committee, p. 251.

43. Affidavit of David Dubinsky to the McClellan Committee, August 9, 1957, included in Appendix A-1, Minutes of the August 1957 Meeting of the AFL-CIO Executive Council, AFL-CIO Executive Council Minutes, Box 36, RG4-006, Meany Papers.

44. Paul J. Tierney to Robert F. Kennedy, Re: Local 102 UAW, Paper Locals Case, Serial No. 18-6-195, March 20, 1957, McClellan Committee Records.

45. The quote from Lester Washburn's testimony before the McClellan Committee. Joseph Loftus, "Dubinsky Union Used Dio as Agent, Inquiry Is Told," *New York Times*, August 2, 1957, p. 1.

46. For an example of these exchanges, see: William F. Schnitzler to Herman Kenin, June 8, 1961; Herman Kenin to William F. Schnitzler, June 29, 1961. For a more surreal version of this exchange, see Douglas Nesbitt's response on behalf of the International Association of Siderographers, the smallest national union in the AFL-CIO. With thirty-two members organized into three locals, Nesbitt told the Ethical Practices Committee staff member, "Since every member is known to me personally, and to every other member of the International, it would be almost impossible for anyone to try to take over the Association." Moreover, with only $600 in yearly revenue and health or pension funds, no paid officers, and no office or office equipment, it wasn't clear to Nesbitt that anybody would want take over his union. Douglas Nesbitt to Wesley Reedy, September 9, 1963. All correspondence in Folder 110/23, Box 23, RG1-038, Meany Papers.

47. M.A. Hutchinson to George Meany, March 10, 1958, Folder 110-24, Box 24, RG1-038, Meany Papers.

48. See financial spreadsheet entitled "Free Teamster Defense Fund," December 15, 1961, to March 16, 1962, Folder 127-10; William Kirchner to George Meany, February 14, 1963, Folder 127-10; both in Box 127, RG1-038, Meany Papers.

49. Goulden, *Meany*, pp. 254–55.

50. Interview transcripts in binder marked DD 13 & DD 14, pp. 24–26, in Box 2, ILGWU Collection 6036/012, Kheel Center.

51. Robinson, *George Meany and His Times*, pp. 214–16.

52. Flier entitled "Dressmakers' General Strike Declared Today, 10 AM Sharp," Wednesday, March 5, 1958, Folder 4B, Box 297, David Dubinsky Papers, President's Records, 1932–1966, International Ladies' Garment Workers' Union Papers, ILGWU Collection 5780/002, Kheel Center.

53. "Pa. Strikers Hear Dubinsky Hit Hoodlums," *New York Post*, April 15, 1958, news clipping in Folder 4E, Box 297, Dubinsky Papers, President's Records, ILGWU Collection 5780/002, Kheel Center.

54. News Release, International Ladies' Garment Workers' Union, April 17, 1958, Folder 4B, Box 297, Dubinsky Papers, President's Records, ILGWU 5780/002.

55. News Release, International Ladies' Garment Workers' Union, May 24, [1959], Folder 4a, Box 297, Dubinsky Papers, President's Records, ILGWU Collection 5780/002, Kheel Center.

56. Notes on a conference between Julius Hochman, Emil Schlesinger, and Lazare Teper, January 25, 1958, Folder 2, Box 20, Joint Dress Board Managers' Correspondence, ILGWU Collection 5780/047, Kheel Center.

57. Julius Hochman, Report to Joint Board, September 4, 1957, Folder 3, Box 6, Joint Board of the Dress and Waistmakers' Union of Greater New York, Managers' Correspondence, 1909–1978, ILGWU Collection 5780/047, Kheel Center.

58. Examples of the standard depiction of David Dubinsky and the ILG can be found in: Dubinsky and Raskin, *David Dubinsky*; and Bernstein, *Turbulent Years*. Also see Hill, "The Mob and Labor Management," pp. 68–82.

59. Hochman, Report to Joint Board.

60. Hochman, Report to Joint Board.

61. Reference to bullet fired into Jack Retowski's house in, No author, typed memo, April 2, 1958, Folder 7, Box 297, "full of fear" in Min Matheson to David Dubinsky, no date, Folder 4B, Box 297; both in ILGWU Collection 5780/002, Kheel Center.

62. Wolensky et al., *Fighting for the Union Label*, p. 257.

63. An untitled personal chronology of the strike that details Dubinsky's direct role in the negotiations and refers to himself in the first person, "me." Time line of negotiations with PGMA, March-April 1958. Folder 4B, Box 297, ILGWU Collection 5780/002, Kheel Center.

64. Michael J. McInerney to File, Subject: Abe Chait, Burton Chait, Sara Chait, September 4, 1958, Serial No. 18-173-270, Case File 173, McClellan Committee Records.

65. "Union Will No Longer Negotiate With PGMA," *Wilkes-Barre Record*, April 4, 1958, news clipping in Folder 4E, Box 297, ILGWU Collection 5780/002, Kheel Center; Wolensky et al., *Fighting for the Union Label*, pp. 176–77.

66. Wolensky et al., *Fighting for the Union Label*, pp. 180–82; Melman, "Cause and Effect of the ILGWU Dress Industry General Strike," pp. 28–31.

67. Min Matheson to William Ball, April 10, 1959; Min Matheson to David Dubinsky, April 28, 1959; both in Folder 4a, Box 297, ILGWU Collection 5780/002, Kheel Center; "Dress Strike Hearing: 5 Held Under Bail in Dress Plant Strike," *Evening News* [Wilkes-Barre newspaper], April 3, 1959, news clipping in Folder 4E, Box 297, ILGWU Collection 5780/002, Kheel Center.

68. News Release, International Ladies' Garment Workers' Union, May 24, [1959], Folder 4a, Box 297, Dubinsky Papers, President's Records, ILGWU Collection 5780/002, Kheel Center; A.H. Raskin Interview with David Dubinsky and Charles [Sasha] Zimmerman, pp. 6–7, Box 2, A.H. Raskin Collection 6036/012, Kheel Center.

69. David Dubinsky to William P. Rogers, May 22, 1959; William P. Rogers to David Dubinsky, May 29, 1959, both in Folder 4a, Box 297, ILGWU Collection 5780/002, Kheel Center; in regard to number of racketeering investigations, see "Labor Racketeering," *Fortune*, July 1955, pp. 50, 54.

70. Robert F. Kennedy to Harold Brislin, September 9, 1958, Serial No. 18-193-514, McClellan Committee Records.

71. David Witwer, "The Different Meanings of Corruption in the Context of the Teamsters Union," *Journal of Labor Research* 21, no. 2 (2000), pp. 287–303.

72. Andrew Wender Cohen, *The Racketeer's Progress: Chicago and the Struggle for the Modern American Economy, 1900–1940* (Cambridge: Cambridge University Press, 2004), p. 260.

73. Witwer, "Westbrook Pegler and the Anti-union Movement," pp. 527–52.

74. Witwer, *Corruption and Reform in the Teamsters Union*, p. 103.

75. David Witwer, "The Racketeer Menace and Antiunionism in the Mid-Twentieth Century U.S.," pp. 124–47; the quote is from p. 132.

76. Elizabeth A. Fones-Wolf, *Selling Free Enterprise*, p. 268.

77. Alan K. McAdams, *Power and Politics in Labor Legislation* (New York: Columbia University Press, 1964), pp. 2–4, 52–54, 68–71; Fones-Wolf, *Selling Free Enterprise*, pp. 258–61; William H. Miernyk, *Trade Unions in the Age of Affluence* (New York: Random House, 1965), pp. 13–14; Melvyn Dubofsky, *The State and Labor in Modern America* (Chapel Hill: University of North Carolina Press, 1994), pp. 218–21; Witwer, *Corruption and Reform in the Teamsters Union*, pp. 204–11.

78. Fones-Wolf, *Selling Free Enterprise*, pp. 52–54, 68–71; Miernyk, *Trade Unions in the Age of Affluence*, pp. 112–23; McAdams, *Power and Politics in Labor Legislation*, pp. 52–54, 68–99, 212–13; Lee, *Eisenhower & Landrum-Griffin*, pp. 18–44, 74–116; David Witwer, "The Landrum-Griffin Act: A Case Study in the Possibilities and Problems in an Anti-union Corruption Law," *Criminal Justice Review* 27, no. 2 (2002), pp. 301–20.

79. "Meany Bids Labor Fight Union Curbs," *New York Times*, June 2, 1959, p. 28.

80. Report of Charles S. Zimmerman, General Manager, Joint Board of Dress & Waistmakers Union, to the General Executive Board Meeting, August 22, 1960, ILGWU Collection 5780/047, Joint Board Dress & Waistmakers' Union of Greater New York, Managers' Correspondence, Box 5, Folder 9, Kheel Center.

Afterword: The Enemy Within

1. Joseph Loftus, "Meany Declares Terms to the Senate," *New York Times*, August 13, 1957, p. 19.

2. "Dubinsky Says He Fought Dio: Didn't Hire Him," *Chicago Tribune*, August 12, 1957, p. A4; Minutes of the Meeting of the Executive Council of the AFL-CIO, August 12 through August 15, Drake Hotel, Chicago, Illinois, AFL-CIO Executive Council Minutes, pp. 1–2, Box 36, RG4-006, Meany Papers.

3. Witwer, *Shadow of the Racketeer*, pp. 5–6.

4. Westbrook Pegler, "Dubinsky Now Disowns Thug Who Rated Forty-Hack Funeral and Martyr Treatment," *Lebanon Daily News*, August 17, 1957, p. 6.

5. Westbrook Pegler, "There's No Denying 'Martyrs' Record," August 30, 1957, clipping in *New York Journal American* Newspaper Morgue, Briscoe Center for American History, University of Texas, Austin, Texas (hereafter Briscoe Center).

6. "Funeral for Willie," *Time*, May 23, 1949, p. 24.

7. Westbrook Pegler, "Criminal Record of Labor Martyr," *New York Journal American*, August 16, 1957, clipping in *NYJA* Newspaper Morgue, Briscoe Center.

8. The quote by a fellow member of the union's picket crew is from Cal Yagid Interrogation, May 25, 1949; similar assertions, including that Lurye always needed money, came from Albert Cipriani Interrogation, no date; both in New York County District Attorney's Case File, Indictment No. 1405, People vs. Benedicto Macri, New York City Municipal Archives, New York.

9. Westbrook Pegler, "Dubinsky Now Disowns Thug Who Rated Forty-Hack Funeral and Martyr Treatment," *Lebanon Daily News*, August 17, 1957, p. 6; Westbrook Pegler, "New York's Needleworkers Had to Take Payless Holiday for Martyred Hoodlum," *Lebanon Daily News*, August 15, 1957, p. 14; Westbrook Pegler, "Dubinsky's Boss Picket Killed for Double-Cross," *Lebanon Daily News*, August 18, 1957, p. 20; Westbrook Pegler, "David and Peg: Dubinsky Tried Hard on the Dio Record," *Lebanon Daily News*, August 22, 1957, p. 6; Westbrook Pegler, "A Union Organizer Was Murdered," *New York Journal American*, August 22, 1957, clipping in *NYJA* Newspaper Morgue, Briscoe Center. David Dubinsky's papers include the actual criminal record that Pegler handed over to him that day along with notations, in Comments on Police Rents on Police Record, August 15, 1957, Folder 12B, Box 319, David Dubinsky Papers, President's Records, ILGWU Collection 5780/002, Kheel Center.

10. Lewis Nichols, "In and Out of Books," *New York Times*, August 14, 1960, p. BR8; Joseph Loftus, "Counsel's Own Story: The Enemy Within," *New York Times*, February 28, 1960, p. BR22.

11. See for example: *Blood Feud*, the 1983 television miniseries directed by Mike Newell and produced by Twentieth Century Fox; or most recently, James Neff, *Vendetta: Bobby Kennedy Versus Jimmy Hoffa* (New York: Little, Brown, 2015).

12. McAdams, *Power and Politics in Labor Legislation*, p. 69.

13. McAdams, *Power and Politics in Labor Legislation*, pp. 69–70.

14. Guy Farmer, *Management Rights and Union Bargaining Power* (New York: Industrial Relations Consultants, 1965), p. 34.

15. Samuel C. Patterson, *Labor Lobbying and Labor Reform: The Passage of the Landrum-Griffin Act* (New York: Bobbs-Merrill Company, 1966); the quote is from p. 34.

16. Paul Kamerick to Robert F. Kennedy, Subject: Garment Industry: Interview with Mrs. Min (Lurye) Matheson, May 6, 1958, File 18-193-103, McClellan Committee Records.

17. Report of Charles S. Zimmerman, General Manager, Joint Board of Dress & Waistmakers Union, to the General Executive Board Meeting, August 22, 1960.

18. Harrison E. Salisbury, "Newspaper in Little Rock Wins Two Pulitzer Prizes," *New York Times*, May 6, 1958: 1.

19. Gerald W. Johnson, *The Lines Are Drawn: American Life Since the First World War as Reflected in the Pulitzer Prize Cartoons* (Philadelphia: Lippincott, 1958), p. 216.

20. Goulden, *Meany*, pp. 294–99; Roscoe Born, "Meany Hits Rayburn on Labor Reform Act," *Wall Street Journal*, September 15, 1959, p. 12; Roscoe Born, "Labor Sits It Out: AFL-CIO Won't Back Anyone for Presidency," *Wall Street Journal*, January 18, 1960, p. 1.

21. Lawrence Richards, *Union-Free America: Workers and Antiunion Culture* (Urbana: University of Illinois Press, 2008), p. 87.

22. Kathleen Weldon, "Public Attitudes About Labor Unions, 1936–Today," *Huffington Post*, August 29, 2014, http://www.huffingtonpost.com/kathleen -weldon/public-attitudes-about-la_b_5716177.html, accessed July 25, 2017.

INDEX

Johnson, Gerald, 235
Johnson, Malcolm, 137
Joselit, Jenna Weissman, 18
Judy Lee Dance Frocks, 65

Kansas City Massacre (June 1933),
72
Kaplan, Arthur, 194–95
Kempton, Murray, 11, 154
Kennedy, John F., 223
Kennedy, Robert F.: and Hoffa, 232–33;
and McClellan Committee hearings,
13, 146–47, 159, 164, 180–82, 186,
188, 202–3, 232
King, Martin Luther, Jr., 50
Kings County District Attorney's Office,
113
Klar, Gabriel, 125
Kleinman, Leo, 65
Knox Coal Company, 97
Ku Klux Klan, 35
Kutlow, Ben, 77

La Cosa Nostra (Mafia), 76, 114, 131
labor beat journalists, 131–45, 154,
228–29; anti-communism, 132,
134–35, 136, 139; calls for
congressional probes into
racketeering, 137–39, 141–50; Frank,
134–35; Johnson, 137; Mollenhoff on
Hoffa and Teamsters corruption,
137–39, 146; Pegler on Lurye's
criminal record, 228–30; Pegler's
critiques of labor power, 133–35, 188,
222; Riesel and Dioguardi, 144–45,
152–59; Riesel and the acid attack,
131–59; Stark's model of reporting,
133–34
labor racketeering: and the Ethical
Practices Committee of the AFL-CIO,
195–215, 225; FBI investigations of
the garment industry, 60–66, 72–73,
76, 79, 122–23; Garment District and
New York garment industry, 17–22,
53–80, 108–10, 175; ILG's anti-
racketeering strategies, 7–14, 20–28,
59–62, 124–26, 191–95, 216–17, 225;
labor beat journalists on, 131–45,
154, 228–30; Lens's analysis of,
108–10; Meany's views on, 196–99,
208–10, 215, 224; mythic norms and
operational codes of professional
behavior, 54, 59, 79–80, 209–10, 212,
215, 230–31; paper locals, 163–80;
term "racketeering," 76, 222; union

leaders' strategic arrangements with
mob bosses, 110, 118–30, 216–21,
227–29, 231. See also McClellan
Committee hearings on labor
racketeering
Lambert, William, 138
Landrum-Griffin Act (1959), 215, 221,
223–25, 233–35
Lasky, Louis, 167–68
Laundry Workers Union, 164, 205, 206,
208
Lee, William, 45–46
Lens, Sydney, 108–10, 128, 258n10
Levine, Joe, 170–71
Levy, Alton, 152
Lichtenstein, Nelson, 2
Life magazine, 46, 145, 161, 184–85
Liuzzo, Viola, 50
Lombardy Dress Company, 19
Look magazine, 137
Los Angeles Times, 3, 140
Lovestone, Jay, 86, 91
Lucchese, Thomas ("Three Finger
Brown"), 74, 77, 119, 123, 191–93,
219
Lucchese crime family, 74, 119, 176, 177,
191
Lurye, Bernice, 83
Lurye, Max, 82, 84–85
Lurye, Maxine, 83
Lurye, Min. *See* Matheson, Min Lurye
Lurye, Sie, 83
Lurye, William: corruption and criminal
record, 111–12, 228–30; Macri's
indictment and murder trial, 106–8,
110–13, 116–17; murder of, 8–14,
20–21, 30, 53–54, 67, 79, 81–84,
118–19, 132, 228–30; police
investigation and indictments, 67,
105–8, 110; and sister Min Matheson,
81–84, 229

Macri, Benedicto: indictment and
murder trial, 110–13, 116–17; and
Lurye's murder, 53–54, 79, 106–8,
110–13, 116–17, 230; surrender to
Winchell, 110–11; ties to Anastasia's
Mafia, 106, 114–16
Macri, James, 114
Mangano, Vincent, 114, 115
Mangano crime family, 114–15
Mann Act, 228
Marinelli, Albert, 67
Masiello, John, 123
Matheson, Bill, 92–93, 102

ABOUT THE AUTHORS

Before attending graduate school **David Witwer** worked in the Labor Racketeering Bureau of the New York County District Attorney's Office and served as a staff researcher at the New York State Organized Crime Task Force, where he contributed to the report *Corruption and Racketeering in the New York City Construction Industry*. Later he worked at the Office of Investigation, created after the federal government's court settlement with the Teamsters Union in 1991, and charged with purging mob-connected union officials. Since receiving his PhD in history from Brown University he has published two books and over a dozen articles on aspects of the history of labor racketeering, including *Corruption and Reform in the Teamsters Union* (University of Illinois Press, 2003), which was named a *Choice* magazine Outstanding Academic Book, and *Shadow of the Racketeer: Scandal in Organized Labor* (University of Illinois Press, 2009), which won the journal *Labor History*'s Best Book Prize for 2009. He is a professor of history and American studies at Penn State Harrisburg and also serves as director of the Honors Programs there.

Catherine Rios holds an MFA from Columbia University in screenwriting and a BFA from the Rhode Island School of Design. She is an award-winning filmmaker and writer, and was a fellow with the Sundance Institute Screenwriting Intensive program in Philadelphia. Her short story "Open Season" received first prize in fiction from the *Orchid Literary Review*, was performed in the Reading Aloud program at the InterAct Theatre in Philadelphia, and received a Pennsylvania Fellowship for the Arts Award in Literature. She is an associate professor of humanities and communications and the associate director of the School of Humanities at Penn State Harrisburg. This is her third collaboration with David Witwer, which includes a dramatic treatment based on the research of this book.

PUBLISHING IN THE
PUBLIC INTEREST

Thank you for reading this book published by The New Press. The New Press is a nonprofit, public interest publisher. New Press books and authors play a crucial role in sparking conversations about the key political and social issues of our day.

We hope you enjoyed this book and that you will stay in touch with The New Press. Here are a few ways to stay up to date with our books, events, and the issues we cover:

- Sign up at www.thenewpress.com/subscribe to receive updates on New Press authors and issues and to be notified about local events
- Like us on Facebook: www.facebook.com/newpressbooks
- Follow us on Twitter: www.twitter.com/thenewpress

Please consider buying New Press books for yourself; for friends and family; or to donate to schools, libraries, community centers, prison libraries, and other organizations involved with the issues our authors write about.

The New Press is a 501(c)(3) nonprofit organization. You can also support our work with a tax-deductible gift by visiting www .thenewpress.com/donate.